A MORE PERFECT UNION

A MORE PERFECT UNION

◆

Documents in U.S. History

THIRD EDITION

Volume I: To 1877

PAUL F. BOLLER, JR.

Professor Emeritus, Texas Christian University

RONALD STORY

University of Massachusetts, Amherst

Houghton Mifflin Company   **Boston**

Dallas   Geneva, Illinois   Palo Alto   Princeton, New Jersey

To Martin and Eliza

Sponsoring Editor: John Weingartner
Project Editor: Celena Sun
Senior Production Coordinator: Renée Le Verrier
Senior Manufacturing Coordinator: Marie Barnes
Marketing Manager: Diane Gifford

Cover: Columbia waving the Phrygian banner, copper weathervane made before 1867. Courtesy of Steve Miller, American Folk Art.

ISBN: 0-395-59171-6

Library of Congress: 91-72006

ABCDEFGHIJ-AH-954321

CONTENTS

◆

CHAPTER FOUR
◆ ─────────────────────

The Age of Reform

◆ CHAPTER FIVE
─────────────────

Rebels, Yankees, and Freedmen

PREFACE

◆

Our two-volume reader, *A More Perfect Union: Documents in U.S. History,* presents students with the original words of speeches and testimony, political and legal writings, and literature that have reflected, precipitated, and implemented pivotal events of the past four centuries. The readings in Volume I cover the era from the founding of the Virginia and Massachusetts Bay colonies to Reconstruction. Volume II begins with the post-Civil War period, repeating some of the first volume's final readings, and concludes with contemporary selections. We are pleased with the reception that *A More Perfect Union* has received, and we have worked toward refining the contents of this new edition.

About a third of the material is new to this edition. New selections in Volume I include, for example, "Address to John Smith" by Powhatan and "The Examination of Anne Hutchinson" from the seventeenth century and Lydia Maria Child's "That Class of Americans Called Africans" and Elizabeth Palmer Peabody's "Plan of Brook Farm" from the nineteenth century. Many new selections have been added to Volume II. Among them are "Chief Joseph's Story" and Robert Hunt's "Bessemer Steel" from the late nineteenth century as well as Harry Blackmun's opinion in *Roe v. Wade* and George Bush on the war with Iraq.

The readings in these volumes represent a blend of social and political history, along with some cultural and economic trends, suitable for introductory courses in American history. We made our selections with three thoughts in mind. First, we looked for famous documents with a lustrous place in the American tradition—or the Gettysburg Address, for example, or Franklin D. Roosevelt's First Inaugural Address. These we chose for their great mythic quality, as expressions of fundamental sentiments with which students should be familiar. Second, we looked for writings that caused something to happen or had an impact when they appeared. Examples include the Virginia slave statutes, Thomas Paine's *The Crisis,* the Emancipation Proclamation, and Earl Warren's opinion in *Brown* v. *Board of Education of Topeka*—all of them influential pieces, some of them famous as well. Third, we looked for documents that seemed to reflect important attitudes or developments. Into this group fall Thomas Hart Benton's racial views as well as the writings of Upton Sinclair on industrial Chicago and of Martin Luther King, Jr. on Vietnam. In this category, where the need for careful selection from a wide field was most apparent, we looked especially for thoughtful pieces with a measure of fame and influence. Horace Mann's statement on schools reflected common attitudes; it also caused something to happen and is a well-known reform statement. We have also tried to mix a few unusual items into the stew, as with the "Report of the Joint Committee on Reconstruction" and a *Playboy* interview with Germaine Greer.

We have edited severely in places, mostly when the document is long or contains extraneous material or obscure references. We have also, in some cases, modernized spelling and punctuation.

Each document has a lengthy headnote that summarizes the relevant trends of the era, provides a specific setting for the document, and sketches the life of the author. There are also "Questions to Consider" to guide students through the prose and suggest ways of thinking about the selections. In addition, we have eliminated the Counterpoints. Reviewers wanted to see more selections and believed the Counterpoints to be less useful.

We would like to thank the following people who reviewed the manuscript for one or both volumes:

John K. Alexander, University of Cincinnati; George Flynn, Texas Tech University; Marty Haas, Adelphi University; Michael Krenn, University of Miami; Lisa Lane, Miracosta College; C. Elizabeth Raymond, University of Nevada-Reno; James Oliver Robertson, University of Connecticut; Henry J. Sage, Northern Virginia Community College; Robert Smith, University of Toledo; and John Scott Wilson, University of South Carolina.

We also wish to express our appreciation to the editorial staff of Houghton Mifflin Company for their hard and conscientious work in producing these volumes. We owe a particular debt of gratitude to Celena Sun, who was a model of efficiency, intelligence, and tact throughout the project; to John Weingartner and Jeff Greene, who advised without commanding; and to Jean Woy, under whose auspices earlier editions of this collection first saw the light of day and whose continued presence at Houghton Mifflin was both energizing and reassuring.

P.F.B.
R.S.

A MORE PERFECT UNION

A recruiting flyer. An illustration from an early 17th-century British pamphlet seeking settlers for Virginia, or "Nova Britannia"—New Britain.

Planters and Puritans

1

◆

CONTACT

Englishmen came to Virginia in 1607 with one overriding purpose: to find gold and find it quickly. If possible, they would achieve this goal by raiding Spanish treasure galleons; more likely, they would force the so-called Indians to mine it for them, as the Spaniards had in Mexico and Peru. "Our gilded refiners with their golden promises made all men their slaves in hope of recompense," complained Captain John Smith, the settlement's military leader and chronicler. "There was no talk, no hope, but dig gold, wash gold, refine gold, load gold."

Unfortunately for the English, the Chesapeake Bay region proved not only too distant from the Spanish Main for raiding but also barren of precious metal. The Virginia Company, which was organized militarily, was short of provisions and top-heavy with "gentlemen adventurers" and luxury craftsmen without the skill or will to grow crops. The company lost half its men within two years, and without help from the native American population, the remainder would also have perished.

The Chesapeake region was inhabited mostly by Powhatans, a confederacy of ten thousand people in one hundred and thirty villages. Their shrewd leader, Chief Powhatan, bore the tribal name. Powhatan might easily have refused to help the hapless English. European-born diseases had afflicted the tribal population even before these English arrived. European raiders, English and Spanish, had attacked and burned Powhatan villages. But there were also reasons to offer help. The Powhatans, reared in a collective, uncompetitive ethos, were generous—both among themselves and with nonthreatening neighbors, as the tiny English band probably appeared at first. Chief Powhatan was looking for allies in a territorial dispute with nonconfederacy tribes. The English, who carried edged metal weapons and primitive firearms, appeared likely recruits.

Reduced to eating "dogs, cats, rats, and mice" (and eventually cadavers and one another), the English should have received Powhatan's gifts of corn and meat with gratitude. But Captain Smith was an aggressive mercenary soldier who had once been enslaved by "infidel" Turks and was deeply suspicious of "infidel Indians," particularly given the defenseless state of the English settlement. He tended to see even acts of generosity as the mere treachery of "wild cruel Pagans."

Smith preferred to take by force what he needed rather than to receive it by gift. While engaged in raiding forays, he sometimes found himself trapped by Powhatan's forces. On one such occasion, Powhatan sought to demonstrate his authority by arranging a mock execution of Smith. He had Pocahontas, his young daughter, halt the proceedings by throwing herself upon the prisoner in a symbolic adoption gesture. Smith, perhaps understandably, misinterpreted the gesture as an expression of love for the English, thus supplying one of the earliest Anglo-American fables.

Powhatan delivered the address reprinted below during an encounter with Smith in the winter of 1608, when the English were again desperate for provisions. The speech first appeared in Smith's *A Map of Virginia, with a Description of the Countrey, the Commodities, People, Government, and Religion,* published in London in 1612. Transcribed into Elizabethan English by men barely familiar with Native American ways and language, the passage nevertheless seems a clear and straightforward rendering of Powhatan's concerns and hopes.

The chief, whom Smith estimated to be about sixty years old in 1607, was himself the son of a chief from south of the Chesapeake, possibly from Spanish Florida. When Powhatan saw the English continually raiding villages despite his overtures to John Smith, this accomplished statesman and stern ruler determined to starve the English into submission through intermittent war. His policy was partially successful. English weakness and the marriage of Pocahontas to settler John Rolfe in 1614 brought an uneasy truce that lasted until Powhatan's death in 1618. However, his successor, Opechankanough, saw the English as competitors for land rather than as raiders for food. In 1622 he launched an attack that killed a third of the settlers. The bankruptcy of the Virginia Company, the conversion of Virginia to a royal colony, and a rapid increase in European settlement soon followed. By 1669, when the first Virginia census was taken, the Powhatans themselves numbered barely 2,000.

Questions to Consider. Do Powhatan's opening remarks contain anything to substantiate his reputation for shrewd statecraft? According to Powhatan, why had his people refused to give corn to the English? What arguments did Powhatan use in trying to persuade the English not to wage war against him? What did he mean by the word that the English translated as *love*? Was Powhatan aware that Captain Smith was a much younger man? Why did Powhatan want John Smith and his men to come unarmed for talks? Why did the English fail to respond to so promising and open-handed an appeal?

◆

Address to John Smith (1608)

POWHATAN

Captain Smith, some doubt I have of your coming hither, that makes me not so kindly seek to relieve you as I would; for many do inform me, your coming is not for trade, but to invade my people and possess my Country, who dare not come to bring you corn, seeing you thus armed with your men. To cheer [relieve] us of this fear, leave aboard your weapons, for here they are needless, we being all friends and forever Powhatans. . . .

Captain Smith, you may understand that I, having seen the death of all my people thrice, and not one living of those three generations but myself, I know the difference of peace and war better than any in my Country. But now I am old, and ere long must die. My brethren, namely Opichapam, Opechankanough, and Kekataugh, [and] my two sisters, and their two daughters, are distinctly each others' successors. I wish their experiences no less than mine, and your love to them, no less than mine to you: but this brute [noise] from Nansamund, that you are come to destroy my Country, so much affrighteth all my people, as they dare not visit you. What will it avail you to take that which perforce, you may quietly have with love, or to destroy them that provide you food? What can you get by war, when we can hide our provision and flee to the woods, whereby you must famish, by wronging us your friends? And why are you thus jealous of our love, seeing us unarmed, and both do, and are willing still to feed you with what you cannot get but by our labors?

Think you I am so simple not to know it is better to eat good meat, lie well, and sleep quietly with my women and children, laugh, and be merry with you, have copper, hatchets, or what I want being your friend; than be forced to flee from all, to lie cold in the woods, feed upon acorns, roots and such trash, and be so hunted by you that I can neither rest, eat nor sleep, but my tired men must watch, and if a twig but break, everyone cry, there comes Captain Smith: then must I flee I know not wither, and thus with miserable fear end my miserable life, leaving my pleasures to such youths as you, which through your rash unadvisedness, may quickly as miserably end, for want of that you never know how to find? Let this therefore assure you of our loves, and every year our friendly trade shall furnish you with corn; and now also, if you would come in friendly manner to see us, and not thus with your guns and swords as to invade your foes.

From Edward Arber, ed., *Travels and Works of Captain John Smith* (Edinburgh, 1910) I: 132–136.

An Indian gathering. A 16th century-English depiction of Native Americans around a campfire during the earliest days of European exploration in the Chesapeake region. (North Carolina Division of Archives and History)

2

◆

FIRST RIGHTS AND PRIVILEGES

The first representative body in the New World was the Virginia Assembly, or House of Burgesses. This development came about when the directors of the Virginia Company, a joint-stock corporation of British investors, decided to allow more freedom in order to attract more colonists. The directors scrapped the colony's military and communal organization when the little settlement at Jamestown, established in 1607, failed to produce a profit and came close to collapsing due to disease and starvation. The company directors distributed land to the settlers, arranged to transport craftsmen and servants, as well as women, to the colony, and authorized the election of a general assembly to help govern the colony. On July 30, 1619, twenty-two burgesses, chosen by the settlers, met for the first time with the governor and the council, appointed by the company.

The document authorizing the House of Burgesses has been lost, but an "ordinance" of 1621 (reproduced below) is believed to reproduce the provisions of 1619. Largely the work of Sir Edwin Sandys, one of the leading directors of the Virginia Company, the ordinance provided for a Council of State, appointed by the company, as well as for an assembly elected by the people. The Virginia Assembly had the power to "make, ordain, and enact such general Laws and Orders, for the Behoof of the said Colony, and the good Government thereof, as shall, from time to time, appear necessary or requisite," subject to the company's approval. The new governmental arrangements, together with the discovery that tobacco could be a lucrative crop, soon made Virginia a thriving enterprise, and these arrangements were continued after Virginia became a royal colony in 1624.

Questions to Consider. In examining the ordinance's description of the two councils for governing Virginia, it is helpful to consider the following questions: How large was the Council of State? How was it chosen? What responsibilities did it possess? How did the responsibilities of the General Assembly compare in importance with those of the Council of State? Who possessed the ultimate authority in Virginia?

◆

The Virginia Ordinance of 1619

An ordinance and Constitution of the Treasurer, Council, and Company in England, for a Council of State and General Assembly. . . .

To all People, to whom these Presents shall come, be seen, or heard the Treasurer, Council, and Company of Adventurers and Planters for the city of *London* for the first colony of *Virginia*, send Greeting. . . .

We . . . the said Treasurer, Council, and Company, by Authority directed to us from his Majesty under the Great Seal, upon mature Deliberation, do hereby order and declare, that, from henceforward, there shall be TWO SUPREME COUNCILS in *Virginia*, for the better Government of the said Colony aforesaid.

The one of which Councils, to be called THE COUNCIL OF STATE (and whose Office shall chiefly be assisting, with their Care, Advise, and Circumspection, to the said Governor) shall be chosen, nominated, placed and displaced, from time to time, by Us, the said Treasurer, Council, and Company, and our Successors: Which Council of State shall consist, for the present, only of these Persons, as are here inserted, *viz.* Sir *Francis Wyat*, Governor of *Virginia*, Captain *Francis West*, Sir *George Yeardley*, Knight, Sir *William Neuce*, Night Marshal of *Virginia*, Mr. *George Sandys*, Treasurer, Mr. *George Thorpe*, Deputy of the College, Captain *Thomas Neuce*, Deputy for the Company, Mr. *Pawlet*, Mr. *Leech*, Captain *Nathaniel Powel*, Mr. *Harwood*, Mr. *Samuel Macock*, Mr. *Christopher Davison*, Secretary, *Doctor Pots*, Physician to the Company, Mr. *Roger Smith*, Mr. *John Berkley*, Mr. *John Rolfe*, Mr. *Ralph Hamer*, Mr. *John Pountis*, Mr. *Michael Lapworth*. Which said Counsellors and Council we earnestly pray and desire, and in his Majesty's Name strictly charge and command, that (all Factions, Partialities, and sinister Respect laid aside) they bend their Care and Endeavors to assist the said Governor; first and principally in the Advancement of the Honour and Service of God, and the Enlargement of his Kingdom amongst the Heathen People; and next, in erecting of the said Colony in due obedience to his Majesty, and all lawful Authority from his Majesty's Directions; and lastly, in maintaining the said People in Justice and *Christian* Conversation amongst themselves, and in Strength and Ability to withstand their Enemies. And this Council, to be always, or for the most Part, residing about or near the Governor.

From F. N. Thorpe, ed., *The Federal and State Constitutions* (7 v., Government Printing Office, Washington, D.C., 1909), VII: 3810–3812.

The other Council, more generally to be called by the Governor, once yearly, and no oftener, but for very extraordinary and important occasions, shall consist, for the present, of the said Council of State, and of two Burgesses out of every Town, Hundred, or other particular Plantation, to be respectively chosen by the Inhabitants; Which Council shall be called THE GENERAL ASSEMBLY, wherein (as also in the said Council of State) all Matter shall be decided, determined, and ordered, by the greater Part of the Voices then present; reserving to the Governor always a Negative Voice. And this General Assembly shall have free Power to treat, consult, and conclude, as well of all emergent Occasions concerning the Public Weal of the said Colony and every Part thereof, as also to make, ordain, and enact such general Laws and Orders, for the Behoof of the said Colony, and the good Government thereof, as shall, from time to time, appear necessary or requisite. . . .

Whereas in all other Things, we require the said General Assembly, as also the said Council of State, to imitate and follow the Policy of the Form of Government—Laws, Customs, and Manner of Trial, and other administration of Justice, used in the Realm of *England*, as near as may be, even as ourselves, by his Majesty's Letters Patent, are required.

Provided, that no Law or Ordinance, made in the said General Assembly, shall be or continue in Force or Validity, unless the same shall be solemnly ratified and confirmed, in a General Quarter Court of the said Company here in England and so ratified, be returned to them under our Seal; It being our Intent to afford the like Measure also unto the said Colony, that after the Government of the said Colony shall once have been well framed, and settled accordingly, which is to be done by Us, as by Authority derived from his Majesty, and the same shall have been so by Us declared, no Orders of Court afterwards shall bind the said Colony, unless they be ratified in like Manner in the General Assemblies. IN WITNESS whereof we have here unto set our Common Seal, the 24th of *July* 1621, and in the Year of the Reign of our Sovereign Lord, JAMES, King of *England, &c.*

3

♦

THE PURITAN VISION

In 1630 began the Great Migration of Puritans to America. That summer, under the direction of John Winthrop, a fleet of seventeen ships carrying about one thousand men and women crossed the Atlantic to Massachusetts Bay. A few months later, the settlers founded a colony on the site of the present city of Boston. Within a few years Massachusetts Bay Colony was the largest of all the English colonies on the American mainland.

John Winthrop, a college-educated squire from Groton Manor, Suffolk, had been elected governor of the new colony even before the settlers left England. Though not a clergyman, he was a devout Puritan. During the passage he delivered a lecture called "A Model of Christian Charity" to his coreligionists on the flagship *Arbella*. In it he reminded them of their Puritan ideals and outlined the religious and social purposes by which he expected them to organize their settlement in the New World. He wanted Massachusetts Bay Colony to be a model "Christian commonwealth," that is, a kind of "city upon a hill" for the rest of the world to admire and perhaps imitate. The settlers, he said, had a special commission from God to establish such a community in the New World. The new colony was to be dedicated to the glory of God rather than to worldly success. The "care of the public," he declared, "must oversway all private respects," and the settlers must strive at all times "to do justly, to love mercy, to walk humbly with our God."

For almost two decades Winthrop dominated Massachusetts Bay Colony. John Cotton, Boston's leading clergyman, called him "a brother . . . who has been to us a mother," but he was a father as well. He was convinced he was destined to rule and was an exacting parent. Born to wealth in Suffolk in 1588, he was educated at Trinity College, Cambridge, became prominent in the legal profession, and served as justice of the peace and lord of Groton Manor before heading the expedition to America. A strong leader who opposed both religious dissent and popular rule in Massachusetts, Winthrop served as governor for twelve years; when not governor he served as deputy governor and member of the governing council. He regarded democracy as "the meanest and worst form of government," and most people agreed with him in those days. When criticized tor highhandedness, he managed to convince his critics that "liberty" meant not the right to do as one pleased but, rather, emancipation from selfish desires and obedience to the moral law. A journal he kept from the inception of the colony until his death in 1649 is a rich source for the early history of Massachusetts Bay Colony.

Questions to Consider. In his lecture to the settlers, Winthrop spoke of the "law of the Gospel." In what ways did he make the Bible the basis of his plans for Massachusetts Bay Colony? How close were relations between church and state to be in the new settlement? Which was to come first: the individual or the community? What principles of behavior did he consider essential to the success of the enterprise? What did he mean by his statement that the Puritans were operating under a "special overruling providence"? What did he think would be the fate of the colonists if they failed to carry out the high purposes he had outlined for them?

◆

A Model of Christian Charity (1630)

JOHN WINTHROP

This law of the Gospel propounds likewise a difference of seasons and occasions. There is a time when a Christian must sell all and give to the poor as they did in the apostles' times; there is a time also when a Christian, though they give not all yet, must give beyond their ability, as they of Macedonia (II Cor. 8). Likewise, community of perils calls for extraordinary liberality, and so doth community in some special service for the church. Lastly, when there is no other means whereby our Christian brother may be relieved in this distress, we must help him beyond our ability, rather than tempt God in putting him upon help by miraculous or extraordinary means.

1. For the persons, we are a company professing ourselves fellow members of Christ, in which respect only, though we were absent from each other many miles, and had our employments as far distant, yet we ought to account ourselves knit together by this bond of love, and live in the exercise of it, if we would have comfort of our being in Christ.

2. For the work we have in hand, it is by mutual consent, through a special overruling providence and a more than an ordinary approbation of

From *The Winthrop Papers* (5 v., Massachusetts Historical Society, Boston, 1931), II: 282–295. Reprinted by permission.

John Winthrop, second governor of Massachusetts. This engraving (undated) shows Winthrop in the prime of life. He was forty-two when he succeeded Matthew Cradock as governor of Massachusetts in 1629. The next year he came to America on the **Arbella** with a fleet of seventeen ships carrying close to one thousand men and women. He settled at Charlestown first and began building a house there, but soon changed his mind and moved to Boston, where he spent the rest of his life. Winthrop's term as governor was one year, and he was re-elected three times. But when John Cotton, prominent Boston clergyman, announced that competent magistrates ought to be re-elected continually, the freemen showed their independence by choosing someone else in 1634. They turned to Winthrop again, however, in 1642, and from 1645 to 1649, the year of his death, he was re-elected anually. (American Antiquarian Society)

the churches of Christ, to seek out a place of cohabitation and consortship, under a due form of government both civil and ecclesiastical. In such cases as this, the care of the public must oversway all private respects by which not only conscience but mere civil policy doth bind us; for it is a true rule that particular estates cannot subsist in the ruin of the public.

3. The end is to improve our lives to do more service to the Lord, the comfort and increase of the body of Christ whereof we are members, that ourselves and posterity may be the better preserved from the common corruptions of this evil world, to serve the Lord and work out our salvation under the power and purity of His holy ordinances.

4. For the means whereby this must be effected, they are twofold: a conformity with the work and the end we aim at; these we seek are extraordinary, therefore we must not content ourselves with usual ordinary means. Whatsoever we did or ought to have done when we lived in England, the same must we do, and more also where we go. That which the most in their churches maintain as a truth in profession only, we must bring into familiar and constant practice: as in this duty of love we must love brotherly without dissimulation; we must love one another with a pure heart fervently, we must bear one another's burdens, we must not look only on our own things but also on the things of our brethren. Neither must we think that the Lord will bear with such failings at our hands as He doth from those among whom we have lived. . . .

Thus stands the cause between God and us; we are entered into covenant with Him for this work; we have taken out a commission, the Lord hath given us leave to draw our own articles. We have professed to enterprise these actions upon these and these ends; we have hereupon besought Him of favor and blessing. Now if the Lord shall please to hear us and bring us in peace to the place we desire, then hath He ratified this covenant and sealed our Commission, [and] will expect a strict performance of the articles contained in it. But if we shall neglect the observation of these articles which are the ends we have propounded, and dissembling with our God, shall fall to embrace this present world and prosecute our carnal intentions, seeking great things for ourselves and our posterity, the Lord will surely break out in wrath against us, be revenged of such a perjured people, and make us know the price of the breach of such a covenant.

Now the only way to avoid this shipwreck and to provide for our posterity is to follow the counsel of Micah: to do justly, to love mercy, to walk humbly with our God. For this end, we must be knit together in this work as one man. We must entertain each other in brotherly affection; we must be willing to abridge ourselves of our superfluities for the supply of others' necessities; we must uphold a familiar commerce together in all meekness, gentleness, patience and liberality. We must delight in each other, make others' condition our own, rejoice together, mourn together, labor and suffer together: always having before our eyes our commission and community in the work, our community as members of the same body. So shall we keep the unity of the spirit in the bond of peace, the Lord will be our God and delight to dwell among us, as His own people, and will command a blessing upon us in all our ways, so that we shall see much more of His wisdom, power, goodness, and truth than formerly we have been acquainted with. We shall find that the God of Israel is among us, when ten of us shall be able to resist a thousand of our enemies, when He shall make us a praise and glory, that men shall say of succeeding plantations: "The Lord make it like that of New England." For we must consider that we shall be as a city upon a hill, the eyes of all people are upon us. So that if we shall deal falsely with our God in this work we have undertaken, and so cause Him to withdraw His present help from us, we shall be made a story and a by-word through the world: we shall open the mouths of enemies to speak evil of the ways of God and all professors for God's sake; we shall shame the faces of many of God's worthy servants, and cause their prayers to be turned into curses upon us, till we be consumed out of the good land whither we are going.

And to shut up this discourse with that exhortation of Moses, that faithful servant of the Lord, in his last farewell to Israel (Deut. 30): Beloved, there is now set before us life and good, death and evil, in that we are commanded this day to love the Lord our God, and to love one another, to walk in His ways and to keep His commandments and His ordinance and His laws and the articles of our covenant with Him, that we may live and be multiplied, and that the Lord our God may bless us in the land whither we go to possess it: but if our hearts shall turn away so that we will not obey, but shall be seduced and worship . . . other gods, our pleasures and profits, and serve them, it is propounded unto us this day, we shall surely perish out of the good land whither we pass over this vast sea to possess it.

> *Therefore, let us choose life,*
> *that we, and our seed,*
> *may live; by obeying His*
> *voice and cleaving to Him,*
> *for He is our life and*
> *our prosperity.*

4

◆

THE UNDERSIDE OF PRIVILEGE

In 1619 a Dutch trader brought twenty "Negars" from Africa and sold them in Jamestown. For a long time, however, black slavery, though common in Spanish and Portuguese colonies in the New World, was not important in Virginia. For many years white indentured servants from England performed most of the labor in the colony; after three decades there were still only about three hundred blacks in the English colonies. By the end of the seventeenth century, however, transporting Africans to America had become a profitable business for English and American merchants, and the slave trade had grown to enormous proportions.

In Virginia the planters used Africans as cheap labor on their plantations and also employed them as household servants, coachmen, porters, and skilled workers. Their status was indeterminate at first, and they may have been treated somewhat like indentured servants for some time. As tobacco became important, however, and the number of blacks working on plantations soared, the position of blacks declined rapidly. The Virginia Assembly began enacting laws governing their behavior and regulating their relations with whites. The statutes, some of which are reproduced here, do not show whether racial prejudice and discrimination preceded slavery, followed it, or, more likely, accompanied it. But they do dramatize the fact that in Virginia, as elsewhere, the expansion of freedom and self-government for European Americans could go hand in hand with the exploitation and oppression of African-Americans.

Questions to Consider. How strictly did the Virginia lawmakers attempt to control the behavior of Africans in the colony? How severe were the punishments provided for offenders against the law? What penalties were provided for the "casual killing" of slaves? What appeared to be the greatest fear of the Virginia lawmakers?

◆

Virginia Slavery Legislation (1630–1691)

[1630]   Hugh David to be soundly whipped, before an assembly of Ne-groes and others for abusing himself to the dishonor of God and shame of Christians, by defiling his body in lying with a negro; which fault he is to acknowledge next Sabbath day.

[1640]   Robert Sweet to do penance in church according to laws of England, for getting a negro woman with child and the woman whipt.

[1661]   *Be it enacted* That in case any English servant shall run away in company with any negroes who are incapable of making satisfaction by addition of time, *Be it enacted* that the English so running away in company with them shall serve for the time of the said negroes absence as they are to do for their own by a former act.

[1668]   Whereas some doubts, have arisen whether negro women set free were still to be accompted tithable according to a former act, *It is declared by this grand assembly* that negro women, though permitted to enjoy their Freedom yet ought not in all respects to be admitted to a full fruition of the exemptions and impunities of the England, and are still liable to payment of taxes.

[1669]   Whereas the only law in force for the punishment of refractory servants resisting their master, mistress or overseer cannot be inflicted upon negroes, nor the obstinancy of many of them by other than violent means supprest, *Be it enacted and declared by this grand assembly*, if any slave resist his master (or other by his master's order correcting him) and by the extremity of the correction should chance to die, that his death shall not be accompted Felony, but the master (or that other person appointed by the master to punish him) be acquit from molestation, since it cannot be presumed that prepensed malice (which alone makes murder Felony) should induce any man to destroy his own estate.

[1680]   *It is hereby enacted by the authority aforesaid,* that from and after the publication of this law, it shall not be lawful for any negro or other slave to carry or arm himself with any club, staff, gun, sword, or any other weapon of defence or offence, nor to go to depart from his master's ground without a certificate from his master, mistress or overseer, and such per-mission not to be granted but upon particular and necessary occasions; and every negro or slave so offending not having a certificate as aforesaid shall be sent to the next constable, who is hereby enjoined and required to give the said negro twenty lashes on his bare back well laid on, and so

From William Hening, ed., *The Laws of Virginia, 1619–1792* (13 v., Samuel Pleasants, Rich-mond, 1809–1823).

sent home to his said master, mistress or overseer. *And it is further enacted by the authority aforesaid* that if any negro or other slave shall presume to lift up his hand in opposition against any christian, shall for every such offense, upon due proof made thereof by the oath of the party before a magistrate, have and receive thirty lashes on his bare back well laid on.

[1691]   *It is hereby enacted,* that in all such cases upon intelligence of any such negroes, mulattoes, or other slaves lying out, two of their majesties' justices of the peace of that county, whereof one to be of the quorum, where such negroes, mulattoes or other slave shall be, shall be impowered and commanded, and are hereby impowered and commanded, to issue out their warrants directed to the sheriff of the same county to apprehend such negroes, mulattoes, and other slaves, which said sheriff is hereby likewise required upon all such occasions to raise such and so many forces from time to time as he shall think convenient and necessary for the effectual apprehending such negroes, mulattoes and other slaves, and in case any negroes, mulattoes or other slave or slaves lying out as aforesaid shall resist, run away, or refuse to deliver and surrender him or themselves to any person or persons that shall be by lawful authority employed to apprehend and take such negroes, mulattoes or other slaves that in such cases it shall and may be lawful for such person and persons to kill and destroy such negroes, mulattoes, and other slave or slaves by gun or any other ways whatsoever.

5

♦

FAITH AND DISSENT

Although John Winthrop's "Christian commonwealth" flourished for several decades, it did not do so without difficulty. Location (near a forest that enticed settlers westward and an ocean that tugged them back east) was one problem: enemies (Spaniards and Native Americans) were another. But the colony also had internal troubles. Some of these stemmed from the fact that many tradesmen, sailors, and other inhabitants were not professing Congregationalists. Other troubles can be traced to stress within the Puritan community itself. As early as 1635, for example, colonial leaders, including Winthrop, banished a popular young minister named Roger Williams for spreading two "dangerous opinions." Williams believed that Englishmen should not settle North America unless the "Indians" gave their permission. Even worse, in the eyes of his judges, he taught that church and state should be totally separate lest the one corrupt the other and both corrupt the individual's striving for true faith. Other dissidents faced excommunication, fines, imprisonment, and sometimes death.

In this community, there was no more zealous Puritan than Anne Hutchinson. The daughter of a learned English clergyman, Hutchinson had migrated to Boston with her husband in 1634, following a favorite Puritan minister. Taking seriously the rule that Saints (or members of the true Church), should study God's word, she invited people into her home to discuss scripture and sermons. Hutchinson extended her invitations to women she met in her work as midwife as well as to ministers and prominent merchants. Among the sermons they discussed were those of ministers whom she criticized for preaching salvation through "works" (good behavior) rather than "grace" (faith). This doctrine implied that people could save themselves through good deeds rather than by relying on God's will. It seemed to imply that God is not all-powerful and to encourage the sin of human pride, positions that were anathema to most good Puritans.

Hutchinson's activities unsettled not only the ministers she criticized but John Winthrop and other political leaders. They brought her to trial in 1637 for "traducing the ministers." The magistrates disliked criticism of the ministry, a pillar of the Massachusetts establishment. Moreover, to urge "grace" over "works" *too* hotly was to imply that

God considered polite behavior, including obedience to the law, un-
important—a position the magistrates considered dangerous to society.
Indeed, as the following excerpts from the record of Hutchinson's
interrogation make clear, to urge "grace" too hotly was to claim divine
inspiration. Such a claim constituted a heresy that struck at the very
heart of congregational Puritanism and the Christian commonwealth—
at least as understood by the leadership of Massachusetts Bay. Moreover, Hutchinson was female in a patriarchal world, which clearly
disturbed her accusers and underscored her guilt.

In 1638 the Massachusetts General Court found Anne Hutchinson
guilty and banished her from the colony; a short time later her church
excommunicated her as well. She and her family, including most of
her fifteen children, then moved to an island off the coast of Rhode
Island. Following the death of her husband in 1642, Hutchinson moved
her family to Long Island in the New Netherlands (later New York).
In 1643, she and several of her children perished in an Indian raid.

Questions to Consider. When John Winthrop accused Anne Hutchinson of holding opinions that "troubled the peace of the commonwealth and the churches," to what opinions was he referring? What
was it about Hutchinson's meetings at her home that upset Winthrop?
Why was Deputy Governor Dudley distressed that Hutchinson might
have accused Puritan ministers of preaching a "covenant of works"?
Why did he compare her to a "Jesuit"? When Governor Winthrop
("the Court") exclaimed "Very well, very well" after the exchanges
concerning Hutchinson's criticism of the ministers, had she won the
point, or had he? Hutchinson delivered a long statement to demonstrate
her innocence, but it clearly agitated the magistrates, particularly when
she referred to "immediate revelation." What did they think she
was claiming? Why did they think this was dangerous to society? Did
Anne Hutchinson's beliefs, her practices, or her manner most aggravate
her examiners?

◆

The Examination of Anne Hutchinson (1637)

Mr. Winthrop, governor. Mrs. Hutchinson, you are called here as one of
those that have troubled the peace of the commonwealth and the churches
here; you are known to be a woman that hath had a great share in the
promoting and divulging of those opinions that are causes of this trouble,

From Thomas Hutchinson, *History of the Colony and Province of Massachusetts Bay* (Boston, 1767).

Anne Hutchinson. A 20th-century Massachusetts memorial to Anne Hutchinson. (Gift to the Commonwealth by the Anne Hutchinson Memorial Association and Massachusetts State Federation of Women's Clubs. Photo courtesy Massachusetts State Library)

and to be nearly joined not only in affinity and affection with some of those the court had taken notice of and passed censure upon. But you have spoken divers things as we have been informed very prejudicial to the honour of the churches and ministers thereof, and you have maintained a meeting and an assembly in your house that hath been condemned by the general assembly as a thing not tolerable nor comely in the sight of God nor fitting for your sex; and notwithstanding that was cried down, you have continued the same. Therefore we have thought good to send for you to understand how things are. . . .

Mrs. Hutchinson. I am called here to answer before you but I hear no things laid to my charge.

Gov. I have told you some already and more I can tell you. *(Mrs. H.)* Name one Sir.

Gov. Have I not named some already?

Mrs. H. What have I said or done?

Gov. Why for your doings, this you did harbour and countenance those that are parties in this faction that you have heard of. *(Mrs. H.)* That's matter of conscience, Sir.

Gov. Your conscience you must keep, or it must be kept for you. . . .

Gov. Why do you keep such a meeting at your house as you do every week upon a set day?

Mrs. H. It is lawful for me so to do, as it is all your practices; and can you find a warrant for yourself and condemn me for the same thing? The ground of my taking it up was, when I first came to this land, because I did not go to such meetings as those were, it was presently reported that I did not allow of such meetings but held them unlawful, and therefore in that regard they said I was proud and did despise all ordinances. Upon that, a friend came unto me and told me of it and I to prevent such aspersions took it up, but it was in practice before I came; therefore I was not the first.

Gov. For this, that you appeal to our practice you need no confutation. If your meeting had answered to the former it had not been offensive, but I will say that there was no meeting of women alone. But your meeting is of another sort, for there are sometimes men among you.

Mrs. H. There was never any man with us.

Gov. Well, admit there was no man at your meeting and that you was sorry for it, there is no warrant for your doings; and by what warrant do you continue such a course?

Mrs. H. I conceive there is a clear rule in Titus, that the elder women should instruct the younger; and then I must have a time wherein I must do it.

Gov. All this I grant you, I grant you a time for it; but what is this to the purpose that you, Mrs. Hutchinson, must call a company together from their callings to come to be taught of you?

Mrs. H. Will it please you to answer me this and to give me a rule, for then I will willingly submit to any truth? If any come to my house to be instructed in the ways of God, what rule have I to put them away?

Gov. But suppose that a hundred men come unto you to be instructed, will you forbear to instruct them?

Mrs. H. As far as I conceive I cross a rule in it.

Gov. Very well and do you not so here?

Mrs. H. No Sir, for my ground is they are men.

Gov. Men and women all is one for that, but suppose that a man should come and say, "Mrs. Hutchinson, I hear that you are a woman that God hath given his grace unto and you have knowledge in the word of God. I pray instruct me a little." Ought you not to instruct this man?

Mrs. H. I think I may.—Do you think it not lawful for me to teach women, and why do you call me to teach the court?

Gov. We do not call you to teach the court but to lay open yourself.

Mr. Dudley, dep. gov. Here hath been much spoken concerning Mrs. Hutchinson's meetings and among other answers she saith that men come not there. I would ask you this one question then, whether never any man was at your meeting?

Gov. There are two meetings kept at their house.

Dep. Gov. How; is there two meetings?

Mrs. H. Ey Sir, I shall not equivocate, there is a meeting of men and women, and there is a meeting only for women.

Dep. Gov. Are they both constant?

Mrs. H. No, but upon occasions they are deferred.

Mr. Endicot. Who teaches in the men's meetings, none but men? Do not women sometimes?

Mrs. H. Never as I heard, not one. . . .

Dep. Gov. Now it appears by this woman's meeting that Mrs. Hutchinson hath so forestalled the minds of many by their resort to her meeting that now she hath a potent party in the country. Now if all these things have endangered us as from that foundation, and if she in particular hath disparaged all our ministers in the land that they have preached a covenant of works, . . . why this is not to be suffered. And therefore being driven to the foundation, and it being found that Mrs. Hutchinson is she that hath depraved all the ministers and hath been the cause of what is fallen out, why we must take away the foundation and the building will fall.

Mrs. H. I pray, Sir, prove it that I said they preached nothing but a covenant of works.

Dep. Gov. Nothing but a covenant of works? Why, a Jesuit may preach truth sometimes.

Mrs. H. Did I ever say they preached a covenant of works, then?

Dep. Gov. If they do not preach a covenant of grace clearly, then they preach a covenant of works.

Mrs. H. No Sir, one may preach a covenant of grace more clearly than another, so I said.

Dep. Gov. We are not upon that now, but upon position.

Mrs. H. Prove this then, Sir, that you say I said.

Dep. Gov. When they do preach a covenant of works, do they preach truth?

Mrs. H. Yes Sir, but when they preach a covenant of works for salvation, that is not truth.

Dep. Gov. I do but ask you this: when the ministers do preach a covenant of works, do they preach a way of salvation?

Mrs. H. I did not come hither to answer to questions of that sort.

Dep. Gov. Because you will deny the thing.

Mrs. H. Ey, but that is to be proved first.

Dep. Gov. I will make it plain that you did say that the ministers did preach a covenant of works.

Mrs. H. I deny that.

Dep. Gov. And that you said they were not able ministers of the new testament. . . .

Mrs. H. If ever I spake that, I proved it by God's word.

Court. Very well, very well. . . .

Mrs. H. If you please to give me leave, I shall give you the ground of what I know to be true. Being much troubled to see the falseness of the constitution of the church of England, I had like to have turned separatist; whereupon I kept a day of solemn humiliation and pondering of the thing; this scripture was brought unto me—he that denies Jesus Christ to be come in the flesh is antichrist—This I considered of, and in considering found that the papists did not deny him to be come in the flesh, nor we did not deny him—who then was antichrist? Was the Turk antichrist only? The Lord knows that I could not open scripture; he must by his prophetical office open it unto me. So after that, being unsatisfied in the thing, the Lord was pleased to bring this scripture out of the Hebrews. He that denies the testament denies the testator, and in this did open unto me and give me to see that those which did not teach the new covenant had the spirit of antichrist, and upon this he did discover the ministry unto me and ever since. I bless the Lord, he hath let me see which was the clear ministry and which the wrong. Since that time I confess I have been more choice, and he hath let me to distinguish between the voice of my beloved and the voice of Moses, the voice of John Baptist and the voice of antichrist, for all those voices are spoken of in scripture. Now if you do condemn me for speaking what in my conscience I know to be truth, I must commit myself unto the Lord.

Mr. Nowell. How do you know that that was the spirit?

Mrs. H. How did Abraham know that it was God that bid him offer his son, being a breach of the sixth commandment?

Dep. Gov. By an immediate voice.

Mrs. H. So to me by an immediate revelation.

Dep. Gov. How! an immediate revelation.

Mrs. H. By the voice of his own spirit to my soul. I will give you another scripture, Jer. 46. 27,28—out of which the Lord shewed me what he would do for me and the rest of his servants.—But after he was pleased to reveal himself to me, I did presently like Abraham run to Hagar. And after that, he did let me see the atheism of my own heart, for which I begged of the Lord that it might not remain in my heart; and being thus, he did shew me this (a twelvemonth after) which I told you of before. Ever since that time I have been confident of what he hath revealed unto me. . . .You see this scripture fulfilled this day, and therefore I desire you that as you tender the Lord and the church and commonwealth to consider and look what you do. You have power over my body, but the Lord Jesus hath power over my body and soul; and assure yourselves thus much, you do as much as in you lies to put the Lord Jesus Christ from you; and if you go on in this course you begin, you will bring a curse upon you and your posterity, and the mouth of the Lord hath spoken it.

Dep. Gov. What is the scripture she brings?

Mr. Stoughton. Behold I turn away from you.

Mrs. H. But now having seen him which is invisible, I fear not what man can do unto me.

Gov. Daniel was delivered by miracle. Do you think to be deliver'd so too?

Mrs. H. I do here speak it before the court. I look that the Lord should deliver me by his providence.

Mr. Harlakenden. I may read scripture and the most glorious hypocrite may read them and yet go down to hell.

Mrs. H. It may be so. . . .

Mr. Endicot. I would have a word or two with leave of that which hath thus far been revealed to the court. I have heard of many revelations of Mr. Hutchinson's, but they were reports, but Mrs. Hutchinson I see doth maintain some by this discourse; and I think it is a special providence of God to hear what she hath said. Now there is a revelation you see which she doth expect as a miracle. She saith she now suffers, and let us do what we will she shall be delivered by a miracle. I hope the court takes notice of the vanity of it and heat of her spirit.

6

◆

PURITAN TWILIGHT

Men and women of the seventeenth century believed in the invisible spirit world far more than most people today can comprehend, and the New England Puritans were no different. Most of the Puritans were farmers whose livelihoods depended on the inexplicable ebbs and flows of disease and weather. Like all farmers and peasants of their time, they looked for signs of divine will to explain why rain did or did not fall or why calves were born healthy or dead. And in Massachusetts Bay, as Saints (members of the true Church), they sought constantly for hopeful signs—shooting stars or a bird killing and devouring a snake or rodent—of God's continuing favor for their Holy enterprise.

But spiritual belief had a dark side. If the invisible spirit of God was everywhere, so, too, was the invisible spirit of Satan. For the Puritans, Satan was a constant presence, a powerful, evil, menacing force constantly seeking to undo the work of Christ and the lives of Christians. Sometimes the Devil himself was present, employing his own "evil hand" to kill farm animals, cause haystacks to burn, sicken children. More commonly, Satan employed followers: witches or, occasionally, their male counterparts, wizards. In Europe in the 1500s and 1600s, tens of thousands perished at the the burning stake for witchcraft, and a few were hanged in early New England.

Thus it was not in itself startling when accusations of witchcraft surfaced in early 1692 in Salem Village, a little rural community just west of the bustling port of Salem Town. But things soon became startling. Most outbreaks of witchcraft in New England were minor affairs that flared briefly and then subsided. In Salem Village, however, the outbreak did not subside. It spread wider and wider, eventually encompassing hundreds of people in the local area and numerous figures from the commercial and political elites of nearby Salem Town and even of the provincial capital, Boston. And not only were hundreds accused. Dozens of them stood trial for the crime of witchcraft, and of these a full score or more went to their deaths on the sinister gallows atop Witch's Hill. Only the belated intervention of the colony's most powerful ministers and officeholders finally brought the killing to a halt late in 1692.

The ghastly business had begun when a group of adolescent girls started telling fortunes with a West Indian slave, then went into bizarre hysterical seizures, and finally turned to accusations of witchcraft to relieve their torment. When adult relatives and friends of the girls joined the cry, the village found itself awash in mystery, terror, and recrimination. Soon standing in the center of the fray was the local minister, Samuel Parris. Several of the afflicted girls were living in Parris's house when the outbreak began, and members of his congregation—actual Saints able to partake of Sabbath communion—had fallen under suspicion. So it was fitting for Parris to warn his parishioners of Satan's legions and to offer guidance as to the character of the witches lurking not just around them but also in their very midst.

Parris preached, as he always did, in the plain, direct, unadorned style that was the hallmark of Puritan preaching, the form used repeatedly since the 1630s to bring parishioners close to God's Word and purposes. In 1692 Parris scarcely needed adornment to make his point. His sermon "Christ Knows How Many Devils There Are," an outline of which is excerpted below, in fact resembled the woeful "jeremiads," the dire warnings that ministers had used for years to assail the corruption of faith by worldliness and lust. In style and content, if not in its obsession with witches, Parris's sermon was thoroughly familiar. But just as the Salem affair was New England's last significant witchhunt, so Parris's sermon was one of its last jeremiads. Neither witchcraft nor jeremiad, it seems, could withstand the materialism of the eighteenth century.

Samuel Parris was born in 1653 in London, the younger son of a speculator in West Indian goods. Seeing little future for himself in England, Parris sailed in about 1680 for Boston, where he tried trading with the Indies himself before turning to the ministry as a calling. He arrived in Salem Village in late 1689—just in time to play his fateful role in the accusations and executions of the purported witches. Parris's overzealousness in what amounted to a local civil war made it impossible for him to play a healing role once the trials stopped. Although he received the support of a majority of villagers during various campaigns to remove him, he finally resigned in 1696. He tried briefly to continue his ministry elsewhere, but fighting witches and corruption was out of fashion. He wound up a schoolmaster and petty tradesman in Sudbury, Massachusetts, where he died in 1720.

Questions to Consider. What was Samuel Parris's motive in preaching this particular sermon? Why might he have felt obligated to preach it at this particular time? Did he really believe in witchcraft? What according to Parris, were the chief evils of witches and wizards? If you had been sitting in the meetinghouse that Sunday, what kind of person would you have suspected of witchcraft? Was it significant that Salem Village lay very near the commercial port of Salem Town? What would John Winthrop have thought about Parris's sermon?

◆

Christ Knows How Many Devils There Are (1692)

SAMUEL PARRIS

27 March 1691/92, Sacrament day.

Occasioned by dreadful Witchcraft broke out here a few weeks past, and one Member of this Church, and another of Salem, upon public examination by Civil Authority vehemently suspected for she-witches, and upon it committed,

John 6: 70. "Have not I chosen you twelve, and one of you is a Devil.". . .

Doctrine: *Our Lord Jesus Christ knows how many Devils there are in his Church, and who they are.*

1. There are devils as well as saints in Christ's Church.
2. Christ knows how many of these devils there are.
3. Christ knows who these devils are.

Proposition 1: There are devils as well as saints in Christ's church. Here three things may be spoken to: (1) Show you what is meant here by *devils;* (2) That there are such devils in the church; (3) That there are also true saints in such churches.

(1). What is meant here by *devils?* "One of you is a devil." Answer: By *devil* is ordinarily meant any wicked angel or spirit. Sometimes it is put for the prince or head of the evil spirits, or fallen angels. Sometimes it is used for vile and wicked persons—the worst of such, who for their villainy and impiety do most resemble devils and wicked spirits. Thus Christ in our text calls Judas a devil: for his great likeness to the devil. "One of you is a devil": i.e., a devil for quality and disposition, not a devil for nature— for he was a man, etc.—but a devil for likeness and operation (John 8: 38, 41, 44—"Ye are of your father the devil.").

(2). There are such devils in the church. Not only sinners, but notorious sinners; sinners more like to the devil than others. So here in Christ's little Church. (Text.) This also Christ teacheth us in the parable of the tares (Matth. 13: 38), where Christ tells us that such are the children of the

From Paul Boyer and Stephen Nissenbaum: *Salem Village Witchcraft: A Documentary Record of Local Conflict in Colonial New England.* (Belmont, Calif., Wadsworth Publishing, 1972) pp. 129–130. Reprinted by permission of the authors.

Accusation of a witch. This twentieth-century rendering captures the tensions and terror that pervaded the Salem Village Meetinghouse during the witchcraft trials of 1692. A minimum of 234 people were accused of being witches in seventeenth-century New England. Of these, authorities executed 36. Salem Village, with its 19 executions, thus accounted for over half of all New England's executions, obviously a horrendous outbreak of fear and death for so small a place. About three-quarters of those accused were women, and two-thirds of these women were over forty years old—sinister reinforcement of the stereotype identifying the witch as an aged crone. (Courtesy Essex Institute, Salem, MA)

wicked one—i.e., of the devil. Reason: Because hypocrites are the very worst of men—*corruptio optimi est pessimi.* Hypocrites are the sons and heirs of the devil, the free-holders of hell—whereas other sinners are but tenants. When Satan repossesseth a soul, he becomes more vile and sinful (Luke 11: 24–26). As the jailer lays loads of iron on him that hath escaped. None are worse than those who have been good, and are naught; and might be good, but will be naught. . . .

Proposition 2: Christ knows how many of these devils there are in his churches. As in our text there was one among the twelve. And so in our churches God knows how many devils there are: whether one, two, three, or four in twelve—how many devils, how many saints. He that knows whom he has chosen (John 13: 18), he also knows who they are that have not chosen him, but prefer farms and merchandise above him and above his ordinances (2 Tim. 4: 10). . . .

Use 1. Let none then build their hopes of salvation merely upon this: that they are church members. This you and I may be, and yet devils for all that (Matth. 8: 11–12—"Many shall come from the east and west, and shall sit down, etc. And however we may pass here, a true difference shall be made shortly, etc.").

Use 2. Let none then be stumbled at religion, because too often there are devils found among the saints. You see, here was a true church, sincere converts and sound believers; and yet here was a devil among them.

Use 3. Terror to hypocrites who profess much love to Christ but indeed are in league with their lusts, which they prefer above Christ. Oh! remember that you are devils in Christ's account. Christ is lightly esteemed of you, and you are vilely accounted for by Christ. Oh! if there be any such among us, forbear to come this day to the Lord's table, lest Satan enter more powerfully into you—lest while the bread be between your teeth, the wrath of the Lord come pouring down upon you (Psalm 78: 30–31). . . .

Use 5. Examine we ourselves well, what we are—what we church members are. We are either saints or devils: the Scripture gives us no medium. The Apostle tells us we are to examine ourselves (2 Cor. 13: 5). Oh! it is a dreadful thing to be a devil, and yet to sit down at the Lord's table (1 Cor. 10: 21). Such incur the hottest of God's wrath (as follows—v. 22). Now, if we would not be devils, we must give ourselves wholly up to Christ, and not suffer the predominancy of one lust—and particularly that of covetousness, which is made so light of, and which so sorely prevails in these perilous times. Why, this one lust made Judas a devil (John 12: 6, Matth. 26: 15). And no doubt it has made more devils than one. For a little pelf [money], men sell Christ to his enemies, and their souls to the devil. But there are certain sins that make us devils; see that we be not such:

1. A liar or murderer (John 8: 44)
2. A slanderer or an accuser of the godly
3. A tempter to sin
4. An opposer of godliness, as Elymos (Acts 13: 8 etc.)
5. Envious persons as witches
6. A drunkard (I Sam. 1: 15–16)
7. A proud person

Finis textus

7

◆

AN IMPERIAL PRESENCE

The Navigation Act of 1696 systematized various regulatory laws passed by Parliament during the preceding half-century. The act made clearer than ever the aim of British mercantilist policy: to advance the interests of English merchants, shippers, shipbuilders, and producers and to make England, not other parts of the Empire, wealthy. There were, to be sure, some benefits for Americans. The English government paid bounties to producers of naval stores and indigo in America and saw to it that American tobacco had a preferential position in England. The British navy, moreover, protected the colonies as well as the mother country. But there were disadvantages as well as advantages. Mercantilism hurt the northern colonies, which concentrated on shipping and trade, more than it did the southern colonies, which engaged primarily in agriculture, and American enterprisers, eager to forge ahead on their own, found British policies increasingly irksome.

Since earlier laws had been only loosely enforced, the Navigation Act of 1696 tried to address the enforcement problem directly by providing for a variety of inspection and customs officials and making clear which ports were legal for Imperial shippers and which were not. But in the first half of the eighteenth century Britain was engaged in wars with France and again failed to crack down on Americans who ignored the laws. After winning the French and Indian War in 1760 and taking over Canada from France by treaty in 1763, however, Britain turned its fullest attention to American economic activities. When Britain began to enact legislation (such as the Sugar Act of 1764 and the Stamp Act of 1765) that seemed designed to raise money as well as control trade, the reaction was violent. Americans denied that Britain had the right to regulate their economy and began calling for economic autonomy. American merchants moved increasingly to protest, evasion of the law, resistance, and, in the end, outright rebellion.

Questions to Consider. Some parts of the Navigation Act excerpted here deal mainly with trade routes and shipping. What specific English economic interests were addressed? If the Act had been passed seventy-five years earlier or seventy-five years later, do you think it would have contained the same provisions? Did these provisions reflect mainly the way the Empire was put together as of 1696 or mainly economic developments within England? The act contains several enforcement provisions. Of these, which ones were most likely to cause political trouble eventually? Might this act have been enforced without causing political trouble? Does this act, as some have argued, appear to contain the seeds of the American Revolution?

◆

The Navigation Act of 1696

II. Be it enacted . . . That after the five and twentieth day of March, 1698, no goods or merchandizes whatsoever shall be imported into, or exported out of, any colony or plantation to his Majesty, in Asia, Africa, or America, belonging, or in his possession,. . . or shall be laden in, or carried from any one port or place in the said colonies or plantations to any other port or place in the same [or] the kingdom of England . . . in any ship or bottom, but what is or shall be of the built of England, [or] Ireland, or the said colonies or plantations, and wholly owned by the people thereof, or any of them, and navigated with the masters and three fourths of the mariners of the said places only . . . under pain of forfeiture of ship and goods. . . .

VI. [And] be it further enacted . . . That the officers for the collecting and managing his Majesty's revenue, and inspecting the plantation trade, in any of the said plantations, shall have the same powers and authorities, for visiting and searching of ships, and taking their entries, and for seizing and securing or bringing on shore any of the goods prohibited to be imported or exported . . . or for which any duties are payable or ought to have been paid . . . as are provided for the officers of the customs in England [and also] to enter houses or warehouses, to search for and seize any such goods. . . .

IX. And it is further enacted . . . That all laws, by-laws, usages or customs, at this time, or which hereafter shall be in practice . . . in any of the said plantations, which are in any wise repugnant to the before mentioned laws, or any of them, so far as they do relate to the said plantations, or any of them, or which are any ways repugnant to this present act, or to any other law hereafter to be made in this kingdom, so far as such law shall relate to and mention the said plantations, are illegal, null and void. . . .

XIV. And whereas several ships and vessels laden with tobacco, sugars, and other goods of the growth and product of his Majesty's plantations in

From Danby Pickering, *The Statutes at Large from the Magna Charta to the End of the Eleventh Parliament of Great Britain, anno. 1761* (46 v., J. Bentham, Cambridge, 1806), 9: 428–430.

America, have been discharged in . . . Scotland and Ireland, contrary to the laws and statutes now in being, under pretence that the said ships and vessels were driven thither by stress of weather or for want of provisions . . . be it enacted . . . That from and after the first day of December, 1696, it shall not be lawful, on any pretence whatsoever, to put on shore in . . . Scotland or Ireland, any goods or merchandize of the growth or product of any of his Majesty's plantations aforesaid, unless the same shall have been first landed in the kingdom of England . . . and paid the rates and duties wherewith they are chargeable by law. . . .

XVI. And be it further enacted . . . That all persons and their assignees, claiming any right or propriety in any islands or tracts of land upon the continent of America, by charters or letters patents, shall not at any time hereafter aliene [transfer], sell or dispose of any of the said islands, tracts of lands or proprieties, other than to the natural-born subjects of England [and] Ireland . . . without the license and consent of his Majesty . . . ; and all governors nominated and appointed by any such persons or proprietors, who shall be entitled to make such nomination, shall be allowed and approved of by his Majesty . . . and shall take the oaths enjoined by this or any other act to be taken by the governors or commanders in chief in other of his Majesty's colonies and plantations, before their entering upon their respective governments, under the like penalty, as his Majesty's governors and commanders in chief are by the said acts liable to.

The break from England. A 1790 engraving of a Revolutionary leader reading the Declaration of Independence to a cluster of citizens in July, 1776. One man is tossing his tricorner hat in a cheer. Most listeners remain seriously intent as they digest this portentous news.

CHAPTER TWO

◆

Strides Toward Independence

8

◆

SELF-IMPROVEMENT

Benjamin Franklin was amazingly versatile. He was at various times printer, journalist, editor, educator, satirist, reformer, scientist, inventor, political activist, and diplomat. He was also a successful businessman. His printing business did so well that he was able to retire from active work while in his forties and devote the rest of his life to public service, humanitarian causes, and science and invention. His most famous and rewarding publication was *Poor Richard's Almanac,* which he published annually from 1733 to 1758. In addition to weather and astronomical information, Franklin's *Almanac* also printed mottoes and proverbs touting the virtues of diligence, temperance, moderation, and thrift. "Keep thy shop and thy shop will keep thee," advised Franklin. "Early to bed, and early to rise, makes a man healthy, wealthy, and wise." God, after all, "helps them that help themselves."

Franklin filled his *Almanac* with self-help proverbs because they were popular. But he also believed they worked. He himself had risen from the obscurity of working-class Boston to become a notable Pennsylvanian through self-discipline and improvement—by training himself to think clearly, speak correctly, and write elegantly and to labor diligently in his print shop.

Franklin believed the self-help maxims would work for communities as well as for individuals. He was the quintessential community organizer and was responsible for the establishment of Philadelphia's first public library and its first fire company. Among his other accomplishments were an academy that became the University of Pennsylvania and the first scientific society and the first hospital in British North America.

Perhaps Franklin's earliest civic initiative was an improvement society, the "Junto," whose members met each Friday to discuss some point of morals, politics, or science. The society's members, mostly young craftsmen, discussed each of the following twenty-four "standing queries" at every Junto meeting, with "a pause between each while one might fill and drink a glass of wine." Discussion must have been sober enough, however. From the Junto came numerous spin-off improvement societies, the library and other public projects, and, eventually, much of the civic leadership of eighteenth-century Pennsylvania.

Born in Boston in 1706, the son of a candlemaker, Benjamin Franklin was apprenticed at the age of twelve to his brother, a printer. At seventeen, having mastered the trade, Franklin ran away to Philadelphia and soon established a thriving printing establishment of his own. Not only did he become famous as a writer and publisher, he also represented the colonies in England from 1757 to 1775 and served as minister to France during the war for independence. For his pioneering work in the field of electricity, he was as famous in Europe as in America. In his *Autobiography,* which he wrote for his son in 1777, he dwelt on his early years, to make it, he said, "of more general use to young readers, as exemplifying strongly the effects of prudent and imprudent conduct in the commencement of a life of business." He remained active until his death in 1790, becoming president of the executive council of Pennsylvania at the age of seventy-nine and representing his state in the Constitutional Convention, which met in Philadelphia in 1787.

Questions to Consider. Why might young male workers who enjoyed a good time want to discuss "queries" of this kind at their meetings? Do the twenty-four queries seem to have been drawn up in any particular order? Which query strikes you as most interesting, surprising or absurd? Do organizations like the Junto exist today? Would the queries have to be amended to be useful today? What sort of society were the Junto members hoping to create? Was this a good way to create it?

◆

The Junto Queries (1729)

BENJAMIN FRANKLIN

Have you read over these queries this morning, in order to consider what you might have to offer the Junto touching any one of them viz:?

1. Have you met with anything in the author you last read, remarkable, or suitable to be communicated to the Junto, particularly in history, morality, poetry, physic, travels, mechanic arts, or other parts of knowledge?

2. What new story have you lately heard agreeable for telling in conversation?

3. Hath any citizen in your knowledge failed in his business lately, and what have you heard of the cause?

From John Bigelow, editor, *The Complete Works of Benjamin Franklin.* New York and London. G.P. Putnam & Sons, 1887. Volume I, ppg. 319–322.

Benjamin Franklin. Franklin as portrayed by a London painter in 1762, at the pinnacle of the Pennsylvanian's fame as a writer, scientist, and statesman. Franklin considered this an accurate likeness and ordered a hundred copies of an engraving taken from the portrait. (Portrait by Mason Chamberlain, 1762, oil on paper; The Mr. and Mrs. Wharton Sinkler Collection of The Philadelphia Museum of Art)

4. Have you lately heard of any citizen's thriving well, and by what means?

5. Have you lately heard how any present rich man, here or elsewhere, got his estate?

6. Do you know of a fellow-citizen, who has lately done a worthy action, deserving praise and imitation; or who has lately committed an error, proper for us to be warned against and avoid?

7. What unhappy effects of intemperance have you lately observed or heard; of imprudence, of passion, or of any other vice or folly?

8. What happy effects of temperance, prudence, of moderation, or of any other virtue?

9. Have you or any of your acquaintance been lately sick or wounded? if so, what remedies were used, and what were their effects?

10. Whom do you know that are shortly going on voyages or journeys, if one should have occasion to send by them?

11. Do you think of anything at present, in which the Junto may be serviceable to *mankind*, to their country, to their friends, or to themselves?

12. Hath any deserving stranger arrived in town since last meeting, that you have heard of?; and what have you heard or observed of his character or merits?; and whether, think you, it lies in the power of the Junto to oblige him, or encourage him as he deserves?

13. Do you know of any deserving young beginner lately set up, whom it lies in the power of the Junto anyway to encourage?

14. Have you lately observed any defect in the laws of your *country*, of which it would be proper to move the legislature for an amendment?; or do you know of any beneficial law that is wanting?

15. Have you lately observed any encroachment on the just liberties of the people?

16. Hath anybody attacked your reputation lately?; and what can the Junto do towards securing it?

17. Is there any man whose friendship you want, and which the Junto, or any of them, can procure for you?

18. Have you lately heard any member's character attacked, and how have you defended it?

19. Hath any man injured you, from whom it is in the power of the Junto to procure redress?

20. In what manner can the Junto or any of them, assist you in any of your honorable designs?

21. Have you any weighty affair on hand in which you think the advice of the Junto may be of service?

22. What benefits have you lately received from any man not present?

23. Is there any difficulty in matters of opinion, of justice, and injustice, which you would gladly have discussed at this time?

24. Do you see anything amiss in the present customs or proceedings of the Junto, which might be amended?

9

◆

A Right to Criticize

In 1735 came the first great battle over freedom of the press in America. Two years earlier, John Peter Zenger, publisher of the outspoken *New-York Weekly Journal,* began printing articles satirizing corruption and highhandedness in the administration of William Cosby, the new royal governor of New York, and he also distributed song sheets praising those who would "boldly despise the haughty knaves who keep us in awe." In 1734 Cosby arranged for Zenger to be arrested, charged with seditious libel, and thrown in prison. He also ordered copies of the *New-York Weekly Journal* burned in public. When Zenger's case came before the court in 1735, Andrew Hamilton, a prominent Philadelphian who was the most skillful lawyer in America, agreed to defend him. According to English law, a printed attack on a public official, even if true, was considered libelous; and the judge ruled that the fact that Zenger had criticized the New York governor was enough to convict him. But Hamilton argued that no one should be punished for telling the truth; Zenger, he pointed out, had told the truth and should not be convicted of libel. In "a free government," he insisted, the rulers should "not be able to stop the people's mouths when they feel themselves oppressed." Liberty, he added, is the "only bulwark against lawless power." Hamilton was so eloquent in his plea that in the end the jury voted "not guilty" and spectators in the courtroom cheered the verdict.

After his release, Zenger printed a complete account of the trial in his paper (some of which appears below) and also arranged to have it printed separately as a pamphlet. The report of the trial aroused great interest in Britain as well as in America and went through many editions. Hamilton's plea to the jury on behalf of "speaking and writing the truth" was one of the landmarks in the struggle for a free press in America. Though other royal judges did not accept the principle enunciated by Hamilton, the decision in the Zenger case did set an important precedent against judicial tyranny in libel suits. Gouverneur Morris, a statesman and diplomat from New York, called it "the morning star of that liberty which subsequently revolutionized America."

Zenger did not speak on his own behalf during the trial. But he had planned, if found guilty, to make a speech reminding the jurors that he and his parents had "fled from a country where oppression, tyranny, and arbitrary power had ruined almost all the people." Zenger, who was born in Germany in 1697, came to America, along with many other German immigrants, when he was twelve years old and was indentured to William Bradford, "the pioneer printer of the middle colonies." In 1726 he set up a printing shop of his own, publishing tracts and pamphlets mainly of a religious nature, and in 1730 he published the first arithmetic text in New York. A few years after his famous trial he became public printer for the colony of New York and a little later for New Jersey as well. He died in 1746.

Questions to Consider. In the following exchange between the prosecuting attorney and Hamilton, Zenger's lawyer, why did Hamilton place such emphasis on the word *false*? What complaint did he make about his effort to present evidence to the court on behalf of his client? What did he mean by saying that "the suppression of evidence ought always to be taken for the strongest evidence"? Why did he think Zenger's case was so important? Do you consider his final appeal to the jury a convincing one?

◆

John Peter Zenger's Libel Trial (1735)

Mr. Attorney. . . . The case before the court is whether Mr. Zenger is guilty of libeling His Excellency the Governor of New York, and indeed the whole administration of the government. Mr. Hamilton has confessed the printing and publishing, and I think nothing is plainer than that the words in the information [indictment] are scandalous, and tend to sedition, and to disquiet the minds of the people of this province. And if such papers are not libels, I think it may be said there can be no such thing as a libel.

Mr. Hamilton. May it please Your Honor, I cannot agree with Mr. Attorney. For though I freely acknowledge that there are such things as libels, yet I must insist, at the same time, that what my client is charged with is not a libel. And I observed just now that Mr. Attorney, in defining a libel, made use of the words "scandalous, seditious, and tend to disquiet the people." But (whether with design or not I will not say) he omitted the word "false."

Mr. Attorney. I think I did not omit the word "false." But it has been said already that it may be a libel, notwithstanding it may be true.

Mr. Hamilton. In this I must still differ with Mr. Attorney; for I depend upon it, we are to be tried upon this information now before the court and

From J. P. Zenger, *The Tryal of J. P. Z. of New York* (London, 1738), 10–17.

THE·TRIAL·OF·JOHN·PETER·ZENGER·FOR·LIBEL
RESULTING·IN·THE·VICTORY·FOR·FREE·PRESS·AUG·4·1735

The trial of John Peter Zenger. This tapestry depicts the New York courtroom in August 1735, when a jury acquitted the printer of a charge of libel. Crown officers and attorneys wore white-powdered wigs, as officials did in England, to emphasize their authority. Since imperial bureaucrats such as these not only were distant geographically from the real center of British power in London but also had to deal with obstreperous colonials such as Zenger, they may have taken even more care than their counterparts at home to keep their wigs white and imposing as symbols of British authority. (A Bicentennial Gift to America from a Grateful Armenian-American People, 1978, The Metropolitan Museum of Art) jury, and to which we have pleaded not guilty, and by it we are charged with printing and publishing a certain false, malicious, seditious, and scandalous libel. This word "false" must have some meaning, or else how came it there?. . .

Mr. Chief Justice. You cannot be admitted, Mr. Hamilton, to give the truth of a libel in evidence. A libel is not to be justified; for it is nevertheless a libel that it is true. . . .

Mr. Hamilton. I thank Your Honor. Then, gentlemen of the jury, it is to you we must now appeal, for witnesses, to the truth of the facts we have offered, and are denied the liberty to prove. And let it not seem strange that I apply myself to you in this manner. I am warranted so to do both by law and reason.

The law supposes you to be summoned out of the neighborhood where the fact [crime] is alleged to be committed; and the reason of your being taken out of the neighborhood is because you are supposed to have the best knowledge of the fact that is to be tried. And were you to find a verdict against my client, you must take upon you to say the papers referred to in the information, and which we acknowledge we printed and published, are false, scandalous, and seditious. But of this I can have no apprehension. You are citizens of New York; you are really what the law supposes you to be, honest and lawful men. And, according to my brief, the facts which we offer to prove were not committed in a corner; they are notoriously known to be true; and therefore in your justice lies our safety. And as we are denied the liberty of giving evidence to prove the truth of what we have published, I will beg leave to lay it down, as a standing rule in such cases, that the suppressing of evidence ought always to be taken for the strongest evidence; and I hope it will have weight with you. . . .

I hope to be pardoned, sir, for my zeal upon this occasion. It is an old and wise caution that when our neighbor's house is on fire, we ought to take care of our own. For though, blessed be God, I live in a government [Pennsylvania] where liberty is well understood, and freely enjoyed, yet experience has shown us all (I'm sure it has to me) that a bad precedent in one government is soon set up for an authority in another. And therefore I cannot but think it mine, and every honest man's duty, that (while we pay all due obedience to men in authority) we ought at the same time to be upon our guard against power, wherever we apprehend that it may affect ourselves or our fellow subjects.

I am truly very unequal to such an undertaking on many accounts. And you see I labor under the weight of many years, and am borne down with great infirmities of body. Yet old and weak as I am, I should think it my duty, if required, to go to the utmost part of the land, where my service could be of any use, in assist—to quench the flame of prosecutions upon informations, set on foot by the government, to deprive a people of the right of remonstrating (and complaining too) of the arbitrary attempts of men in power. Men who injure and oppress the people under their administration provoke them to cry out and complain; and then make that very complaint the foundation for new oppressions and prosecutions. I wish I could say there were no instances of this kind.

But to conclude. The question before the court and you, gentlemen of the jury, is not of small nor private concern. It is not the cause of a poor printer, nor of New York alone, which you are now trying. No! It may, in its consequence, affect every freeman that lives under a British government on the main[land] of America. It is the best cause. It is the cause of liberty. And I make no doubt but your upright conduct, this day, will not only entitle you to the love and esteem of your fellow citizens; but every man who prefers freedom to a life of slavery will bless and honor you, as men who have baffled the attempt of tyranny, and, by an impartial and un-corrupt verdict, have laid a noble foundation for securing to ourselves, our posterity, and our neighbors, that to which nature and the laws of our country have given us a right—the liberty both of exposing and opposing arbitrary power (in these parts of the world, at least) by speaking and writing truth. . . .

10

◆

THE GREAT AWAKENING

Jonathan Edwards was upset by the "extraordinary dullness in religion" he observed around him. During the first part of the eighteenth century, as the population of the colonies increased and Americans developed a thriving trade with other parts of the world, they became increasingly worldly in their outlook. It wasn't that they abandoned religion; what they abandoned was the stern, harsh religion that Edwards considered essential to salvation. Edwards, like John Winthrop, was a devout Puritan. He believed human beings were incorrigible sinners, filled with greed, pride, and lust, and that a just God had condemned them to eternal damnation for their transgressions. But God was merciful as well as just. Because Jesus had atoned for man's sins by dying on the cross, God agreed to shed his grace on some men and women and elect them for salvation. The individual who was chosen for salvation experienced God's grace while being converted. For Edwards the conversion experience was the greatest event in a person's life. After conversion, the individual dedicated himself to the glory of God and possessed a new strength to resist temptation.

In his sermons, Edwards, pastor of the Congregational church in Northampton, Massachusetts, tried to impress on people the awful fate that awaited them unless they acknowledged their sinfulness and threw themselves upon the mercy of God. During the last part of 1734 Edwards delivered a series of sermons that moved his congregation deeply. In them he gave such vivid descriptions of human depravity and the torments awaiting the unredeemed in the next world that people in the congregation wept, groaned, and begged for mercy. Edward's sermons produced scores of conversions. During the winter and spring over three hundred people were converted and admitted to full membership in the church. "This town," wrote Edwards joyfully, "never was so full of Love, nor so full of Joy, nor so full of distress as it has lately been." The religious revival that Edwards led in Northampton was only one of many revivals sweeping America at this time—in New England, in the Middle Colonies, and in the South. The Great Awakening, as the revivalist movement was called, affected the Presbyterians as well as the Congregationalists, and also swept through other denominations, keeping the churches in turmoil from about 1734 to 1756. The Great Awakening did produce a renewed interest in religion, but not always in Edwards's austere Puritanism. Edwards led revivals only in New England. George Whitefield, an English associate of John Wesley, the founder of Methodism, came to America, toured the colonies, and led revivals wherever he went. He helped make the Great Awakening an intercolonial movement. It was the first movement in which all the colonies participated before the American Revolution.

Edwards, who was born in East Windsor, Connecticut, in 1703, was a precocious lad. He wrote a treatise on spiders at age twelve and entered Yale College at age thirteen. The son of a Congregational minister, he experienced conversion as a young man, dedicated his life to the church, and pursued theological studies at Yale after graduation. In 1726 he became associate pastor of the Congregational church in Northampton, and in 1729 he was appointed pastor. For twenty-one years he labored hard in Northampton, studying, writing, and preaching; he also launched his ambitious plan for publishing treatises on all of the great Puritan doctrines. He wrote, too, a psychological analysis of the conversion experience, based on his study of the revivals that took place in Northampton and elsewhere. He delivered his famous sermon, "Sinners in the Hands of an Angry God" in Enfield, Connecticut, in 1741. In 1750 he took his family to Stockbridge, Massachusetts. There he spent the rest of his life, preaching and serving as missionary to the Native Americans. In 1758 he was appointed president of the College of New Jersey (Princeton), but he died of smallpox before beginning his duties there.

Questions to Consider. Edwards delivered his sermons in a quiet, though impassioned, tone of voice and looked at the back wall of the church, not the congregation, while preaching. How, then, was he able, in a sermon like "Sinners in the Hands of an Angry God," to arouse the rapt attention of the people? In what ways did he set forth the sovereignty of God, a prime doctrine of the Puritans? Do you think there is any inconsistency in his belief that only a few people (the elect) are saved and his insistence that everybody strive for salvation? In what ways might the Great Awakening have fostered antiestablishment, anti-imperial attitudes among the American colonists?

◆

Sinners in the Hands of an Angry God (1741)

JONATHAN EDWARDS

. . . This that you have heard is the case of every one of you that are out of Christ. That world of misery, that lake of burning brimstone, is extended abroad under you. There is the dreadful pit of the glowing flames of the wrath of God; there is hell's wide gaping mouth open; and you have nothing to stand upon, nor any thing to take hold of; there is nothing between you and hell but the air; 'tis only the power and mere pleasure of God that holds you up.

You probably are not sensible of this; you find you are kept out of hell, but don't see the hand of God in it, but look at other things, as the good state of your bodily constitution, your care of your own life, and the means you use for your own preservation. But indeed these things are nothing; if God should withdraw his hand, they would avail no more to keep you from falling, than the thin air to hold up a person that is suspended in it.

Your wickedness makes you as it were heavy as lead, and to tend downwards with great weight and pressure towards hell; and, if God should let you go, you would immediately sink, and swiftly descend and plunge into the bottomless gulf; and your healthy constitution, and your own care and prudence, and best contrivance, and all your righteousness, would have no more influence to uphold you and keep you out of hell, than a spider's web would have to stop a falling rock. Were it not that so is the sovereign pleasure of God, the earth would not bear you one moment; for you are a burden to it; the creation groans with you; the creation is made subject to the bondage of your corruption, not willingly; the sun don't willingly shine upon you, to give you light to serve sin and Satan; the earth don't willingly yield her increase to satisfy your lusts, nor is it willingly a stage for your wickedness to be acted upon; the air don't willingly serve you for breath to maintain the flame of life in your vitals, while you spend your life in the service of God's enemies. God's creatures are good, and were made for men to serve God with, and don't willingly subserve to any other purpose, and groan when they are abused to purposes so directly contrary to their nature and end. And the world would spue you out, were it not for the sovereign hand of him who hath subjected it in hope. There are the black clouds of God's wrath now hanging directly over your heads, full of the dreadful storm, and big with thunder; and, were it not for the restraining hand of God, it would immediately burst forth upon you. The

From Samuel Austin, ed., *The Works of President Edwards* (6 v., Isaiah Thomas, Worcester, 1808), II. 72–79.

sovereign pleasure of God for the present stays his rough wind; otherwise it would come with fury, and your destruction would come like a whirl-wind, and you would be like the chaff of the summer threshing-floor.

The wrath of God is like great waters that are dammed for the present; they increase more and more, and rise higher and higher, till an outlet is given; and the longer the stream is stopt, the more rapid and mighty is its course when once it is let loose. 'Tis true, that judgment against your evil works has not been executed hitherto; the floods of God's vengeance have been withheld; but your guilt in the mean time is constantly increasing, and you are every day treasuring up more wrath; the waters are continually rising, and waxing more and more mighty; and there is nothing but the mere pleasure of God that holds the waters back that are unwilling to be stopt, and press hard to go forward. If God should only withdraw his hand from the floodgate, it would immediately fly open, and the fiery floods of the fierceness and wrath of God would rush forth with inconceivable fury, and would come upon you with omnipotent power; and if your strength were ten thousand times greater than it is, yea ten thousand times greater than the strength of the stoutest, sturdiest, devil in hell, it would be nothing to withstand or endure it.

The bow of God's wrath is bent, and the arrow made ready on the string; and justice bends the arrow at your heart, and strains the bow; and it is nothing but the mere pleasure of God, and that of an angry God, without any promise or obligation at all, that keeps the arrow one moment from being made drunk with your blood.

Thus are all you that never passed under a great change of heart, by the mighty power of the spirit of God upon your souls; all that were never born again, and made new creatures, and raised from being dead in sin, to a state of new, and before altogether unexperienced light and life. How-ever you may have reformed your life in many things, and may have had religious affections, and may keep up a form of religion in your families and closets, and in the house of God, and may be strict in it, you are thus in the hands of an angry God; 'tis nothing but his mere pleasure that keeps you from being this moment swallowed up in everlasting destruction.

However unconvinced you may now be of the truth of what you hear, by and by you will be fully convinced of it. Those that are gone from being in the like circumstances with you, see that it was so with them; for de-struction came suddenly upon most of them, when they expected nothing of it, and while they were saying, peace and safety. Now they see, that those things that they depended on for peace and safety, were nothing but thin air and empty shadows.

The God that holds you over the pit of hell, much as one holds a spider or some loathesome insect over the fire, abhors you, and is dreadfully provoked; his wrath towards you burns like fire; he looks upon you as worthy of nothing else but to be cast into the fire; he is of purer eyes than to bear to have you in his sight; you are ten thousand times so abominable in his eyes as the most hateful venomous serpent is in ours. You have offended him infinitely more than ever a stubborn rebel did his prince; and yet 'tis nothing but his hand that holds you from falling into the fire every moment. 'Tis to be ascribed to nothing else, that you did not go to hell the last night; that you was suffered to awake again in this world, after you closed your eyes to sleep. And there is no other reason to be given why you have not dropt into hell since you arose in the morning, but that God's hand has held you up. There is no other reason to be given why you haven't gone to hell since you have sat here in the House of God, provoking his pure eyes by your sinful wicked manner of attending his solemn worship; yea, there is nothing else that is to be given as a reason why you don't this very moment drop down into hell.

O Sinner! Consider the fearful danger you are in. 'Tis a great furnace of wrath, a wide and bottomless pit, full of the fire of wrath, that you are held over in the hand of that God, whose wrath is provoked and incensed as much against you as against many of the damned in hell. You hang by a slender thread, with the flames of divine wrath flashing about it, and ready every moment to singe it, and burn it asunder; and you have no interest in any mediator, and nothing to lay hold of to save yourself, nothing to keep off the flames of wrath, nothing of your own, nothing that you ever have done, nothing that you can do, to induce God to spare you one moment. . . .

How dreadful is the state of those that are daily and hourly in danger of this great wrath, and infinite misery! But this is the dismal case of every soul in this congregation that has not been born again, however moral and strict, sober and religious they may otherwise be. Oh that you would consider it, whether you be young or old! There is reason to think, that there are many in this congregation, now hearing this discourse, that will actually be the subjects of this very misery to all eternity. We know not who they are, or in what seats they sit, or what thoughts they now have. It may be they are now at ease, and hear all these things without much disturbance, and are now flattering themselves that they shall escape. If we knew that there was one person, and but one, in the whole congregation, that was to be the subject of this misery, what an awful thing would it be to think of! If we knew who it was, what an awful sight would it be to see such a person! How might all the rest of the congregation lift up a lamentable and bitter cry over him! But alas! instead of one, how many is it likely will remember this discourse in hell? And it would be a wonder if some that are now present should not be in hell in a very short time, before this year is out; and it would be no wonder if some person that now sits here in some seat of this meeting-house, in health, and quiet and secure, should be there before to-morrow morning.

11

♦

MULTIPLICITY AND ABUNDANCE

Between 1749 and 1754 more than thirty thousand Germans came to Pennsylvania. Soon they came to constitute about one-third of the colony's population. Most Germans coming to America at this time were indentured servants (that is, they were contracted to work for a master for a certain period of time before striking off on their own). They were also known as "redemptioners." To pay for the trip across the Atlantic they sold their labor for a period of two to seven years. On reaching America they "redeemed" themselves by working for a farmer or merchant until they had paid off the debt they had contracted. Slaves were scarce in Pennsylvania, and there was a great demand for redemptioners to work as farm laborers, skilled craftsmen, and domestic servants. Unfortunately, there was much skullduggery in the redemption system. Although redemptioners from England received written contracts or indentures specifying the service they owed, German immigrants received only verbal assurances from shipmasters and merchants as to their future obligations. Once they reached America their labor was auctioned off to the highest bidder, they had nothing to say about their terms of service, and they were often exploited.

Gottlieb Mittelberger, a native of Württemberg, arrived in Philadelphia late in 1750. He was one of about five hundred passengers aboard the ship *Osgood*. Mittelberger settled in a German community not far from Philadelphia and became organist and schoolmaster there. But less than four years later he returned to Germany, where he spent the rest of his life. In 1756 he published a little volume entitled *Journey to Pennsylvania* describing life in the New World. He filled his book with statistics, geographical information, and anecdotes, but he also had much to say about conditions among German immigrants like himself in America.

Mittelberger was especially critical of "Newlanders" (agents of shipmasters charged with recruiting redemptioners) who traveled about Germany exaggerating the opportunities for immigrants in the "New Land." Not only was Mittelberger distressed by the exploitation of the redemptioners, he was also bothered by the disregard for rank in Pennsylvania, by the laxity in religion, and by the free and easy manners of the back-country Pennsylvanians whom he encountered. Immigrants from Germany belonged to a variety of religious sects, and in Pennsylvania they were free to practice their religion as they pleased. Mittelberger was struck by the bounteous freedom which the colony offered its inhabitants, but feared it might jeopardize social stability. Mittelberger's book did not stop the flow of Germans to America. Though conditions in America were not as glorious as the Newlanders portrayed them, life was still considerably better there than in Germany, which was ravaged by war, famine, and poverty.

Questions to Consider. In the following extract from *Journey to Pennsylvania* Mittelberger recorded his observations of religious and economic life in Pennsylvania in the early 1750s. What impressed him the most about religion in the colony? Did he entirely approve of it? How much economic freedom did he find in the colony? How much opportunity to get ahead did he think existed there? What comments did he make on the size of America as compared with that of Europe? Do you think his overall impression of America was a favorable one?

◆

Journey to Pennsylvania (1756)

GOTTLIEB MITTELBERGER

In Pennsylvania there exist so many varieties of doctrines and sects that it is impossible to name them all. Many people do not reveal their own particular beliefs to anyone. Furthermore there are many hundreds of adults who not only are unbaptized, but who do not even want baptism. Many others pay no attention to the Sacraments and to the Holy Bible, or even to God and His Word. Some do not even believe in the existence of a true God or Devil, Heaven or Hell, Salvation or Damnation, the Resurrection of the Dead, the Last Judgment and Eternal Life, but think that everything visible is of merely natural origin. For in Pennsylvania not only is everyone allowed to believe what he wishes; he is also at liberty to express these beliefs publicly and freely.

Thus when young people not raised in the fundamentals of religion must go into service for many years with such freethinkers and unbelievers and are not permitted by these people to attend any church or school, especially when they live far away from them, then such innocent souls do not reach a true knowledge of the Divine and are brought up like heathen or Indians. . . .

Reprinted by permission of the publishers from *Journey to Pennsylvania* by Gottlieb Mittelberger, trans. & ed. by Oscar Handlin, Cambridge, Mass.: The Belknap Press of Harvard University Press, Copyright © 1960 by the President and Fellows of Harvard College.

Philadelphia. A view of the city in 1754, when the "City of Brotherly Love," still dominated by Quaker merchants, was the most flourishing commercial center of British North America. (Courtesy Historical Society of Pennsylvania)

   To come back to Pennsylvania again. It offers people more freedom than the other English colonies, since all religious sects are tolerated there. One can encounter Lutherans, members of the Reformed Church, Catholics, Quakers, Mennonites or Anabaptists, Herrenhüter or Moravian Brothers, Pietists, Seventh-Day Adventists, Dunkers, Presbyterians, New-born, Freemasons, Separatists, Freethinkers, Jews, Mohammedans, Pagans, Negroes, and Indians. But the Evangelicals and the Reformed constitute the majority. There are several hundred unbaptized people who don't even wish to be baptized. Many pray neither in the morning nor in the evening, nor before or after meals. In the homes of such people are not to be found any devotional books, much less a Bible. It is possible to meet in one house, among one family, members of four or five or six different sects.

Freedom in Pennsylvania extends so far that everyone's property—commercial, real estate, and personal possessions—is exempt from any interference or taxation. For owning a hundred morgen [Dutch unit of land] one is assessed an annual tax of not more than one English shilling. This is called ground-rent or quit-rent. One shilling is worth approximately eighteen kreuzer in German money. What is peculiar is that single men and women must pay two to five shillings annually, in proportion to their earnings, the reason for this being that they have none but themselves to look after. In Philadelphia the money raised in this way is used to purchase lights by which the streets of the city are illuminated every night. . . .

In Pennsylvania no profession or craft needs to constitute itself into a guild. Everyone may engage in any commercial or speculative ventures, according to choice and ability. And if someone wishes or is able to carry on ten occupations at one and the same time, then nobody is allowed to prevent it. And if, for example, a lad learns his skill or craft as an apprentice or even on his own, he can then pass for a master and may marry whenever he chooses. It is an admirable thing that young people born in this new country are easily taught, clever, and skillful. For many of them have only to look at and examine a work of skill or art a few times before being able to imitate it perfectly. Whereas in Germany it would take most people several years of study to do the same. But in America many have the ability to produce even the most elaborate objects in a short span of time. When these young people have attended school for half a year, they are generally able to read anything.

The province of Pennsylvania is a healthy one; for the most part it has good soil, good air and water, lots of high mountains, and lots of flat land. There are many woods, and where these are not inhabited, there is natural forest through which flow many small and large rivers. The land is also very fertile, and all kinds of grain flourish.

The province is well populated, inhabited far and wide, and various new towns have been founded here and there, namely Philadelphia, Germantown, Lancaster, Reading, Bethlehem, and New Frankfort. Many churches have also been built in this region, but it takes a great many people two, three, four, five, and up to ten hours to get to church. But everyone, men and women, ride to church on horseback, even though they could walk the distance in half an hour. This is also customary at weddings and funerals. At times at such formal country weddings or funerals, it is possible to count up to four hundred or five hundred persons on horseback. One can easily imagine that on such occasions, just as at Holy Communion, nobody appears in black crepe or in a black cloak. . . .

Concerning the size of America, people in Pennsylvania say that this part of the world is supposed to be far larger than Europe, and that it would be impossible to explore it completely on account of the lack of roads, and because of the forests, and the rivers, great and small. Pennsylvania is not an island, as some simpletons in Germany believe it to be. I took the opportunity of talking about the size of this part of the world with an English traveler, who had been with the savages far inland. He told me that he had been with the Indians in the country, trading for skins and furs, more than 700 miles from Philadelphia, that is a journey of 233 Swabian [Swabia = German duchy] hours. He had spoken about this topic with a very aged Indian who gave him to understand in English that he and his brother had at one time traveled straight across the country and through the bush toward the setting sun, starting out from the very place where the meeting with the English traveler took place. And according to their calculations they had journeyed 1,600 English miles. But when they realized that they had no hope of reaching the end of the country they had turned back again. . . .

In the province of Pennsylvania three principal roads have been constructed, all of which lead from Philadelphia into the country as far as it is inhabited. The first runs from Philadelphia to the right hand by the Delaware to New Frankfort; the second or middle road runs toward Germantown, Reading, and Tulpehocken, extending across the Blue Mountains; the third road runs to the left toward Lancaster and Bethlehem, where there is a monastery and convent full of Dunker Brethren and Sisters. The men do not shave their beards; many among them have beards half an ell [an old English unit of length] in length. They wear cowls like the Capuchin monks, in winter of the same cloth or at least the same color, in summer, however, of fine white linen. The Sisters dress in the same manner. These people are not baptized until they are grown up and can testify to their faith, when it is done by dunking in deep water. They keep Saturdays instead of Sundays as holidays. Their convent Sisters, however, frequently bring forth living fruit with much patience.

12

♦

A SHATTERED EMPIRE

On June 7, 1776, Richard Henry Lee, delegate from Virginia to the Second Continental Congress meeting in Philadelphia, proposed a resolution calling for independence from Great Britain. Three days later Congress appointed a committee of five to prepare a statement giving reasons for independence. The committee appointed a sub-committee, consisting of John Adams and Thomas Jefferson, to draft such a statement. The subcommittee met, according to Adams, and Jefferson suggested that Adams write up a statement. "I will not," said Adams emphatically. "You should do it," said Jefferson. "Oh, no," persisted Adams. "Why will you not?" asked Jefferson. "You ought to do it." "I will not," said Adams stubbornly. "Why?" cried Jefferson. "Reasons enough," said Adams. "What can be your reasons?" Jefferson wanted to know. Explained Adams: "Reason first—you are a Virginian, and a Virginian ought to appear at the head of this business. Reason second—I am obnoxious, suspected, and unpopular. You are very much otherwise. Reason third—you can write ten times better than I can." "Well," said Jefferson, "if you are decided, I will do as well as I can." In the end, Jefferson wrote the Great Declaration, minor changes being made by Adams and Benjamin Franklin, and after the Continental Congress made some additional changes in it, the delegates voted to adopt it on July 4. Two days earlier Congress had accepted Lee's resolution for independence. But July 4, not July 2, soon became the great day for patriotic celebrations.

Jefferson's "peculiar felicity of expression," according to John Adams, made him the ideal choice for writing the Declaration. In simple, lucid, logical language, Jefferson explained to the world what he thought the American people were fighting for: to establish a government based not on force and fraud, but on the freely given consent of the people and dedicated to safeguarding the basic rights of all citizens. Jefferson's Declaration made it clear that the American Revolution was more than a fight for independence. "Take away from the Declaration of Independence its self-evident truths," said Adams, "and you rob the North American Revolution of all its moral principles, and proclaim it a foul and unnatural rebellion." After the United States achieved its independence in 1783, the Declaration continued to inspire countless reformers seeking to make their country a better place in which to live: abolitionists, feminists, farmers, and working people. The Declaration also influenced reformers and revolutionaries in other parts of the world—Europe, Asia, and Africa—during the nineteenth and twentieth centuries.

Questions to Consider. In 1858, when Massachusetts lawyer Rufus Choate contemptuously dismissed the Declaration as a collection of "glittering generalities," Ralph Waldo Emerson exclaimed indignantly: "Glittering generalities! Say, rather, blazing ubiquities!" Do you agree with Choate or with Emerson? What are the main generalities set forth in the first two paragraphs of the Declaration? How valid do you think Jefferson's assertions are about equality, "unalienable Rights," and the right of the people to "alter or abolish" their governments? What were Jefferson's major charges against King George III? Do you think he was successful in his attempt to make a long list of abuses and usurpations by the king? Why did he attack the king and avoid any mention of Parliament? What did he say about the English people and why? Do you find any inconsistencies or omissions in the Declaration?

---◆---

The Declaration of Independence (1776)

THOMAS JEFFERSON

When in the Course of human events, it becomes necessary for one people to dissolve the political bands which have connected them with another, and to assume among the Powers of the earth, the separate and equal station to which the Laws of Nature and of Nature's God entitle them, a decent respect to the opinions of mankind requires that they should declare the causes which impel them to the separation.

We hold these truths to be self-evident, that all men are created equal, that they are endowed by their Creator with certain unalienable Rights, that among these are Life, Liberty and the pursuit of Happiness. That to secure these rights, Governments are instituted among Men, deriving their just powers from the consent of the governed. That whenever any Form of Government becomes destructive of these ends, it is the Right of the People to alter or to abolish it, and to institute new Government, laying its foundation on such principles and organizing its powers in such form, as to them shall seem most likely to effect their Safety and Happiness.

From F. N. Thorpe, ed., *The Federal and State Constitutions* (7 v., Government Printing Office, Washington, D.C., 1909), I: 3.

Prudence, indeed, will dictate that Governments long established should not be changed for light and transient causes; and accordingly all experience hath shown, that mankind are more disposed to suffer, while evils are sufferable, than to right themselves by abolishing the forms to which they are accustomed. But when a long train of abuses and usurpations, pursuing invariably the same Object evinces a design to reduce them under absolute Despotism, it is their right, it is their duty, to throw off such Government, and to provide new Guards for their future security.—Such has been the patient sufferance of these Colonies; and such is now the necessity which constrains them to alter their former Systems of Government. The history of the present King of Great Britain is a history of repeated injuries and usurpations, all having in direct object the establishment of an absolute Tyranny over these States. To prove this, let Facts be submitted to a candid world.

He has refused his Assent to Laws, the most wholesome and necessary for the public good.

He has forbidden his Governors to pass Laws of immediate and pressing importance, unless suspended in their operation till his Assent should be obtained; and when so suspended, he has utterly neglected to attend to them.

He has refused to pass other Laws for the accommodation of large districts of people, unless those people would relinquish the rights of Representation in the Legislature, a right inestimable to them and formidable to tyrants only.

He has called together legislative bodies at places unusual, uncomfortable, and distant from the depository of their Public Records, for the sole purpose of fatiguing them into compliance with his measures.

He has dissolved Representative Houses repeatedly, for opposing with manly firmness his invasions on the rights of the people.

He has refused for a long time, after such dissolutions, to cause others to be elected; whereby the Legislative Powers, incapable of Annihilation, have returned to the People at large for their exercise; the State remaining in the mean time exposed to all the dangers of invasion from without, and convulsions within.

He has endeavored to prevent the population of these States; for that purpose obstructing the Laws of Naturalization of Foreigners; refusing to pass others to encourage their migration hither, and raising the conditions of new Appropriations of Lands.

He has obstructed the Administration of Justice, by refusing his Assent to Laws for establishing Judiciary Powers.

He has made Judges dependent on his Will alone, for the tenure of their offices, and the amount and payment of their salaries.

He has erected a multitude of New Offices, and sent hither swarms of Officers to harass our People, and eat out their substance.

He has kept among us, in times of peace, Standing Armies without the Consent of our legislature.

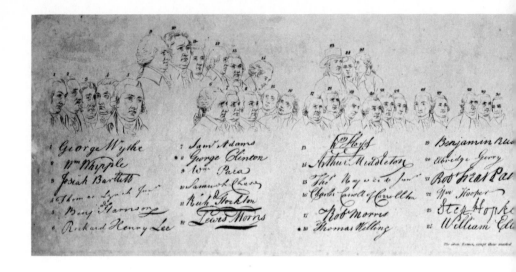

The signatures of the Declaration of Independence. (Print Collection, Miriam and Ira D. Wallach Division of Art, Prints and Photographs, The New York Public Library)

He has affected to render the Military independent of and superior to the Civil Power.

He has combined with others to subject us to a jurisdiction foreign to our constitution, and unacknowledged by our laws; giving his Assent to their acts of pretended legislation:

For quartering large bodies of armed troops among us:

For protecting them, by a mock Trial, from Punishment for any Murders which they should commit on the Inhabitants of these States:

For cutting off our Trade with all parts of the world:

For imposing taxes on us without our Consent:

For depriving us in many cases, of the benefits of Trial by Jury:

For transporting us beyond Seas to be tried for pretended offences:

For abolishing the free System of English Laws in a neighbouring Province, establishing therein an Arbitrary government, and enlarging its Boundaries so as to render it at once an example and fit instrument for introducing the same absolute rule into these Colonies:

For taking away our Charters, abolishing our most valuable Laws, and altering fundamentally the Forms of our Governments:

For suspending our own Legislature, and declaring themselves invested with Power to legislate for us in all cases whatsoever.

He has abdicated Government here, by declaring us out of his Protection and waging War against us.

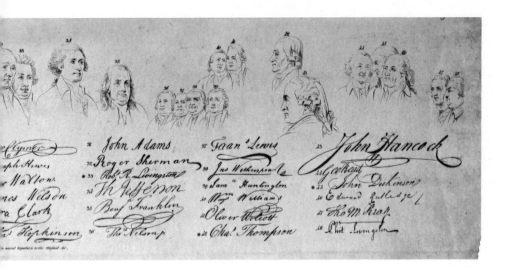

He has plundered our seas, ravaged our Coasts, burnt our towns, and destroyed the lives of our people.

He is at this time transporting large armies of foreign mercenaries to complete the works of death, desolation and tyranny, already begun with circumstances of Cruelty & perfidy scarcely paralleled in the most barbarous ages, and totally unworthy the Head of a civilized nation.

He has constrained our fellow Citizens taken Captive on the high Seas to bear Arms against their Country, to become the executioners of their friends and Brethren, or to fall themselves by their Hands.

He has excited domestic insurrections amongst us, and has endeavoured to bring on the inhabitants of our frontiers, the merciless Indian Savages, whose known rule of warfare, is an undistinguished destruction of all ages, sexes and conditions.

In every state of these Oppressions We have Petitioned for Redress in the most humble terms: Our repeated Petitions have been answered only be repeated injury. A Prince, whose character is thus marked by every act which may define a Tyrant, is unfit to be the ruler of a free People.

Nor have We been wanting in attention to our British brethren. We have warned them from time to time of attempts by their legislature to extend an unwarrantable jurisdiction over us. We have reminded them of the circumstances of our emigration and settlement here. We have appealed to their native justice and magnanimity, and we have conjured them by the ties of our common kindred to disavow these usurpations, which would inevitably interrupt our connections and correspondence. They too have been deaf to the voice of justice and of consanguinity. We must, therefore, acquiesce in the necessity, which denounces our Separation, and hold them, as we hold the rest of mankind, Enemies in War, in Peace Friends.

We, therefore, the Representatives of the united States of America, in General Congress, Assembled, appealing to the Supreme Judge of the world for the rectitude of our intentions, do, in the Name, and by Authority of the good People of these Colonies, solemnly publish and declare, That these United Colonies are, and of Right ought to be Free and Independent States; that they are Absolved from all Allegiance to the British Crown, and that all political connection between them and the State of Great Britain, is and ought to be totally dissolved; and that as Free and Independent States, they have full Power to levy War, conclude Peace, contract Alliances, establish Commerce, and to do all other Acts and Things which Independent States may of right do. And for the support of this Declaration, with a firm reliance on the Protection of Divine Providence, we mutually pledge to each other our Lives, our Fortunes and our Sacred Honor.

13

◆

IDEOLOGY AND AGITATION

On December 18, 1776, George Washington wrote his brother discouragingly: "Between you and me, I think our affairs are in a very bad situation. . . . If every nerve is not strained up to the utmost to recruit the new army with all possible expedition, I think the game is up." A few days later Thomas Paine published the first number of *The Crisis,* a pamphlet calling attention to the heartbreaking difficulties the Americans faced in their struggle with Britain and appealing for renewed dedication to the Revolutionary cause. Paine said he wrote in "a passion of patriotism." His essay quickly "rallied and reanimated" the people, according to one observer, and before long "hope succeeded to despair, cheerfulness to gloom, and firmness to irresolution." In twelve more issues of *The Crisis* Paine continued his impassioned fight against apathy, indifference, and defeatism in American ranks. He wrote additional numbers about American problems after the Yorktown victory in 1781.

Paine, a British corset maker and excise officer, was an ardent supporter of the American cause from almost the beginning. Shortly after arriving in Philadelphia in November 1774, he became editor of the *Pennsylvania Magazine,* discovered he had great gifts as a journalist, and in January 1776 published a little pamphlet entitled *Common Sense,* urging Americans to convert their resistance to British oppression into a fight for national independence. Before long thousands of copies of his pamphlet were circulating in the colonies and Washington arranged to have passages from it read to his troops. The first best-seller in history, *Common Sense* persuaded many Americans who were wavering that separation from Britain was both possible and desirable.

Paine pioneered in a new kind of journalism. He avoided the elegant and ornate kind of writing fashionable in aristocratic circles and wrote simply, naturally, and forcefully. He used homely metaphors, introduced everyday words and phrases into his essays, translated foreign phrases for his readers, interspersed his logical arguments with lively anecdotes, and brought a sense of immediacy to his writings by including personal, on-the-spot reports. He was, in short, writing for the plain people from whom he himself had come. His influence on the thinking of countless people was enormous.

Paine, born in England of Quaker parents in 1737, lived in obscurity until he came to America in 1774. He became editor of the *Pennsylvania Magazine* and quickly identified himself with the American cause. After the American Revolution he went to France, supported the revolution that broke out there in 1789, and published *The Rights of Man* (1791–1792), a work defending the principles of the French Revolution. He also wrote *The Age of Reason* (1793–1795), criticizing both atheism and orthodox Christianity and calling for a religion based on reason. Though sympathetic to the French Revolution, Paine opposed the execution of King Louis XVI and was appalled by the Reign of Terror that accompanied the Revolution. In the end he was thrown in prison and sentenced to the guillotine; but he was saved by the intervention of the American minister in France, James Monroe. In 1802 he returned to America; but his attacks on George Washington while in France and his religious radicalism made him an outcast. He died in New York, lonely, poverty-stricken, and largely forgotten, in 1809.

Questions to Consider. Paine is eminently quotable. Do you find any passages in the essay below that seem especially eloquent? Do you think Paine's appeal rests on substance as well as style? How did he attempt to whip up enthusiasm for the American cause despite reverses on the battlefield? Do you think his handling of Tories, that is, Americans who were sympathetic to Britain, was effective? Do you think he was just to the Loyalists, to King George III, and to General William Howe? Were his appeals to God likely to impress religious people in America? What parts of the essay do you think George Washington chose to have read to his troops?

◆

The Crisis, Number One (1776)

THOMAS PAINE

These are the times that try men's souls. The summer soldier and the sunshine patriot will, in this crisis, shrink from the service of his country; but he that stands it NOW, deserves the love and thanks of man and woman. Tyranny, like hell, is not easily conquered; yet we have this consolation with us, that the harder the conflict, the more glorious the triumph. What we obtain too cheap, we esteem too lightly: 'Tis dearness only that gives every thing its value. Heaven knows how to put a proper price upon

From Daniel E. Wheeler, ed., *Life and Writings of Thomas Paine* (10 v., V. Parke and Co., New York, 1915), III: 1–16.

Destruction of the Royal Statue in New York City. The passions of the Revolutionary era, fanned by the writings of Tom Paine and other propagandists, led to the systematic destruction of symbols of British authority, including this gilded lead statue of George III in New York. The Americans later molded the lead into bullets. The engraving, in an unintended irony, shows African slaves doing the actual work of destruction as their masters, patriots all, look complacently on. In fact, militiamen and other free citizens performed the deed.

its goods; and it would be strange indeed, if so celestial an article as FREEDOM should not be highly rated. Britain, with an army to enforce her tyranny, has declared that she has a right (*not only to* TAX) but "*to* BIND *us in* ALL CASES WHATSOEVER," and if being *bound in that manner*, is not slavery, then is there not such a thing as slavery upon earth. Even the expression is impious, for so unlimited a power can belong only to GOD. . . .

I have as little superstition in me as any man living, but my secret opinion has ever been, and still is, that God Almighty will not give up a people to military destruction, or leave them unsupportedly to perish, who had so earnestly and so repeatedly sought to avoid the calamities of war, by every decent method which wisdom could invent. Neither have I so much of the infidel in me, as to suppose that HE has relinquished the government of the world, and given us up to the care of devils; and as I do not, I cannot see on what grounds the king of Britain can look up to Heaven for help against us: A common murderer, a highwayman, or a house-breaker has a good a pretence as he. . . .

I shall not now attempt to give all the particulars of our retreat to the Delaware; suffice it for the present to say, that both officers and men, though greatly harassed and fatigued, frequently without rest, covering, or provision, the inevitable consequences of a long retreat, bore it with a manly and a martial spirit. All their wishes were one, which was, that the country would turn out and help them to drive the enemy back. Voltaire has remarked that King William never appeared to full advantage but in difficulties and in action; the same remark may be made on George Washington, for the character fits him. There is a natural firmness in some minds which cannot be unlocked by trifles, but which, when unlocked, discovers a cabinet of fortitude; and I reckon it among those kind of public blessings, which we do not immediately see, that GOD hath blest him with uninterrupted health, and given him a mind that can even flourish upon care.

I shall conclude this paper with some miscellaneous remarks on the state of our affairs; and shall begin with asking the following question, Why is it that the enemy have left the New-England provinces, and made these middle ones the seat of war? The answer is easy: New-England is not infested with tories, and we are. I have been tender in raising the cry against these men, and used numberless arguments to shew them their danger, but it will not do to sacrifice a world to either their folly or their baseness. The period is now arrived, in which either they or we must change our sentiments, or one or both must fall. And what is a tory? Good GOD! what is he? I should not be afraid to go with an hundred whigs against a thousand tories, were they to attempt to get into arms. Every tory is a coward, for a servile, slavish, self-interested fear is the foundation of toryism; and a man under such influence, though he may be cruel, never can be brave.

But, before the line of irrecoverable separation be drawn between us, let us reason the matter together: Your conduct is an invitation to the enemy, yet not one in a thousand of you has heart enough to join him. [General William] Howe is as much deceived by you as the American cause is injured by you. He expects you will all take up arms, and flock to his standard with muskets on your shoulders. Your opinions are of no use to him, unless you support him personally, for 'tis soldiers, and not tories, that he wants.

I once felt all that kind of anger, which a man ought to feel, against the mean principles that are held by the tories: A noted one, who kept a tavern at Amboy, was standing at his door, with as pretty a child in his hand, about eight or nine years old, as most I ever saw, and after speaking his mind as freely as he thought was prudent, finished with this unfatherly expression, *"Well! give me peace in my day."* Not a man lives on the continent but fully believes that a separation must some time or other finally take place, and a generous parent should have said, *"If there must be trouble, let it be in my day that my child may have peace;"* and this single reflection, well applied, is sufficient to awaken every man to duty. Not a place upon earth might be so happy as America. Her situation is remote from all the wrangling world, and she has nothing to do but to trade with them. A man may easily distinguish in himself between temper and principle, and I am as confident, as I am that GOD governs the world, that America will never be happy till she gets clear of foreign dominion. Wars, without ceasing, will break out till that period arrives, and the continent must in the end be conqueror; for though the flame of liberty may sometimes cease to shine, the coal never can expire. . . .

Not all the treasures of the world, so far as I believe, could have induced me to support an offensive war, for I think it murder; but if a thief break into my house, burn and destroy my property, and kill or threaten to kill me, or those that are in it, and to *"bind me in all cases whatsoever,"* to his absolute will, am I to suffer it? What signifies it to me, whether he who does it, is a king or a common man; my countryman or not my countryman? whether it is done by an individual villain, or an army of them? If we reason to the root of things we shall find no difference; neither can any just cause be assigned why we should punish in the one case and pardon in the other. Let them call me rebel, and welcome. I feel no concern from it; but I should suffer the misery of devils, were I to make a whore of my soul by swearing allegiance to one whose character is that of a sottish, stupid, stubborn, worthless, brutish man. I conceive likewise a horrid idea in receiving mercy from a being, who at the last day shall be shrieking to the rocks and mountains to cover him, and fleeing with terror from the orphan, the widow, and the slain of America.

There are cases which cannot be overdone by language, and this is one. There are persons too who see not the full extent of the evil which threatens them, they solace themselves with hopes that the enemy, if they succeed, will be merciful. It is the madness of folly to expect mercy from those who have refused to do justice; and even mercy, where conquest is the object, is only a trick of war: The cunning of the fox is as murderous as the violence of the wolf; and we ought to guard equally against both. Howe's first object is partly by threats and partly by promise, to terrify or seduce the people to deliver up their arms, and receive mercy. The ministry recommended the same plan to [General Thomas] Gage, and this is what the tories call making their peace: *" a peace which passeth all understanding"* indeed! A peace which would be the immediate forerunner of a worse ruin than any we have yet thought of. Ye men of Pennsylvania, do reason upon these things! Were the back counties to give up their arms, they would fall an easy prey to the Indians, who are all alarmed. This perhaps is what some tories would not be sorry for. Were the home counties to deliver up their arms, they would be exposed to the resentment of the back counties, who would then have it in their power to chastise their defection at pleasure. And were any one state to give up its arms, THAT state must be garrisoned by all Howe's army of Britons and Hessians to preserve it from the anger of the rest. Mutual fear is a principal link in the chain of mutual love, and woe be to that state that breaks the compact. Howe is mercifully inviting you to barbarous destruction, and men must be either rogues or fools that will not see it. I dwell not upon the powers of imagination; I bring reason to your ears; and in language as plain as A, B, C, hold up truth to your eyes.

I thank GOD that I fear not. I see no real cause for fear. I know our situation well, and can see the way out of it. While our army was collected, Howe dared not risk a battle, and it is no credit to him that he decamped from the White Plains, and waited a mean opportunity to ravage the defenceless Jerseys; but it is great credit to us, that, with a handful of men, we sustained an orderly retreat for near an hundred miles, brought off our ammunition, all our field-pieces, the greatest part of our stores, and had four rivers to pass. None can say that our retreat was precipitate, for we were near three weeks in performing it, that the country might have time to come in. Twice we marched back to meet the enemy and remained out till dark. The sign of fear was not seen in our camp, and had not some of the cowardly and disaffected inhabitants spread false alarms through the country, the Jerseys had never been ravaged. Once more we are again collected and collecting; our new army at both ends of the continent is recruiting fast, and we shall be able to open the next campaign with sixty thousand men, well armed and cloathed. This is our situation, and who will may know it. By perseverance and fortitude we have the prospect of a glorious issue; by cowardice and submission, the sad choice of a variety of evils—a ravaged country—a depopulated city—habitations without safety, and slavery without hope—our homes turned into barracks and bawdy-houses for Hessians, and a future race to provide for whose fathers we shall doubt of. Look on this picture and weep over it! and if there yet remains one thoughtless wretch who believes it not, let him suffer it unlamented.

14
◆

SECURING LIBERTY

In May 1787 delegates from every state except Rhode Island met in Philadelphia to revise the Articles of Confederation. But they disregarded their instructions; by mid-September they had drawn up an entirely new frame of government for the nation that had achieved its independence in 1783. The Constitutional Convention was a distinguished gathering; the states sent their ablest men to Philadelphia. George Washington was there; so were Benjamin Franklin, Alexander Hamilton, and James Madison. For many weeks the delegates labored mightily to construct a constitution that would "form a more perfect union" without jeopardizing liberty. In September they completed their work and submitted the Constitution to the states for ratification. At once a great debate commenced. In countless essays, editorials, pamphlets, and handbills the American people discussed the merits and defects of the new instrument of government offered for their consideration. The most famous of all the commentaries on the Constitution appeared in *The Federalist*.

The Federalist Papers consist of eighty-five essays appearing in various New York newspapers between October 1787 and August 1788. Hamilton, who had taken part in the Constitutional Convention, wrote the major portion of them; but James Madison, whose diligence in Philadelphia won him the nickname "Father of the Constitution," wrote a sizable number as well. John Jay, author of the New York State Constitution of 1777, also wrote a few. The essays, which were soon published in book form, discussed the weakness of the Confederation, the powers assigned to the federal government in the new Constitution and the organization of these powers into legislative, executive, and judicial branches of government, and the safeguards that were built into the Constitution to prevent oppression. Thomas Jefferson, who was in Paris at the time as minister to France, wrote to say he read the *Papers* with "care, pleasure, and improvement" and called them the "best commentary on the principles of government which was ever written."

The immediate impact of *The Federalist Papers* was probably not great. Some of the states had completed ratification before many of the essays were published. But the essays may have helped persuade

New York and Virginia to ratify the Constitution, and their long-range influence has been profound. Since their first appearance the *Papers* have become a classic of political science. Scholars, legislators, judges, and Supreme Court justices have looked to them time and again for clues to understanding the Constitution that was accepted by the states in 1788. After the Declaration of Independence and the Constitution they are the nation's most important political statement. *The Federalist,* Number Ten, written by Madison, is perhaps the most famous. In it, Madison points out the inevitability of conflicts of interest (particularly economic interest) in free societies and insists that representative government can keep these conflicts from getting out of hand and endangering both private rights and the public good.

James Madison, son of a Virginia planter, was born in Port Conway, Virginia, in 1751, and attended the College of New Jersey (now Princeton). In 1776 he helped frame Virginia's constitution and declaration of rights. Between 1780 and 1783 he was a member of the Continental Congress; after the Revolution he served in Virginia's House of Delegates, where he sponsored legislation to disestablish the Anglican church and provide for religious freedom. As a member of Virginia's delegation to the Philadelphia convention in 1787 he played a major role in shaping the Constitution; his notes on the debates are our main source for information about what was discussed. As a member of the First Congress under Washington he sponsored legislation establishing the State, Treasury, and War Departments and also introduced the first ten amendments to the Constitution (the Bill of Rights) into the House of Representatives. For eight years he served as Thomas Jefferson's secretary of state and succeeded him as president in 1809. His own presidency was a stormy one. Though a man of peace, he presided over the controversial War of 1812 with Britain ("Mr. Madison's War"), which ended with a treaty settling none of the outstanding disputes between the two countries. While he was president, the Republican party gradually accepted the economic program once sponsored by Hamilton and opposed by Jefferson: a second Bank of the United States, a protective tariff, and a large funded debt. In 1817, Madison retired to his estate at Montpelier to manage his farm, pursue his studies, advise James Monroe, his successor in the White House, and warn against disunion. He died in 1836 at the age of eighty-five.

Questions to Consider. In the extract from *The Federalist,* Number Ten, presented below, Madison began by singling out factions as the chief problem confronting free nations like the United States. How did he define *faction?* He said there are two ways to prevent factions from forming. What are they? Why did he reject both of them? What did he mean by saying that the "latent causes of faction" are found in human nature? Do you think he was right in his statement that "the most common and durable source of factions has been the various and unequal distribution of property"? What examples did he give of various propertied interests? Did Madison think a "pure democracy" could handle the "mischief of faction"? How did he distinguish a republic from a democracy? Why did he think a republican form of government, such as outlined in the U.S. Constitution, could deal effectively with the problem of factions?

♦

The Federalist, Number Ten (1787)

JAMES MADISON

Among the numerous advantages promised by a well-constructed Union, none deserves to be more accurately developed than its tendency to break and control the violence of faction. The friend of popular governments never finds himself so much alarmed for their character and fate as when he contemplates their propensity to this dangerous vice. He will not fail, therefore, to set a due value on any plan which, without violating the principles to which he is attached, provides a proper cure for it. . . .

By a faction I understand a number of citizens, whether amounting to a majority or minority of the whole, who are united and actuated by some common impulse of passion, or of interest, adverse to the rights of other citizens, or to the permanent and aggregate interests of the community.

There are two methods of curing the mischiefs of faction: the one, by removing its causes; the other, by controlling its effects.

There are again two methods of removing the causes of faction: the one, by destroying the liberty which is essential to its existence; the other, by giving to every citizen the same opinions, the same passions, and the same interests.

It could never be more truly said than of the first remedy that it was worse than the disease. Liberty is to faction what air is to fire, an aliment without which it instantly expires. But it could not be a less folly to abolish liberty, which is essential to political life, because it nourishes faction than it would be to wish the annihilation of air, which is essential to animal life, because it imparts to fire its destructive agency.

The second expedient is as impracticable as the first would be unwise. As long as the reason of man continues fallible, and he is at liberty to exercise it, different opinions will be formed. As long as the connection subsists between his reason and his self-love, his opinions and his passions will have a reciprocal influence on each other; and the former will be objects

From *The Federalist* (Colonial Press, New York, 1901), 44–52.

James Madison. A portrait by Charles Wilson Peale, one of the earliest out-standing American artists. (Portrait by Charles Wilson Peale, 1792, oil on canvas; courtesy Thomas Gilcrease Institute of American History and Art, Tulsa, OK)

to which the latter will attach themselves. The diversity in the faculties of men, from which the rights of property originate, is not less an insuperable obstacle to a uniformity of interests. The protection of these faculties is the first object of government. From the protection of different and unequal faculties of acquiring property, the possession of different degrees and kinds of property immediately results; and from the influence of these on the sentiments and views of the respective proprietors ensues a division of the society into different interests and parties.

The latent causes of faction are thus sown in the nature of man; and we see them everywhere brought into different degrees of activity, according to the different circumstances of civil society. A zeal for different opinions concerning religion, concerning government, and many other points, as well of speculation as of practice; an attachment to different leaders ambitiously contending for pre-eminence and power; or to persons of other descriptions whose fortunes have been interesting to the human passions, have, in turn, divided mankind into parties, inflamed them with mutual animosity, and rendered them much more disposed to vex and oppress each other than to co-operate for their common good. So strong is this propensity of mankind to fall into mutual animosities that where no substantial occasion presents itself the most frivolous and fanciful distinctions have been sufficient to kindle their unfriendly passions and excite their most violent conflicts. But the most common and durable source of factions has been the various and unequal distribution of property. Those who hold and those who are without property have ever formed distinct interests in society. Those who are creditors, and those who are debtors, fall under a like discrimination. A landed interest, a manufacturing interest, a mercantile interest, a moneyed interest, with many lesser interests, grow up of necessity in civilized nations, and divide them into different classes, actuated by different sentiments and views. . . .

Shall domestic manufacturers be encouraged, and in what degree, by restrictions on foreign manufacturers? are questions which would be differently decided by the landed and the manufacturing classes, and probably by neither with a sole regard to justice and the public good. The apportionment of taxes on the various descriptions of property is an act which seems to require the most exact impartiality; yet there is, perhaps, no legislative act in which greater opportunity and temptation are given to a predominant party to trample on the rules of justice. Every shilling with which they overburden the inferior number is a shilling saved to their own pockets.

It is in vain to say that enlightened statesmen will be able to adjust these clashing interests and render them all subservient to the public good. Enlightened statesmen will not always be at the helm. Nor, in many cases, can such an adjustment be made at all without taking into view indirect and remote considerations, which will rarely prevail over the immediate interest which one party may find in disregarding the rights of another or the good of the whole.

The inference to which we are brought is that the *causes* of faction cannot be removed and that relief is only to be sought in the means of controlling its *effects*.

If a faction consists of less than a majority, relief is supplied by the republican principle, which enables the majority to defeat its sinister views by regular vote. It may clog the administration, it may convulse the society; but it will be unable to execute and mask its violence under the forms of the Constitution. When a majority is included in a faction, the form of popular government, on the other hand, enables it to sacrifice to its ruling passion or interest both the public good and the rights of other citizens. To secure the public good and private rights against the danger of such a faction, and at the same time to preserve the spirit and the form of popular government, is then the great object to which our inquiries are directed. . . .

By what means is this object attainable? Evidently by one of two only. Either the existence of the same passion or interest in a majority at the same time must be prevented, or the majority, having such coexistent passion or interest, must be rendered, by their number and local situation, unable to concert and carry into effect schemes of oppression. . . .

[A] pure democracy, by which I mean a society consisting of a small number of citizens, who assemble and administer the government in person, can admit of no cure for the mischiefs of faction. A common passion or interest will, in almost every case, be felt by a majority of the whole; a communication and concert results from the form of government itself; and there is nothing to check the inducements to sacrifice the weaker party or an obnoxious individual. Hence it is that such democracies have ever been spectacles of turbulence and contention; have ever been found incompatible with personal security or the rights of property; and have in general been as short in their lives as they have been violent in their deaths. . . .

A republic, by which I mean a government in which the scheme of representation takes place, opens a different prospect and promises the cure for which we are seeking. Let us examine the points in which it varies from pure democracy, and we shall comprehend both the nature of the cure and the efficacy which it must derive from the Union.

The two great points of difference between a democracy and a republic are: first, the delegation of the government, in the latter, to a small number of citizens elected by the rest; secondly, the greater number of citizens and greater sphere of country over which the latter may be extended.

The effect of the first difference is, on the one hand, to refine and enlarge the public views by passing them through the medium of a chosen body of citizens, whose wisdom may best discern the true interest of their country and whose patriotism and love of justice will be least likely to sacrifice it to temporary or partial considerations. Under such a regulation it may well happen that the public voice, pronounced by the representatives of the people, will be more consonant to the public good than if pronounced by the people themselves, convened for the purpose. On the other hand, the effect may be inverted. Men of factious tempers, of local prejudices, or of sinister designs, may, by intrigue, by corruption, or by other means, first obtain the suffrages, and then betray the interests of the people. . . .

In the first place it is to be remarked that however small the republic may be the representatives must be raised to a certain number in order to guard against the cabals of a few; and that however large it may be they must be limited to a certain number in order to guard against the confusion of a multitude. . . .

In the next place, as each representative will be chosen by a greater number of citizens in the large than in the small republic, it will be more difficult for unworthy candidates to practise with success the vicious arts by which elections are too often carried; and the suffrages of the people being more free, will be more likely to center on men who possess the most attractive merit and the most diffusive and established characters. . . .

The other point of difference is the greater number of citizens and extent of territory which may be brought within the compass of republican than of democratic government; and it is this circumstance principally which renders factious combinations less to be dreaded in the former than in the latter. The smaller the society, the fewer probably will be the distinct parties and interests composing it; the fewer the distinct parties and interests, the more frequently will a majority be found of the same party; and the smaller the number of individuals composing a majority, and the smaller the compass within which they are placed, the more easily will they concert and execute their plans of oppression. Extend the sphere and you take in a greater variety of parties and interests. . . .

The influence of factious leaders may kindle a flame within their particular States but will be unable to spread a general conflagration through the other States. A religious sect may degenerate into a political faction in a part of the Confederacy; but the variety of sects dispersed over the entire face of it must secure the national councils against any danger from that source. A rage for paper money, for an abolition of debts, for an equal division of property, or for any other improper or wicked project, will be less apt to pervade the whole body of the Union than a particular member of it, in the same proportion as such a malady is more likely to taint a particular county or district than an entire State.

In the extent and proper structure of the Union, therefore, we behold a republican remedy for the diseases most incident to republican government.

The Harrison campaign. The 1840 presidential campaign of William Henry Harrison, complete with songs, parades, stump speaking, military banners, log cabin symbolism, and all the other hoopla of politics in the "age of the common man." (Franklin D. Roosevelt Library)

CHAPTER THREE

◆

Nationalists and Partisans

15

◆

THE INDUSTRIAL VISION

Under the new Constitution, Congress had the power to tax, borrow, and regulate trade and money. But the president was also important; he could recommend to Congress "such measures" as he thought "necessary and expedient." While George Washington was president, he established many precedents of economic policy and behavior. Probably the most important recommendations made during his presidency came from Secretary of the Treasury Alexander Hamilton. Hamilton's four reports to Congress on economic and financial policies were crucial in shaping the development of the new nation. In them Hamilton sought to make the Constitution's promise of a "more perfect Union" a reality by recommending governmental policies that fostered private enterprise and economic growth.

Hamilton's first three reports had to do with funding the national debt and creating a national bank. Hamilton wanted the federal government to take over the old Revolutionary debt as well as the debts incurred by the states during the Revolution, convert them into bonds, and pay for the interest on the bonds by levying excise taxes on distilled spirits and by imposing customs duties on such imports as tea, coffee, and wine. Congress adopted his funding proposals; it also accepted his plan for a large national bank that could make loans to businesses and issue currency backed by federal bonds. Hamilton's fourth report, "On Manufactures," urged a system of import taxes ("protective tariffs"), better roads and harbors ("internal improvements"), and subsidies ("bounties") in order to spur manufacturing.

Hamilton's four reports, with their emphasis on national rather than state power, on industry rather than agriculture, and on public spending to promote private enterprise, had a tremendous political impact. First, they triggered the birth of the earliest formal party system: Hamiltonian Federalists urging passage of the program and Democratic Republicans, followers of Secretary of State Thomas Jefferson, trying to modify or block it. Second, the reports helped establish the questions of governmental power and the nature of the economy as basic issues of political debate over the next half-century. Finally, Hamilton's reports became a veritable fountainhead for Americans concerned with the enhancement of capitalism and national power. Hamiltonian conservatives did not want an uninvolved government; they wanted to forge a partnership between government and business in which federal policies would actively promote business enterprise.

Congress did not immediately adopt Hamilton's recommendations for manufacturing. Protective tariffs, internal improvements, and bounties came much later and were adopted in a piecemeal fashion. Still, "On Manufactures" is important in its preview of the future. Hamilton was perceptive in foreseeing that America's destiny was an industrial one. Long after he had passed from the scene, industrialism did overtake and surpass agriculture (with the encouragement of the states as well as of the federal government) as the driving force of the American economy.

Hamilton himself was concerned more with the political implications of his reports than with their economic effects. His major aim was to strengthen the Union. This strong nationalism probably came from Hamilton's lack of state loyalties. He was born in 1755 in the West Indies (Hamilton claimed 1757). Orphaned at the age of thirteen, he was sent by relatives to the colony of New York in 1772. After preliminary study in New Jersey, he entered King's College (now Columbia University). When war with Britain broke out, he joined the army; in 1777 George Washington made him his aide-de-camp and personal secretary. After the Revolution he studied law, married well, rose rapidly in New York society, and became a dominant force in the Washington administration and the Federalist party. Overbearing and ambitious as well as bright and energetic, he proceeded to alienate important party leaders such as John Adams, and his career declined steadily after Washington left office. In 1804, Vice President Aaron Burr, a long-time political adversary who had just been defeated in the election for governor of New York, demanded a duel of honor with Hamilton because of some alleged derogatory remarks. On July 11, Burr shot Hamilton at their meeting in a field near Weehawken, New Jersey. He died the following day.

Questions to Consider. Hamilton argued for manufacturing on the grounds that it would attract immigrants and employ women and children. What does this prediction tell us about the availability and condition of labor in early America and about the attitudes of American leaders toward the work force? Hamilton argued not just for the specialization of labor but even more for the easier application of machinery that would result from labor specialization. What two models did he suggest for combining machinery and labor, and what does his simultaneous use of these two very different models indicate about the state of American industry at the time he was writing? Hamilton thought the spirit of capitalist enterprise must be fostered by government. Why, if this spirit was so prevalent, did Hamilton feel the need for special measures to promote it? How compatible was Hamilton's economic nationalism with Madison's political federalism?

◆

On Manufactures (1791)

ALEXANDER HAMILTON

It is now proper to proceed a step further, and to enumerate the principal circumstances, from which it may be inferred that manufacturing establishments not only occasion an augmentation of the produce and revenue of the society, but that they contribute essentially to rendering them greater than they could possibly be without such establishments.

Each of these circumstances has a considerable influence upon the total mass of industrious effort in a community; together, they add to it a degree of energy and effect which is not easily conceived. . . .

1. As to the Division of Labor

It has justly been observed, that there is scarcely any thing of greater moment in the economy of a nation than the proper division of labor. The separation of occupations causes each to be carried to a much greater perfection than it could possibly acquire if they were blended. This arises principally from three circumstances:

1st. The greater skill and dexterity naturally resulting from a constant and undivided application to a single object. It is evident that these properties must increase in proportion to the separation and simplification of objects, and the steadiness of the attention devoted to each; and must be less in proportion to the complication of objects, and the number among which the attention is distracted.

2nd. The economy of time, by avoiding the loss of it, incident to a frequent transition from operation to another of a different nature. This depends on various circumstances: the transition itself, the orderly disposition of the implements, machines, and materials employed in the operation to be relinquished, the preparatory steps to the commencement of a new one, the interruption of the impulse which the mind of the workman acquires from being engaged in a particular operation, the distractions,

From Henry Cabot Lodge, ed., *The Works of Alexander Hamilton* (12 v., G. P. Putnam's Sons, New York, 1904), IV: 70–198.

hesitations, and reluctances which attend the passage from one kind of business to another.

3rd. An extension of the use of machinery. A man occupied on a single object will have it more in his power, and will be more naturally led to exert his imagination, in devising methods to facilitate and abridge labor, than if he were perplexed by a variety of independent and dissimilar operations. Besides this, the fabrication of machines, in numerous instances, becoming itself a distinct trade, the artist who follows it has all the advantages which have been enumerated, for improvement in his particular art; and, in both ways, the invention and application of machinery are extended.

And from these causes united, the mere separation of the occupation of the cultivator from that of the artificer has the effect of augmenting the productive powers of labor, and with them, the total mass of the produce or revenue of a country. In this single view of the subject, therefore, the utility of artificers or manufacturers, towards promoting an increase of productive industry, is apparent.

2. As to an Extension of the Use of Machinery, A Point Which, Though Partly Anticipated, Requires to Be Placed in One or Two Additional Lights

The employment of machinery forms an item of great importance in the general mass of national industry. It is an artificial force brought in aid of the natural force of man; and, to all the purposes of labor, is an increase of hands, an accession of strength, unencumbered too by the expense of maintaining the laborer. . . .

The cotton mill, invented in England, within the last twenty years, is a signal illustration of the general proposition which has been just advanced. In consequence of it, all the different processes for spinning cotton are performed by means of machines, which are put in motion by water, and attended chiefly by women and children—and by a smaller number of persons, in the whole, than are requisite in the ordinary mode of spinning. And it is an advantage of great moment, that the operations of this mill continue with convenience during the night as well as through the day. The prodigious effect of such a machine is easily conceived. To this invention is to be attributed, essentially, the immense progress, which has been so suddenly made in Great Britain, in the various fabrics of cotton.

3. As to the Additional Employment of Classes of the Community Not Originally Engaged in the Particular Business

This is not among the least valuable of the means by which manufacturing institutions contribute to augment the general stock of industry and production. In places where those institutions prevail, besides the persons regularly engaged in them, they afford occasional and extra employment to industrious individuals and families, who are willing to devote the leisure resulting from the intermissions of their ordinary pursuits to collateral labours, as a resource for multiplying their acquisitions or their enjoyments. The husbandman himself experiences a new source of profit and support from the increased industry of his wife and daughters, invited and stimulated by the demands of the neighboring manufactories.

Besides this advantage of occasional employment to classes having different occupations, there is another, of a nature allied to it, and of a similar tendency. This is the employment of persons who would otherwise be idle, and in many cases a burthen on the community, either from the bias of temper, habit, infirmity of body, or some other cause, indisposing or disqualifying them for the toils of the country. It is worthy of particular remark that, in general, women and children are rendered more useful, and the latter more early useful by manufacturing establishments, than they would otherwise be. Of the number of persons employed in the cotton manufactories of Great Britain, it is computed that four sevenths nearly are women and children, of whom the greatest proportion are children, and many of them of a very tender age. . . .

4. As to the Promoting of Emigration from Foreign Countries

Men reluctantly quit one course of occupation and livelihood for another, unless invited to it by very apparent and proximate advantages. Many who would go from one country to another, if they had a prospect of continuing with more benefit the callings to which they have been educated, will often not be tempted to change their situation by the hope of doing better in some other way. Manufacturers who, listening to the powerful invitations of a better price for their fabrics, or their labor, of greater cheapness of provisions and raw materials, of an exemption from the chief part of the taxes, burthens and restraints, which they endure in the Old World, of greater personal independence and consequence, under the operation of a more equal government, and of what is far more precious than mere religious toleration, a perfect equality of religious privileges, would probably flock from Europe to the United States to pursue their own trades or professions, if they were once made sensible of the advantages they would enjoy, and were inspired with an assurance of encouragement and employment, will with difficulty, be induced to transplant themselves, with a view to becoming cultivators of Land.

If it be true, then, that it is in the interest of the United States to open every possible avenue to immigration from abroad, it affords a weighty argument for the encouragement of manufactures; which, for the reasons just assigned, will have the strongest tendency to multiply the inducements to it. . . .

5. As to the Furnishing Greater Scope for the Diversity of Talents and Dispositions, Which Discriminate Men from Each Other

This is a much more powerful means of augmenting the fund of national industry, than may at first sight appear. It is a just observation, that minds of the strongest and most active powers for their proper objects, fall below mediocrity, and labor without effect, if confined to uncongenial pursuits. And it is thence to be inferred, that the results of human exertion may be immensely increased by diversifying its objects. When all the different kinds of industry obtain in a community, each individual can find his proper element, and can call into activity the whole vigor of his nature. And the community is benefited by the services of its respective members, in the manner in which each can serve it with most effect.

If there be any thing in a remark often to be met with, namely, that there is, in the genius of the people of this country, a peculiar aptitude for mechanic improvements, it would operate as a forcible reason for giving opportunities to the exercise of that species of talent, by the propagation of manufactures.

6. As to the Affording a More Ample and Various Field for Enterprise

. . . To cherish and stimulate the activity of the human mind, by multiplying the objects of enterprise, is not among the least considerable of the expedients by which the wealth of a nation may be promoted. Even things in themselves not positively advantageous sometimes become so, by their tendency to provoke exertion. Every new scene which is opened to the busy nature of man to rouse and exert itself, is the addition of a new energy to the general stock of effort.

The spirit of enterprise, useful and prolific as it is, must necessarily be contracted or expanded, in proportion to the simplicity or variety of the occupations and productions which are to be found in a society. It must be less in a nation of mere cultivators, than in a nation of cultivators and merchants; less in a nation of cultivators and merchants, than in a nation of cultivators, artificers and merchants.

7. As to the Creating, in Some Instances, a New, and Securing in All, a More Certain and Steady Demand for the Surplus Produce of the Soil

This is among the most important of the circumstances which have been indicated. It is a principal means by which the establishment of manufactures contributes to an augmentation of the produce or revenue of a country, and has an immediate and direct relation to the prosperity of agriculture.

It is evident that the exertions of the husbandman will be steady or fluctuating, vigorous or feeble, in proportion to the steadiness or fluctuation, adequateness or inadequateness, of the markets on which he must depend for the vent [selling] of the surplus which may be produced by his labor; and that such surplus, in the ordinary course of things, will be greater or less in the same proportion.

For the purpose of this vent, a domestic market is greatly to be preferred to a foreign one; because it is, in the nature of things, far more to be relied upon.

16

♦

BEYOND ENTANGLEMENT

Long before his second term was over, George Washington had decided not to seek a third term. Weary of public life and eager to retire to the peace and quiet of his Mount Vernon estate, he was also anxious for the young nation to prove to the world that it could change rulers peacefully. With the help of James Madison and Alexander Hamilton he prepared a public letter to the American people; on September 19, 1796, a Philadelphia newspaper published it as his "Farewell Address." It was a moving appeal for unity, patriotism, and devotion to the common good. It was also a warning against the major evils Washington thought might wreck the American experiment in self-government.

Washington saw several threats to the new nation's well-being. One was party strife. He was afraid that the acrimonious controversy between Federalists and Republicans over Hamilton's economic policies might tear the nation apart, and he warned against "the baneful effects of the spirit of party." He was also bothered by the way Americans developed "inveterate antipathies against particular nations and passionate attachments for others" without regard for the national interest. When Britain and France went to war in 1793, he issued a proclamation of neutrality, and when British interference with America's neutral rights at sea threatened to produce war, he sponsored the unpopular Jay's treaty in 1795 to keep the peace with Britain. Washington's neutrality policy pleased few people. The Federalists were pro-British and anti-French; they looked on France after the Revolution of 1789 as a threat to property, authority, and order everywhere. Most Republicans, for their part, were anti-British and pro-French; they regarded America's former Revolutionary ally, now a republic, as a comrade-in-arms in the fight against privilege and oppression throughout the world. Washington himself wanted the United States to remain aloof from the wars of Britain and France, if possible, because he thought peace was an absolute necessity for the young developing nation. The United States, he insisted, should keep out of wars not involving its basic national interests and be prepared to fight only in self-defense. He was concerned about the militarism that comes with wars, just as another general-president, Dwight D. Eisenhower, was, over one hundred fifty years later. In one part of the Farewell Address, not included here, Washington urged Americans to avoid "the necessity of those overgrown military establishments, which, under any form of government, are inauspicious to liberty, and which are to be regarded as particularly hostile to republican liberty."

George Washington was born in 1732 on the family tobacco plantation in Westmoreland County, Virginia. Little is known of his childhood; after his father died in 1743 he lived with various relatives, finally coming into the care of his elder half-brother Lawrence, owner of the Mount Vernon estate. At age fifteen he became a surveyor, an occupation he kept until age twenty, when he inherited Mount Vernon upon the death of Lawrence. After this time he obtained various political and militia appointments. He married a wealthy widow, Martha Custis, in 1759 and over the next fifteen years he lived as a gentleman farmer, managing Mount Vernon and growing tobacco with slave labor. He also entered the Virginia House of Burgesses. His years as commander in chief of the Continental Army from 1775–1783 were followed by service in the Constitutional Convention in 1787 and election to the presidency in 1789. Though he was a Virginia planter like Jefferson, he showed himself increasingly sympathetic as president to the ideas of Secretary of the Treasury Hamilton rather than to those of Secretary of State Jefferson. Rejecting pleas to accept a third term, he retired to Mount Vernon in 1797 and died there two years later.

Questions to Consider. Note the specific grounds on which Washington opposed alliances with the nations of the Old World. Did he believe these were permanent considerations or only temporary reflections of the current international turmoil? What types of contact with foreign countries did he view with favor? What did he mean by saying that "habitual hatred" and "habitual fondness" in foreign affairs makes people "in some degree a slave"? Were Washington's anxieties about the impact of international politics on domestic political passions justified? How does his conception of America's place in the world compare with that of modern political leaders?

◆

Farewell Address (1796)

GEORGE WASHINGTON

Observe good faith and justice toward all nations. Cultivate peace and harmony with all. Religion and morality enjoin this conduct. And can it be that good policy does not equally enjoin it? It will be worthy of a free,

From Jared Sparks, ed., *The Writings of George Washington* (12 v., Little, Brown and Co., Boston, 1855), XII: 214–235.

George Washington. Washington speaking in 1797, just after his departure from the presidency, to a group of students at Georgetown Academy (later Georgetown University) in the new national capital in the District of Columbia. (Georgetown University)

enlightened, and, at no distant period, a great nation to give to mankind the magnanimous and too novel example of a people always guided by an exalted justice and benevolence. Who can doubt that in the course of time and things the fruits of such a plan would richly repay any temporary advantages which might be lost by a steady adherence to it? Can it be that Providence has not connected the permanent felicity of a nation with its virtue? The experiment, at least, is recommended by every sentiment which ennobles human nature. Alas! is it rendered impossible by its vices?

In the execution of such a plan nothing is more essential than that permanent, inveterate antipathies against particular nations and passionate attachments for others should be excluded, and that in place of them, just and amicable feelings toward all should be cultivated. The nation which indulges toward another an habitual hatred or an habitual fondness is in some degree a slave. It is a slave to its animosity or to its affection, either of which is sufficient to lead it astray from its duty and its interest. Antipathy in one nation against another disposes each more readily to offer insult and injury, to lay hold of slight causes of umbrage, and to be haughty and intractable when accidental or trifling occasions of dispute occur. . . .

So, likewise, a passionate attachment of one nation for another produces a variety of evils. Sympathy for the favorite nation, facilitating the illusion of an imaginary common interest in cases where no real common interest exists, and infusing into one of the enmities of the other, betrays the former into a participation in the quarrels and wars of the latter without adequate inducement or justification. It leads also to concessions to the favorite nation of privileges denied to others, which is apt doubly to injure the nation making the concessions by unnecessarily parting with what ought to have been retained, and by exciting jealousy, ill will, and a disposition to retaliate in the parties from whom equal privileges are withheld; and it gives to ambitious, corrupted, or deluded citizens (who devote themselves to the favorite nation) facility to betray or sacrifice the interests of their own country without odium, sometimes even with popularity, gilding with the appearances of a virtuous sense of obligation, a commendable deference for public opinion, or a laudable zeal for public good, the base or foolish compliances of ambition, corruption, or infatuation. . . .

Against the insidious wiles of foreign influence (I conjure you to believe me, fellow-citizens) the jealousy of a free people ought to be constantly awake, since history and experience prove that foreign influence is one of the most baneful foes of republican government. But that jealousy, to be useful, must be impartial, else it becomes the instrument of the very influenced to be avoided, instead of a defense against it. Excessive partiality for one foreign nation and excessive dislike of another cause those whom they actuate to see danger only on one side, and serve to veil and even second the arts of influence on the other. Real patriots who may resist the intrigues of the favorite are liable to become suspected and odious, while its tools and dupes usurp the applause and confidence of the people to surrender their interests.

The great rule of conduct for us in regard to foreign nations is, in extending our commercial relations to have with them as little political connection as possible. So far as we have already formed engagements, let them be fulfilled with perfect good faith. Here let us stop.

Europe has a set of primary interests which to us have none or a very remote relation. Hence she must be engaged in frequent controversies, the causes of which are essentially foreign to our concerns. Hence, therefore, it must be unwise in us to implicate ourselves by artificial ties in the ordinary vicissitudes of her politics or the ordinary combinations and collisions of her friendships or enmities.

Our detached and distant situation invites and enables us to pursue a different course. If we remain one people, under an efficient government, the period is not far off when we may defy material injury from external annoyance; when we may take such an attitude as will cause the neutrality, we may at any time resolve upon, to be scrupulously respected; when belligerent nations, under the impossibility of making acquisitions upon us, will not lightly hazard the giving us provocation; when we may choose peace or war, as our interest, guided by justice, shall counsel.

Why forego the advantages of so peculiar a situation? Why quit our own to stand upon foreign ground? Why, by interweaving our destiny with that of any part of Europe, entangle our peace and prosperity in the toils of European ambition, rivalship, interest, humor, or caprice?. . .

Harmony, liberal intercourse with all nations are recommended by policy, humanity, and interest. But even our commercial policy should hold an equal and impartial hand, neither seeking nor granting exclusive favors or preferences; consulting the natural course of things; diffusing and diversifying by gentle means the streams of commerce, but forcing nothing; establishing with powers so disposed, in order to give trade a stable course, to define the rights of our merchants, and to enable the Government to support them, conventional rules of intercourse, the best that present circumstances and mutual opinion will permit, but temporary and liable to be from time to time abandoned or varied as experience and circumstances shall dictate; constantly keeping in view that it is folly in one nation to look for disinterested favors from another; that it must pay with a portion of its independence for whatever it may accept under that character; that by such acceptance it may place itself in the condition of having given equivalents for nominal favors, and yet of being reproached with ingratitude for not giving more. There can be no greater error than to expect or calculate upon real favors from nation to nation. It is an illusion which experience must cure, which a just pride ought to discard.

17

◆

A CALL FOR UNITY

The election of 1800 was a stormy one. During the campaign Democratic-Republican Thomas Jefferson was called a dangerous radical and Federalist John Adams a high-toned royalist. The House of Representatives, voting by states in February 1801, finally picked Jefferson as president on the thirty-sixth ballot. Jefferson called his election "the revolution of 1800." Reacting against what he regarded as monarchical tendencies in the Federalists, he insisted on "republican simplicity" in his administration. He stopped using the fancy carriage of state and rode horseback through the streets of Washington like any other citizen. He refused to wear "court dress" when receiving foreign diplomats, and his casual demeanor shocked some of the diplomatic corps. The British minister was so outraged by the informality of dinners at the Executive Mansion that he began refusing invitations to dine with the president.

Jefferson's first inaugural address, given on March 4, 1801, was a beautifully phrased exposition of his republican philosophy. The American republic, he declared, was founded on the sacred principle of majority rule; but the majority, he added, must respect the rights of the minority. History, Jefferson thought, showed the failure of undemocratic governments. He placed his faith in the future in governments resting on the consent of the people.

Thomas Jefferson was born in 1743 on his father's Virginia tobacco plantation. After he graduated from William and Mary College in 1762, he studied law and entered politics, joining the Virginia House of Burgesses in 1769. In 1775 he became a delegate to the Continental Congress and was chosen to draft the Declaration of Independence. He served as governor of Virginia from 1779 to 1781 and as U.S. minister to France from 1785 to 1789. Insistent, in his correspondence with James Madison, on the necessity of adding a Bill of Rights to the Constitution, he became increasingly disturbed by the policies of Hamilton and Washington and saw his election as president as partial vindication of his own views on the importance of land, liberty, and localism in the new republic. His reputation as a scholar and architect flourished after his retirement from office in 1809, although his personal finances did not. He died, deeply revered as the Sage of Monticello but still an indebted slaveholder, at his Monticello estate on July 4, 1826, fifty years to the day after the adoption of his Declaration of Independence. On the same day John Adams died in Quincy, Massachusetts. Jefferson and Adams had been friends at the time of the American Revolution but became political enemies during the early years of the American republic. They became reconciled later in life and entered into a lively correspondence that has delighted generations of Americans. Just before he died Adams exclaimed: "Thomas Jefferson survives!"

Questions to Consider. In what ways did Jefferson perceive the United States to be different from the countries of Europe? What did he mean by saying that "every difference of opinion is not a difference of principle"? After the bitter political strife of the 1790s, how could Jefferson argue that "we are all Republicans, we are all Federalists"? What role did the accidents of geography—physical separation from Europe and what Jefferson called "a chosen country, with room enough for our descendants"—play in his optimistic expectations? Is it possible to summarize Jefferson's "essential principles of our Government" even more than he was able or willing to do? In view of these principles, how could a Massachusetts Federalist like John Adams believe that Jefferson's election as president would produce "the loathsome steam of human victims offered in sacrifice"?

◆

First Inaugural Address (1801)

THOMAS JEFFERSON

Called upon to undertake the duties of the first executive office of our country, I avail myself of the presence of that portion of my fellow-citizens which is here assembled to express my grateful thanks for the favor with which they have been pleased to look toward me, to declare a sincere consciousness that the task is above my talents, and that I approach it with those anxious and awful presentiments which the greatness of the charge and the weakness of my powers so justly inspire. A rising nation, spread over a wide and fruitful land, traversing all the seas with the rich productions of their industry, engaged in commerce with nations who feel power and forget right, advancing rapidly to destinies beyond the reach of mortal eyes—when I contemplate these transcendent objects, and see the honor,

From James D. Richardson, ed., *A Compilation of the Messages and Papers of the Presidents* (Government Printing Office, Washington, D.C., 1897–1907), I: 309–312.

Thomas Jefferson. President Jefferson by C. B. J. Févret de St.-Mémin, 1804, a year after the acquisition of the Louisiana Territory. (Portrait by Charles Févret de St-Mémin, 1804, black chalk on paper; Worcester Art Museum, Worcester, MA)

the happiness, and the hopes of this beloved country committed to the issue and the auspices of this day, I shrink from the contemplation, and humble myself before the magnitude of the undertaking. Utterly, indeed, should I despair did not the presence of many whom I here see remind me that in the other high authorities provided by our Constitution I shall find resources of wisdom, of virtue, and of zeal on which to rely under all difficulties. To you, then, gentlemen, who are charged with the sovereign functions of legislation, and to those associated with you, I look with encouragement for that guidance and support which may enable us to steer with safety the vessel in which we are all embarked amidst the conflicting elements of a troubled world.

During the contest of opinion through which we have passed the animation of discussions and of exertions has sometimes worn an aspect which might impose on strangers unused to think freely and to speak and to write what they think; but this being now decided by the voice of the nation, announced according to the rules of the Constitution, all will, of course, arrange themselves under the will of the law, and unite in common efforts for the common good. All, too, will bear in mind this sacred principle, that though the will of the majority is in all cases to prevail, that will to be rightful must be reasonable; that the minority possess their equal rights, which equal law must protect, and to violate would be oppression. Let us, then, fellow-citizens, unite with one heart and one mind. Let us restore to social intercourse that harmony and affection without which liberty and even life itself are but dreary things. And let us reflect that, having banished from our land that religious intolerance under which mankind so long bled and suffered, we have yet gained little if we countenance a political intolerance as despotic, as wicked, and capable of as bitter and bloody persecutions. During the throes and convulsions of the ancient world, during the agonizing spasms of infuriated man, seeking through blood and slaughter his long-lost liberty, it was not wonderful that the agitation of the billows should reach even this distant and peaceful shore; that this should be more felt and feared by some and less by others, and should divide opinions as to measures of safety. But every difference of opinion is not a difference of principle. We have called by different names brethren of the same principle. We are all Republicans, we are all Federalists. If there be any among us who would wish to dissolve this Union or to change its republican form, let them stand undisturbed as monuments of the safety with which error of opinion may be tolerated where reason is left free to combat it. I know, indeed, that some honest men fear that a republican government can not be strong, that this Government is not strong enough; but would the honest patriot, in the full tide of successful experiment, abandon a government which has so far kept us free and firm on the theoretic and visionary fear that this Government, the world's best hope, may by possibility want energy to preserve itself? I trust not. I believe this, on the contrary, the strongest Government on earth. I believe it the only one where every man, at the call of the law, would fly to the standard of the law, and would meet invasions of the public order as his own personal concern. Sometimes it is said that man can not be trusted with government of himself. Can he, then, be trusted with the government of others? Or have we found angels in the forms of kings to govern him? Let history answer this question.

Let us, then, with courage and confidence pursue our own Federal and Republican principles, our attachment to union and representative government. Kindly separated by nature and a wide ocean from the exterminating havoc of one quarter of the globe; too high-minded to endure the degradations of the others; possessing a chosen country, with room enough for our descendants to the thousandth and thousandth generation; entertaining a due sense of our own faculties, to the acquisitions of our own industry, to honor and confidence from our fellow-citizens, resulting not from birth, but from our actions and their sense of them; enlightened by a benign religion, professed, indeed, and practiced in various forms, yet all of them inculcating honesty, truth, temperance, gratitude, and the love of man; acknowledging and adoring an overruling Providence, which by all its dispensations proves that it delights in the happiness of man here and his greater happiness hereafter—with all these blessings, what more is necessary to make us a happy and prosperous people? Still one thing more, fellow-citizens—a wise and frugal Government, which shall restrain men from injuring one another, shall leave them otherwise free to regulate their own pursuits of industry and improvement, and shall not take from the mouth of labor the bread it has earned. This is the sum of good government, and this is necessary to close the circle of our felicities.

About to enter, fellow-citizens, on the exercise of duties which comprehend everything dear and valuable to you, it is proper you should understand what I deem the essential principles of our Government, and consequently those which ought to shape its Administration. I will compress them within the narrowest compass they will bear, stating the general principle, but not all its limitations. Equal and exact justice to all men, of whatever state or persuasion, religious or political; peace, commerce, and honest friendship with all nations, entangling alliances with none; the support of the State governments in all their rights, as the most competent administrations for our domestic concerns and the surest bulwarks against antirepublican tendencies; the preservation of the General Government in its whole constitutional vigor, as the sheet anchor of our peace at home and safety abroad; a jealous care of the right of election by the people—a mild and safe corrective of abuses which are lopped by the sword of revolution where peaceable remedies are unprovided; absolute acquiescence in the decisions of the majority, the vital principle of republics, from which is no appeal but to force, the vital principle and immediate parent of despotism; a well-disciplined militia, our best reliance in peace and for the first moments of war, till regulars may relieve them; the supremacy of the civil over the military authority; economy in the public expense, that labor may be lightly burthened; the honest payment of our debts and sacred preservation of the public faith; encouragement of agriculture, and of commerce as its handmaid; the diffusion of information and arraignment of all abuses at the bar of the public reason; freedom of religion; freedom of the press, and freedom of person under the protection of the habeas corpus, and trial by juries impartially selected. These principles form the bright constellation which has gone before us and guided our steps through an age of revolution and reformation. The wisdom of our sages and blood of our heroes have been devoted to their attainment. They should be the creed of our political faith, the text of civic instruction, the touchstone by which to try the services of those we trust; and should we wander from them in moments of error or of alarm, let us hasten to retrace our steps and to regain the road which alone leads to peace, liberty, and safety. . . .

Relying, then, on the patronage of your good will, I advance with obedience to the work, ready to retire from it whenever you become sensible how much better choice it is in your power to make. And may that infinite Power which rules the destinies of the universe lead our councils to what is best, and give them a favorable issue for your peace and prosperity.

18

◆

THE CONSTITUTION PROTECTED

Marbury v. *Madison* was the first case in which the Supreme Court exercised the right of "judicial review" over laws passed by Congress. In February 1803, Chief Justice John Marshall, a staunch Federalist, speaking for the majority of justices on the Supreme Court, announced his opinion in the case. William Marbury had been appointed justice of the peace for the District of Columbia by John Adams in the last hours of his administration. But because Marbury was a Federalist, James Madison, Jefferson's secretary of state, withheld the commission from him. Marbury appealed to the Supreme Court for a writ of mandamus, that is, a court order compelling Madison to deliver the commission.

Marshall did not believe that Madison was justified in denying Marbury his commission as justice of the peace. But in his opinion he declared that the Supreme Court could not force Madison to deliver the commission. The Constitution, he said, in defining the original jurisdiction of the Supreme Court, did not include the issue of writs to executive officers. Nonetheless, section 13 of the Judiciary Act of 1789 did give the Supreme Court the power to issue such writs, and it was under this law that Marbury had applied to the Court. Marshall, however, declared that section 13 of the Judiciary Act was unconstitutional and that therefore the Court could not render judgment. He then went on to assert the right of the Supreme Court to pass on the constitutionality of laws passed by Congress. "It is a proposition too plain to be contested," he declared, "that the constitution controls any legislative act repugnant to it" and that "a legislative act contrary to the constitution is not law." He added, "It is emphatically the province and duty of the judicial department to say what the law is." And he concluded that "a law repugnant to the constitution is void, and that courts, as well as other departments, are bound by that instrument." By claiming for the Court the duty of deciding whether acts of Congress were constitutional, Marshall upheld the prestige of the judiciary, even though he was unable to do anything for Marbury. But it was not until the Dred Scott case, more than half a century later, that the Supreme Court invalidated a Congressional act for the second time.

Born in 1755 to well-to-do Virginians, John Marshall received little formal schooling. He studied law, however, and eventually became active in state politics. His service in the army during the American Revolution helped develop his nationalistic outlook. A distant cousin of Thomas Jefferson but a devoted Federalist nonetheless, Marshall served on a commission to France in 1797 and was elected to Congress in 1799. In 1801 President John Adams named him to the U.S. Supreme Court, where he served as chief justice for the next thirty-four years. Among his notable decisions besides *Marbury v. Madison* were *McCulloch v. Maryland* (1819), which protected federal agencies such as the Bank of the United States from state taxes; *Dartmouth College v. Woodward* (1819), which upheld the sanctity of contracts; and *Gibbons v. Ogden* (1824), which established federal authority over interstate and foreign commerce. In these and other cases Marshall sought to protect the rights of property, increase the power of the federal government, and raise the prestige of the federal judiciary. Personally convivial, gossipy, courtly with women, and generally reveling in the social life of the slaveholding gentry, Marshall in public remained a figure of controversy throughout his career. He died in Philadelphia in 1835.

Questions to Consider. Why, according to Chief Justice Marshall, should the Constitution and its principles be considered permanent? How important was it to Marshall's argument that the U.S. Constitution was written? What alternative did he have in mind, and why did he feel compelled to assert the special character of a written document? Why did he single out the legislative branch as opposed to the executive (or judiciary) as the chief danger to the permanence of the Constitution and its principles? On what grounds, according to Marshall, did the judiciary become the final arbiter of constitutional quarrels with the right to annul legislation? Why was Marshall's decision seen as a political victory for the Federalist party?

◆

Marbury v. *Madison*   (1803)

JOHN MARSHALL

. . . The question whether an act repugnant to the constitution can become the law of the land is a question deeply interesting to the United States; but, happily not of an intricacy proportioned to its interest. It seems only

From 1 *Craven* 137 (1803).

necessary to recognize certain principles supposed to have been long and well established, to decide it.

That the people have an original right to establish for their future government such principles as, in their opinion, shall most conduce to their own happiness, is the basis on which the whole American fabric has been erected. The exercise of this original right is a very great exertion, nor can it nor ought it to be frequently repeated. The principles therefore so established are deemed fundamental. And as the authority from which they proceed is supreme and can seldom act, they are designed to be permanent.

This original and supreme will organizes the government, and assigns to different departments their respective powers. It may either stop here or establish certain limits not to be transcended by those departments.

The government of the United States of the latter description. The powers of the legislature are defined and limited; and that those limits may not be mistaken or forgotten, the constitution is written. To what purpose are powers limited, and to what purpose is that limitation committed to writing, if these limits may, at any time, be passed by those intended to be restrained? The distinction between a government with limited and unlimited powers is abolished if those limits do not confine the persons on whom they are imposed and if acts prohibited and acts allowed are of equal obligation. It is a proposition too plain to be contested, that the constitution controls any legislative act repugnant to it; or the legislature may alter the constitution by an ordinary act.

Between these alternatives there is no middle ground. The constitution is either a superior paramount law, unchangeable by ordinary means, or it is on a level with ordinary legislative acts, and, like other acts, is alterable when the legislature shall please to alter it.

If the former part of the alternative be true, then a legislative act contrary to the constitution is not law; if the latter part be true, then written constitutions are absurd attempts, on the part of the people, to limit a power in its own nature illimitable.

Certainly all those who have framed written constitutions contemplate them as forming the fundamental and paramount law of the nation, and consequently the theory of every such government must be that an act of the legislature repugnant to the Constitution is void.

This theory is essentially attached to a written constitution, and is consequently to be considered, by this court, as one of the fundamental principles of our society. It is not, therefore, to be lost sight of in the further consideration of this subject.

If an act of the legislature repugnant to the constitution is void, does it, notwithstanding its invalidity, bind the courts and oblige them to give it effect? Or, in other words, though it be not law, does it constitute a rule as operative as if it was a law? This would be to overthrow in fact what was established in theory, and would seem, at first view, an absurdity too gross to be insisted on. It shall, however, receive a more attentive consideration.

It is emphatically the province and duty of the judicial department to say what the law is. Those who apply the rule to particular cases must of necessity expound and interpret that rule. If two laws conflict with each other, the courts must decide on the operation of each.

So if a law be in opposition to the constitution; if both the law and the constitution apply to a particular case, so that the court must either decide that case conformably to the law, disregarding the constitution, or conformably to the constitution, disregarding the law, the court must determine which of these conflicting rules governs the case. This is of the very essence of judicial duty.

If, then, the courts are to regard the constitution, and the constitution is superior to any ordinary act of the legislature, the constitution, and not such ordinary act, must govern the case to which they both apply.

Those, then, who controvert the principle that the constitution is to be considered in court as a paramount law, are reduced to the necessity of maintaining that courts must close their eyes on the constitution and see only the law.

This doctrine would subvert the very foundation of all written constitutions. It would declare that an act which, according to the principles and theory of our government, is entirely void, is yet, in practice, completely obligatory. It would declare that if the legislature shall do what is expressly forbidden, such act, notwithstanding the express prohibition, is in reality effectual. It would be giving to the legislature a practical and real omnipotence with the same breath which professes to restrict their powers within narrow limits. It is prescribing limits and declaring that those limits may be passed at pleasure.

That it thus reduces to nothing what we have deemed the greatest improvement on political institutions, a written constitution, would of itself be sufficient, in America, where written constitutions have been viewed with so much reverence, for rejecting the construction. But the peculiar expressions of the constitution of the United States furnish additional arguments in favor of its rejection.

The judicial power of the United States is extended to all cases arising under the constitution.

Could it be the intention of those who gave this power to say that in using it the constitution should not be looked into? That a case arising under the constitution should be decided without examining the instrument under which it arises?

This is too extravagant to be maintained.

In some cases, then, the constitution must be looked into by the judges. And if they can open it at all, what part of it are they forbidden to read or to obey?

There are many other parts of the constitution which serve to illustrate this subject.

It is declared that "no tax or duty shall be laid on articles exported from any state." Suppose a duty on the export of cotton, of tobacco, or of flour, and a suit instituted to recover it, ought judgment to be rendered in such a case? Ought the judges to close their eyes on the constitution, and only see the law?

The constitution declares "that no bill of attainder or *ex post facto* law shall be passed." If, however, such a bill should be passed, and a person should be prosecuted under it, must the court condemn to death those victims whom the constitution endeavors to preserve?

"No person," says the constitution, "shall be convicted of treason unless on the testimony of two witnesses to the same overt act, or on confession in open court."

Here the language of the constitution is addressed especially to the courts. It prescribes, directly for them, a rule of evidence not to be departed from. If the legislature should change that rule, and declare one witness, or a confession out of court, sufficient for conviction, must the constitutional principle yield to the legislative act?

From these, and many other selections which might be made, it is apparent that the framers of the constitution contemplated that instrument as a rule for the government of *courts,* as well as of the legislature. Why otherwise does it direct the judges to take an oath to support it? This oath certainly applies in an especial manner to their conduct in their official character. How immoral to impose it on them if they were to be used as the instruments, and the knowing instruments, for violating what they swear to support!

The oath of office, too, imposed by the legislature, is completely demonstrative of the legislative opinion on this subject. It is in these words: "I do solemnly swear that I will administer justice without respect to persons, and do equal right to the poor and to the rich; and that I will faithfully and impartially discharge all the duties incumbent on me as ———, according to the best of my abilities and understanding, agreeably to *the constitution* and laws of the United States." Why does a judge swear to discharge his duties agreeably to the constitution of the United States, if that constitution forms no rule for his government—if it is closed upon him, and cannot be inspected by him?

If such be the real state of things, this is worse than solemn mockery. To prescribe, or to take this oath, becomes equally a crime.

It is also not entirely unworthy of observation, that in declaring what shall be the *supreme* law of the land, the constitution itself is first mentioned, and not the laws of the United States generally, but those only which shall be made in *pursuance* of the constitution, have that rank.

Thus, the particular phraseology of the constitution of the United States confirms and strengthens the principle, supposed to be essential to all written constitutions, that a law repugnant to the constitution is void, and that courts, as well as other departments, are bound by that instrument.

19

◆

THE WIDE MISSOURI

Thomas Jefferson's presidency did not usher in the wide-eyed revolutionary radicalism that some Federalist party orators had warned against, but "Long Tom" did prove reluctant to have the central government promote trade and manufacturing. More solicitous of states' rights than the Federalists, Jefferson hesitated to assert the government's authority in economic matters. More solicitous of farming than of industry as a way of life, he also hesitated to encourage commerce at the expense of agriculture. Ironically enough, it was precisely this agrarian vision, this belief that America should remain predominantly rural, that led Jefferson to purchase the Louisiana Territory from France in 1803, thus doubling the nation's size by means of a maneuver that some observers felt was unconstitutional and underhanded.

This vision of America as a land of farmers also prompted the president to sponsor the exploration of the upper Louisiana Territory and the great Columbia River region beyond. Jefferson's interest in the West was long-standing—he asked Congress to authorize an expedition into the Pacific Northwest months before the United States actually bought the Louisiana Territory—and besides, he never lost an opportunity to slake his immense thirst for scientific knowledge. What better opportunity could arise? Ever the politician, however, he was also careful to stress (for the benefit of stray Federalist voters) that the venture might open vast new trading horizons as well as vast new agricultural regions.

The leaders of this first expedition were U.S. Army captains Meriwether Lewis, a noted woodsman who had once been Jefferson's private secretary, and William Clark, an Indian fighter from Kentucky. In the spring of 1804, Lewis and Clark started from St. Louis up the Missouri River with a large party in three well-stocked boats "under a gentle breeze"; Lewis, in nominal command, fully shared responsibility with Clark. After wintering in present-day North Dakota in 40°-below temperatures, nine hand-picked men plus a Shoshone and a French-Canadian guide traversed the Rocky Mountains; they survived on horse meat and tallow, and in November reached "this great Pacific Ocean. O the joy!" Back in St. Louis by the following September, Lewis sent the eagerly awaited letter excerpted below, the party's first communication with government and country in a year. Enthusiastically received, this report whetted American interest in the new territory to a keen edge, leading not only to more exploration and extensive fur trading but to formal U.S. interest in the Oregon Territory and its ultimate wresting in 1845 from the grip of long-time foe Great Britain.

Meriwether Lewis, the youthful head of the great expedition, was born in 1774 in Albemarle County, Virginia, not far from Jefferson's home. Although his family eventually settled in the state of Georgia, Lewis returned alone at age thirteen to Virginia where, after sporadic private study, he enlisted in the local militia in time to be sent to help suppress the Pennsylvania Whisky Rebellion in 1794. The next year, lacking better prospects and having acquired a taste for bivouacking, Lewis joined the regular army. But when President Jefferson offered to make him presidential secretary, he eagerly, and wisely, accepted. So close did the two men become that for two years Lewis lived in the executive mansion, helping plan the expedition. He prepared himself to lead it by studying mapmaking, firearms design, and other skills. In late 1806, on the heels of his remarkable expeditionary triumph, Jefferson appointed Lewis governor of the Louisiana Territory. In 1809 while journeying to Washington on administrative business, Lewis died under mysterious circumstances near Nashville, Tennessee.

Questions to Consider. Because Meriwether Lewis was eager to send word to the East, he could not in this first letter afford to compile a full report. He had to make decisions, in other words, about what information to include and what not to include. Are you in any way surprised at the letter's contents? What might he have emphasized that he did not? What impression of the journey and the territory was he trying to leave with his reader? Although addressed to Jefferson personally, the letter was quickly publicized and widely read throughout the United States. Does Lewis seem to have been writing for other eyes as well as Jefferson's? Do you think Lewis understood the implications of his message for future American development and foreign policy?

◆

Report on the Missouri and Columbia Rivers (1806)

MERIWETHER LEWIS

It is with pleasure that I announce to you the safe arrival of myself and party at 12 o'clock today at this place with our papers and baggage. In obedience to your orders we have penetrated the continent of North America to the Pacific Ocean, and sufficiently explored the interior of the country to affirm with confidence that we have discovered the most practicable route which does exist across the continent by means of the navigable branches of the Missouri and Columbia Rivers. . . .

We view this passage across the continent as affording immense advantages to the fur trade, but fear that the advantages which it offers as a communication for the productions of the East Indies to the United States and thence to Europe will never be found equal on an extensive scale to that by way of the Cape of Good Hope; still we believe that many articles not bulky, brittle nor of a very perishable nature may be conveyed to the United States by this route with more facility and at less expense than by that at present practiced.

The Missouri and all its branches from the Cheyenne upwards abound more in beaver and common otter, than any other streams on earth, particularly that proportion of them lying within the Rocky Mountains. The furs of all this immense tract of country including such as may be collected on the upper portion of the River St. Peters, Red River, and the Assinniboin with the immense country watered by the Columbia, may be conveyed to the mouth of the Columbia by the 1st of August in each year and from thence be shipped to, and arrive in Canton [China] earlier than the furs at present shipped from Montreal annually arrive in London. The British N. West Company of Canada were they permitted by the United States might also convey their furs collected in the Athabaske, on the Saskashawan, and south and west of Lake Winnipic by that route within the period before mentioned. The productions of nine-tenths of the most valuable fur country of America could be conveyed by the route proposed to the East Indies.

In the infancy of the trade across the continent, or during the period that the trading establishments shall be confined to the Missouri and its branches, the men employed in this trade will be compelled to convey the

From Reuben Gold Thwaites, ed., *Original Journals of the Lewis and Clark Expedition* (New York, 1904–1905), VII: 334–337.

furs collected in that quarter as low on the Columbia as tide water [near the ocean], in which case they could not return to the falls of the Missouri until about the 1st of October, which would be so late in the season that there would be considerable danger of the river being obstructed by ice before they could reach this place and consequently that the commodities brought from the East Indies would be detained until the following spring; but this difficulty will at once vanish when establishments are also made on the Columbia, and a sufficient number of men employed at them to convey annually the productions of the East Indies to the upper establishment on the Kooskooske, and there exchange them with the men of the Missouri for their furs in the beginning of July. By this means the furs not only of the Missouri but those also of the Columbia may be shipped to the East Indies by the season before mentioned, and the commodities of the East Indies arrive at St. Louis or the mouth of the Ohio by the last of September in each year.

Although the Columbia does not as much as the Missouri abound in beaver and otter, yet it is by no means despicable in this respect, and would furnish a valuable fur trade distinct from any other consideration in addition to the otter and beaver which it could furnish. There might be collected considerable quantities of the skins of three species of bear affording a great variety of colours and of superior delicacy, those also of the tiger cat, several species of fox, martin and several others of an inferior class of furs, besides the valuable sea otter of the coast.

If the government will only aid, even in a very limited manner, the enterprise of her citizens I am fully convinced that we shall shortly derive the benefits of a most lucrative trade from this source, and that in the course of ten or twelve years a tour across the continent by the route mentioned will be undertaken by individuals with as little concern as a voyage across the Atlantic is at present.

The British N. West Company of Canada has for several years carried on a partial trade with the Minnetares, Ahwayhaways and Mandans on the Missouri from their establishments on the Assinniboin at the entrance of Mouse River; at present I have good reason for believing that they intend shortly to form an establishment near those nations with a view to engross the fur trade of the Missouri. The known enterprise and resources of this company, latterly strengthened by an union with their powerful rival the X. Y. Company, renders them formidable in that distant part of the continent to all other traders; and in my opinion if we are to regard the trade of the Missouri as an object of importance to the United States, the strides of this company towards the Missouri cannot be too vigilantly watched nor too firmly and speedily opposed by our government. The embarrassments under which the navigation of the Missouri at present labours from the unfriendly dispositions of the Kancez, the several bands of Tetons, Assinniboins, and those tribes that resort to the British establishments on the Saskashawan is also a subject which requires the earliest attention of our government. As I shall shortly be with you I have deemed it unnecessary here to detail the several ideas which have presented themselves to my mind on those subjects, more especially when I consider that a thorough knowledge of the geography of the country is absolutely necessary to their being understood, and leisure has not yet permitted us to make but one general map of the country which I am unwilling to risk by the mail. . . .

I have brought with me several skins of the sea otter, two skins of the native sheep of America, five skins and skeletons complete of the Bighorn or mountain ram, and a skin of the mule deer besides the skins of several other quadrapeds and birds native of the countries through which we have passed. I have also preserved a pretty extensive collection of plants, and collected nine other vocabularies [of Indian tribes].

I have prevailed on the great chief of the Mandan nation to accompany me to Washington; he is now with my friend and colleague Capt. Clark at this place, in good health and spirits, and very anxious to proceed. . . .

The route by which I purpose traveling from hence to Washington is by way of Cahokia, Vincennes, Louisville, Ky., the Crab Orchard, Abington, Fincastle, Stanton and Charlottesville. Any letters directed to me at Louisville ten days after the receipt of this will most probably meet me at that place. I am very anxious to learn the state of my friends in Albemarle, particularly whether my mother is yet living. I am with every sentiment of esteem your Obt. and very Humble servant.

20

◆

A HEMISPHERIC INTEREST

In the early part of the nineteenth century, Spain's colonies in Latin America revolted, declared their independence, and received diplomatic recognition from the United States. In 1823, however, a group of European powers known as the Holy Alliance talked of sending an expedition to the New World to restore Spain's control over her former colonies. President James Monroe was alarmed at the prospect. So was George Canning, the British foreign minister, who was afraid that British trade with the new American nations might be disrupted by European intervention. Canning asked the United States to join Britain in a declaration warning the European nations against attempts to retake Spain's former colonies by force.

Monroe liked Canning's proposal, but Secretary of State John Quincy Adams argued forcefully for a unilateral statement by the United States. Not only was Adams concerned about intervention in South America, he was also disturbed by Russian expansion (from Alaska, which Russia owned, southward) on the Pacific Coast. He wanted the United States to make it clear to the European powers that all parts of the New World were closed to further colonization, and he wanted to send direct warnings to all the nations involved.

Adams managed to win Monroe to his views. The president agreed to drop the idea of a joint declaration with England in favor of an independent statement. He also adopted Adams's view that the statement should apply the noncolonization principle to the New World as a whole. But he insisted on making the declaration in a public document rather than in notes sent directly to the nations involved.

The Monroe Doctrine, as the declaration came to be called, appeared in Monroe's annual message to Congress on December 2, 1823. The declaration consisted of two sections. The first was a warning to Russia in the Pacific Northwest and contained the following noncolonization principle: "The American continents, by the free and independent condition which they have assumed and maintain, are henceforth not to be considered as subjects for future colonization by any European power." The second section was directed against the powers that might intervene in South America. It declared that the United States would not interfere with "existing colonies or dependencies of any European power" in the New World, but that any attempt to reconquer the independent republics of Latin America would be considered "the manifestation of an unfriendly disposition toward the United States."

Monroe's message pleased most Americans but irritated Europeans; they knew the young nation was not strong enough to back up its words. The British, whose navy was primarily responsible for keeping Europeans from meddling in America, were particularly irked. They realized Monroe's principles could be used against them as well as against other nations. But Monroe's statement was soon forgotten. The expression *Monroe Doctrine* did not become common until the 1850s. And it was not until the late nineteenth century that the Monroe Doctrine itself came to be regarded as one of the cornerstones of American foreign policy.

Monroe was born in Virginia in 1758. After two years of study at the College of William and Mary, he left to take part in the Revolution and was wounded at the battle of Trenton. After leaving the service, he studied law with Jefferson, served in Congress from 1783 to 1786, and was elected to the new U.S. Senate in 1790. From the start an ally of his friend and sponsor, Thomas Jefferson, he went to France in 1803 to help Robert R. Livingston negotiate the Louisiana Purchase. From 1799 to 1800 and in 1811 he was governor of Virginia. He held a cabinet post during the War of 1812 and easily went on to win election to the presidency in 1816 and again in 1820. He was the last of the "Virginia dynasty" to occupy the White House and the last president to wear the wig and knee breeches of eighteenth-century gentlemen. Monroe presided over the nation during a period of reduced sectional and party rivalry known as the Era of Good Feelings, which he did much to produce. He retired to Virginia in 1825, where he succeeded Jefferson as regent of the University of Virginia and, also like Jefferson, sank into genteel poverty. He died while visiting New York City on July 4, 1831, the third president (after John Adams and Jefferson) to die on the anniversary of American independence.

Questions to Consider. Note the extent to which Monroe's message derives from the notion of American separateness and exceptionalism. Note, too, how Thomas Jefferson's roomy chosen country had become with Monroe a good deal roomier just twenty-two years later. As for the security issue that concerned Monroe, how important was it that the European powers were not merely strong but also had political systems different from that of the United States? Was it an alien system or an alien force, or some combination of the two, that disturbed Monroe? How important, finally, were the wishes of "our southern brethren," meaning the Latin Americans, to U.S. policymakers? Why did Monroe refer to them? Does the reference make the American system more justifiable or less so?

◆

The Monroe Doctrine (1823)

JAMES MONROE

At the proposal of the Russian Imperial Government, made through the minister of the Emperor residing here, a full power and instructions have been transmitted to the minister of the United States at St. Petersburg to arrange by amicable negotiation the respective rights and interests of the two nations on the northwest coast of this continent. A similar proposal has been made by His Imperial Majesty to the Government of Great Britain, which has likewise been acceded to. The Government of the United States has been desirous by this friendly proceeding of manifesting the great value which they have invariably attached to the friendship of the Emperor and their solicitude to cultivate the best understanding with his Government. In the discussion to which this interest has given rise and in the arrangements by which they may terminate, the occasion has been judged proper for asserting, as a principle in which the rights and interests of the United States are involved, that the American continents, by the free and independent condition which they have assumed and maintain, are henceforth not to be considered as subjects for future colonization by any European power.

It was stated at the commencement of the last session [of Congress] that a great effort was then making in Spain and Portugal to improve the condition of the people of those countries, and that it appeared to be conducted with extraordinary moderation. It need scarcely be remarked that the result has been so far very different from what was then anticipated. Of events in that quarter of the globe, with which we have so much intercourse and from which we derive our origin, we have always been anxious and interested spectators. The citizens of the United States cherish sentiments the most friendly in favor of the liberty and happiness of their fellow-men on that side of the Atlantic. In the wars of the European powers in matters relating to themselves we have never taken any part, nor does it comport with our policy so to do. It is only when our rights are invaded or seriously menaced that we resent injuries or make preparations for our defense. With the movements in this hemisphere we are of necessity more immediately connected, and by causes which must be obvious to all enlightened and impartial observers.

The political system of the allied powers[1] is essentially different in this

From James D. Richardson, ed., *A Compilation of the Messages and Papers of the Presidents* (Government Printing Office, Washington, D.C., 1897–1907), II: 786–789.

1. **The allied powers:** European monarchies associated in the "Holy Alliance."—*Eds.*

respect from that of America. This difference proceeds from that which exists in their respective Governments; and to the defense of our own, which has been achieved by the loss of so much blood and treasure, and matured by the wisdom of their most enlightened citizens, and under which we have enjoyed unexampled felicity, this whole nation is devoted. We owe it, therefore, to candor and to the amicable relations existing between the United States and those powers to declare that we should consider any attempt on their part to extend their system to any portion of this hemisphere as dangerous to our peace and safety. With the existing colonies or dependencies of any European power we have not interfered and shall not interfere. But with the Governments who have declared their independence and maintained it, and whose independence we have, on great consideration and on just principles, acknowledged, we could not view any interposition for the purpose of oppressing them, or controlling in any other manner their destiny, by any European power in any other light than as the manifestation of an unfriendly disposition toward the United States. In the war between those new Governments and Spain we declared our neutrality at the time of their recognition, and to this we have adhered, and shall continue to adhere, provided no change shall occur which, in the judgment of the competent authorities of this Government, shall make a corresponding change on the part of the United States indispensable to their security . . .

Our policy in regard to Europe, which was adopted at an early stage of the wars which have so long agitated that quarter of the globe, nevertheless remains the same, which is, not to interfere in the internal concerns of any of its powers; to consider the government *de facto* as the legitimate government for us; to cultivate friendly relations with it, and to preserve those relations by a frank, firm, and manly policy, meeting in all instances the just claims of every power, submitting to injuries from none. But in regard to these continents circumstances are eminently and conspicuously different. It is impossible that the allied powers should extend their political system to any portion of either continent without endangering our peace and happiness; nor can anyone believe that our southern brethren, if left to themselves, would adopt it of their own accord. It is equally impossible, therefore, that we should behold such interposition in any form with indifference. If we look to the comparative strength and resources of Spain and those new Governments, and their distance from each other, it must be obvious that she can never subdue them. It is still the true policy of the United States to leave the parties to themselves, in the hope that other powers will pursue the same course. . . .

21

◆

THE SECTIONAL SPECTER

The first great sectional struggle in the United States (after the Missouri crisis over slavery) was over the tariff. Northern industrialists favored high tariffs to protect their products from foreign competition. But the South was an agricultural region, and Southerners complained that protective tariffs raised the price of manufactured goods and prevented them from importing low-priced goods from abroad. On May 20, 1828, Congress passed a tariff bill with rates so high that South Carolina's John C. Calhoun (vice president at the time) called it a "Tariff of Abominations." He presented a lengthy statement of the Southern position on tariffs in which he developed his theory of nullification.

Calhoun believed in the "compact" theory of the Union. He maintained that the Constitution was a contract into which the states had entered of their own free will. The states retained their sovereignty, and the federal government was merely their agent for general purposes. If the federal government exceeded its authority and encroached on the powers of the states, the states had a right to resist. Calhoun thought the constitutionality of acts of Congress should be decided by state conventions called for that purpose. If such a convention declared an act of Congress in violation of the Constitution, that act became null and void within the borders of that state. Calhoun insisted that the Constitution did not give Congress the right to levy protective tariffs and that the states had a right to nullify tariff legislation.

On December 19, 1828, the South Carolina legislature published Calhoun's statement (without mentioning his name) as "South Carolina Exposition and Protest," together with resolutions, reproduced below, condemning the tariff. For the time being, South Carolina contented itself with making this protest, hoping that the tariff would be revised after Andrew Jackson became president. But in July 1832, when a new tariff bill was passed by Congress and signed by Jackson, South Carolinians decided to put Calhoun's theory into practice. On November 4, 1832, a special state convention met in Columbia, adopted an ordinance declaring the tariffs of 1828 and 1832 unconstitutional, and announced that no tariff duties would be collected in the state after February 1, 1833. Jackson at once denounced South Carolina's action and asked Congress to give him authority to use the army and navy, if necessary, to compel South Carolina to obey the law. South Carolina continued defiant. When Congress passed a compromise bill lowering the tariff rate, the "nullies" (as they were called) repealed the nullification ordinance. But they did not disavow the nullification theory.

Calhoun was born in South Carolina in 1782 to an upcountry farmer. After graduating from Yale College, he practiced law briefly. He then married a wealthy Charleston woman and began a political climb that led to Congress, a post in James Monroe's cabinet, and the vice presidency under both John Quincy Adams and Andrew Jackson. He began as a vigorous nationalist, favoring the protective tariff, but moved to states' rights and an antitariff position when it became clear that South Carolina had more to gain from free trade. During the nullification crisis he resigned from the vice presidency in December 1832 for a seat in the Senate. There he became one of the "great triumvirate" (along with Henry Clay and Daniel Webster); an implacable foe of Jackson; and a staunch supporter of South Carolina, the South, and slavery. He died in Washington, D.C., in early 1850.

Questions to Consider. Why was a protective tariff considered so threatening to the Carolinians? Were they fearful of higher prices for imported goods or of reduced markets for their own product, cotton? Why did the "encouragement of domestic industry," originally urged by Alexander Hamilton in 1791, cause such a fierce blowup in 1828 but not before? Was Calhoun trying to speak for all of American agriculture or only for a certain kind? Was it the threat to agriculture or to something else that most disturbed Calhoun? Which of the eight articles of the "Protest" furnishes the best clue to the situation in South Carolina? As to the political issue, why did Calhoun fear what he called "simple consolidated government" as a threat to freedom?

◆

South Carolina Exposition and Protest (1828)

JOHN C. CALHOUN

The Senate and House of Representatives of South Carolina, now met, and sitting in General Assembly, through the Hon. William Smith and the Hon. Robert Y. Hayne, the representatives in the Senate of the United States, do, in the name and on behalf of the good people of the said commonwealth, solemnly PROTEST against the system of protecting duties, lately adopted by the federal government, for the following reasons:—

Jonathan Elliot, ed., *The Debates in the Several State Conventions on the Adoption of the Federal Constitution,* &c (5 v., J. B. Lippincott, Philadelphia, 1836), IV: 580–582.

John C. Calhoun. Calhoun, who served as congressman, vice president under Andrew Jackson, and then senator from South Carolina, started out as a strong nationalist and then became one of the most vigorous states' righters in the nation. He insisted that sovereignty (supreme power) resided in "the people of the several states" rather than in the people making up the nation as a whole, and that the people of the states had the right to nullify any federal laws they thought threatened their state's welfare. Calhoun developed his doctrine of nullification as a reaction against protective-tariff measures designed to encourage Northern industries but which he thought hurt South Carolina and other Southern states with little or no manufacturing. He was also a states' righter because he wanted to safeguard the institution of slavery from interference by antislavery crusaders in the North. (National Portrait Gallery/Smithsonian Institution, Washington, DC)

1st. *Because* the good people of this commonwealth believe that the powers of Congress were delegated to it in trust for the accomplishment of certain specified objects which limit and control them, and that every exercise of them for any other purpose, is a violation of the Constitution as unwarrantable as the undisguised assumption of substantive, independent powers not granted or expressly withheld.

2d. *Because* the power to lay duties on imports is, and in its very nature can be, only a means of effecting objects specified by the Constitution; since no free government, and least of all a government of enumerated powers, can of right impose any tax, any more than a penalty, which is not at once justified by public necessity, and clearly within the scope and purview of the social compact; and since the right of confining appropriations of the public money to such legitimate and constitutional objects is as essential to the liberty of the people as their unquestionable privilege to be taxed only by their own consent.

3d. *Because* they believe that the tariff law passed by Congress at its last session, and all other acts of which the principal object is the protection of manufactures, or any other branch of domestic industry, if they be considered as the exercise of a power in Congress to tax the people at its own good will and pleasure, and to apply the money raised to objects not specified in the Constitution, is a violation of these fundamental principles, a breach of a well-defined trust, and a perversion of the high powers vested in the federal government for federal purposes only.

4th. *Because* such acts, considered in the light of a regulation of commerce, are equally liable to objection; since, although the power to regulate commerce may, like all other powers, be exercised so as to protect domestic manufactures, yet it is clearly distinguishable from a power to do so *eo nomine*,[1] both in the nature of the thing and in the common acception of the terms; and because the confounding of them would lead to the most extravagant results, since the encouragement of domestic industry implies an absolute control over all the interests, resources, and pursuits of a people, and is inconsistent with the idea of any other than a simple, consolidated government.

5th. *Because,* from the contemporaneous exposition of the Constitution in the numbers of the *Federalist,* (which is cited only because the Supreme Court has recognized its authority), it is clear that the power to regulate commerce was considered by the Convention as only incidentally connected with the encouragement of agriculture and manufactures; and because the power of laying imposts and duties on imports was not understood to justify in any case, a prohibition of foreign commodities, except as a means of extending commerce, by coercing foreign nations to a fair reciprocity in their intercourse with us, or for some *bona fide* commercial purpose.

---

1. **eo nomine:** "by that name (Latin)

6th. *Because*, whilst the power to protect manufactures is nowhere expressly granted to Congress, nor can be considered as necessary and proper to carry into effect any specified power, it seems to be expressly reserved to the states, by the 10th section of the 1st article of the Constitution.

7th. *Because* even admitting Congress to have a constitutional right to protect manufactures by the imposition of duties, or by regulations of commerce, designed principally for that purpose, yet a tariff of which the operation is grossly unequal and oppressive, is such an abuse of power as is incompatible with the principles of a free government and the great ends of civil society, justice, and equality of rights and protection.

8th. *Finally*, because South Carolina, from her climate, situation, and peculiar institutions, is, and must ever continue to be, wholly dependent upon agriculture and commerce, not only for her prosperity, but for her very existence as a state; because the valuable products of her soil—the blessings by which Divine Providence seems to have designed to compensate for the great disadvantages under which she suffers in other respects— are among the very few that can be cultivated with any profit by slave labor; and if, by the loss of her foreign commerce, these products should be confined to an inadequate market, the fate of this fertile state would be poverty and utter desolation; her citizens, in despair, would emigrate to more fortunate regions, and the whole frame and constitution of her civil policy be impaired and deranged, if not dissolved entirely.

Deeply impressed with these considerations, the representatives of the good people of this commonwealth, anxiously desiring to live in peace with their fellow-citizens, and to do all that in them lies to preserve and perpetuate the union of the states, and liberties of which it is the surest pledge, but feeling it to be their bounden duty to expose and resist all encroachments upon the true spirit of the Constitution, lest an apparent acquiescence in the system of protecting duties should be drawn into precedent—do, in the name of the commonwealth of South Carolina, claim to enter upon the Journal of the Senate their *protest* against it as unconstitutional, oppressive, and unjust.

22

◆

THE TRAIL OF TEARS

American attitudes toward the Native American nations varied widely in the first part of the nineteenth century. Some people urged a policy of assimilation; others proposed the voluntary removal of the Native Americans to lands in the West. But land-hungry Americans in the South and West wanted to push the indigenous peoples off their ancestral lands by force, and a few even favored extermination. When Andrew Jackson, an old "Indian fighter," became president in March 1829, he adopted a policy of forcing the tribes to move to the trans-Mississippi West. The Removal Act of 1830, passed by Congress with his encouragement, proposed that the tribes trade their lands in the United States for new homes in federal territory west of the Mississippi River.

Native Americans everywhere objected to the removal policy, but there was little they could do about it. In Illinois and Florida, they put up forceful resistance, but after several years of bloody warfare they were finally subdued. In Georgia, the Cherokees, a nation in the northwestern part of the state, tried to protect their rights peacefully. Belying the average white's contention that "Indians are savages," the Cherokees had become skilled in agriculture, built fine homes and roads, accepted Christian missionaries, adopted a constitution, and published books in an alphabet invented by Sequoya, a talented hunter who had become a silversmith and a scholar. The Cherokees had treaty commitments from the U.S. government, but neither President Jackson nor the state of Georgia was willing to respect them. In July 1830, when Georgia decided to take over their lands, the Cherokees made a moving appeal to the American people to respect their "national and individual rights" and permit them "to remain on the land of our fathers."

The Cherokees' appeal was in vain. Although some northeastern humanitarians sympathized with the Cherokees, and the Supreme Court in two decisions written by Chief Justice John Marshall ruled in the Cherokees' favor, the state of Georgia asserted its sovereignty over their territory. Jackson sent an army of 7,000 to drive them westward at bayonet point. Over 4,000 of the 15,000 Cherokees who went west along the Trail of Tears in 1838 perished en route. By the time Jackson left office he could boast that his removal policy was rapidly nearing completion. The "shotgun removal," as it was called, shocked Ralph Waldo Emerson, one of America's greatest writers. "Such a dereliction of all faith and virtue," he cried, "such a denial of justice, and such deafness to screams for mercy were never heard of in time of peace and in the dealing of a nation with its own allies and wards, since the earth was made."

Questions to Consider. In the final section of the appeal, which appears below, note the style in which the Cherokees state their case. Is it coolly argued or does it contain deep-seated feelings? How united were the Cherokees? What rights did they cite? What were their major objections to moving to a new location?

◆

Appeal of the Cherokee Nation (1830)

We are aware that some persons suppose it will be for our advantage to remove beyond the Mississippi. We think otherwise. Our people universally think otherwise. Thinking that it would be fatal to their interests, they have almost to a man sent their memorial to Congress, deprecating the necessity of a removal. This question was distinctly before their minds when they signed their memorial. Not an adult person can be found, who has not an opinion on the subject; and if the people were to understand distinctly, that they could be protected against the laws of the neighboring States, there is probably not an adult person in the nation, who would think it best to remove; though possibly a few might emigrate individually. There are doubtless many who would flee to an unknown country, however beset with dangers, privations and sufferings, rather than be sentenced to spend six years in a Georgia prison for advising one of their neighbors not to betray his country. And there are others who could not think of living as outlaws in their native land, exposed to numberless vexations, and excluded from being parties or witnesses in a court of justice. It is incredible that Georgia should ever have enacted the oppressive laws to which reference is here made, unless she had supposed that something extremely terrific in its character was necessary, in order to make the Cherokees willing to remove. We are not willing to remove; and if we could be brought to this extremity, it would be, not by argument; not because our judgment was satisfied; not because our condition will be improved—but only because we cannot endure to be deprived of our national and individual rights, and subjected to a process of intolerable oppression.

From E. C. Tracy, *Memoir of the Life of Jeremiah Evarts* (Boston, 1845), 149–158.

The Trail of Tears. In Robert Lindneux's dramatic painting, the Cherokee move toward reservation territory west of the Mississippi River in 1838. Some 4,000 of the 15,000 who began the trip died. But 15,000 was actually only a small portion of the 100,000 Indians driven out of the southeastern United States between 1820 and 1845, and 4,000 was only a small portion of the 25,000 to 30,000 killed in the process. (Painting by Robert Lindneux, courtesy Woolaroc Museum of Oklahoma)

We wish to remain on the land of our fathers. We have a perfect and original right to claim this, without interruption or molestation. The treaties with us, and laws of the United States made in pursuance of treaties, guaranty our residence, and our privileges, and secure us against intruders. Our only request is, that these treaties may be fulfilled, and these laws executed.

But if we are compelled to leave our country, we see nothing but ruin before us. The country west of the Arkansas territory is unknown to us. From what we can learn of it, we have no prepossessions in its favor. All the inviting parts of it, as we believe, are preoccupied by various Indian nations, to which it has been assigned. They would regard us as intruders, and look upon us with an evil eye. The far greater part of that region is, beyond all controversy, badly supplied with wood and water; and no Indian tribe can live as agriculturists without these articles. All our neighbors, in case of our removal, though crowded into our near vicinity, would speak a language totally different from ours, and practice different customs. The original possessors of that region are now wandering savages, lurking for prey in the neighborhood. They have always been at war, and would be easily tempted to turn their arms against peaceful emigrants. Were the country to which we are urged much better than it is represented to be, and were it free from the objections which we have made to it, still it is not the land of our birth, nor of our affections. It contains neither the scenes of our childhood, nor the graves of our fathers.

23

◆

Assaulting Monopoly

The Second Bank of the United States (BUS), chartered by Congress in 1816 for twenty years, was a powerful institution. It performed several important functions: it served as a depository for government funds, it marketed government securities, it made loans to businesses, and, by maintaining specie payments (gold and silver) on its bank notes, it provided the country with a sound currency. With headquarters in Philadelphia and twenty-nine branches in other cities, the BUS contained private funds as well as government money. It controlled one-fifth of the bank notes and one-third of the bank deposits and specie of the country. Advocates of "cheap money"—state bankers, land speculators, and some small businessowners—were hostile to the bank because it restricted the amount of paper money in circulation. They hoped to benefit from an abundance of paper currency. But those who favored "hard money" also disliked the bank. Eastern working people were suspicious of wages paid in paper money, and Southern planters and Western farmers tended to look on any money but gold and silver as dishonest. Andrew Jackson, who had an unpleasant experience with banks as a young man, was a hard-money man and distrustful of all banks.

In the spring of 1832, friends of the BUS in Congress, particularly Henry Clay, urged Nicholas Biddle, the bank's president, to seek a renewal of the bank's charter. The charter did not actually expire until 1836, but Clay was sure that Congress would approve a new charter at once. He was right; after investigating the bank's operations, Congress passed a recharter bill by large majorities. But on July 10, 1832, President Jackson vetoed the bill. In his veto message, he denounced the bank bill as an unconstitutional violation of states' rights as well as an endorsement of a dangerous monopoly whose profits came from "the earnings of the American people" and went to the benefit of foreign stockholders and "a few hundred of our own citizens, chiefly of the richest class."

When Jackson ran for reelection in 1832 the BUS was the main campaign issue. Henry Clay, the candidate of the National Republicans, was a strong supporter of the bank, and so were most eastern merchants and businessmen. They insisted that the bank performed an essential function in managing the country's finances. But working people in the East and farmers in the West tended to support Jackson. They felt that Nicholas Biddle followed policies that favored the rich and powerful at the expense of the plain people. Biddle himself continually boasted about the great powers at his disposal and made no secret of his contempt for popular government. During the 1832 campaign he worked hard to defeat Jackson by lending large sums of money to Jackson's opponents. Biddle's behavior convinced the Jacksonians that the BUS represented a dangerous "concentration of power in the hands of a few men irresponsible to the people."

After his triumphant reelection, Jackson decided to move against the bank at once without waiting for its charter to expire. He directed Secretary of the Treasury Roger B. Taney to place government funds in state banks rather than in the BUS, where they were usually deposited. By the end of 1833, some twenty-three state banks, called "pet banks" by Jackson's enemies, were handling funds of the federal government. Jackson's withholding of federal funds effectively killed Biddle's bank, although it remained in operation until its charter expired in 1836. In 1836 it was reorganized as a state bank in Pennsylvania. The decline of the BUS was accompanied by increasing disarray in the nation's economy. In 1837 came a financial panic, followed by the country's worst depression up to that time.

Andrew Jackson was born in 1767 on the Carolina frontier; his parents were poor Scotch-Irish immigrants. But Jackson climbed rapidly to wealth and status through land speculation and law practice. In 1795, before he was thirty, he established the Hermitage, a splendid plantation near Nashville, Tennessee, and he headed for Congress the next year. As major-general of his state's militia, Jackson won a victory over the British at the battle of New Orleans in 1815 that catapulted him to national prominence and led to a Senate seat in 1823 and the presidency in 1828. Known as Old Hickory and famous as a champion of the West and the common man, Jackson quarreled with John C. Calhoun over nullification as well as with Biddle over the BUS. These conflicts added to his popularity and enabled him to build a strong Democratic party based on patronage and personality as well as on appeals to regional and class interests. Having survived the first attempt to assassinate a president when an unemployed housepainter attacked him in 1835, Jackson retired at the end of his second term to the Hermitage, where he died in 1845.

Questions to Consider. Jackson, as you will see, opposed the BUS as a monopoly. Why did he attack monopolies so strongly? Did banks in general trouble Jackson, or only this particular bank? How did his castigation of foreign control strengthen Jackson's position with the people? Note, too, the president's concern for the right of states to tax the bank and of state-chartered banks to prosper. Is it surprising that a vigorous chief executive and strong opponent of nullification should here be a champion of states' rights? With whom was Jackson quarreling in his remarks near the end of the message about "necessary" and "proper"? Consider, finally, Jackson's championing of the low and poor against the high and rich. Did this appeal to class differences, as opposed to occupational or sectional ones, signal a new turn in American politics? If so, why do you suppose it occurred in 1832 rather than, say, in 1816 or 1824? Who were Jackson's poor, anyway?

◆

Bank Veto Message (1832)

ANDREW JACKSON

The bill "to modify and continue" the act entitled "An act to incorporate the subscribers to the Bank of the United States" was presented to me on the 4th July instant. Having . . . come to the conclusion that it ought not to become a law, I herewith return it to the Senate, in which it originated, with my objections.

A bank of the United States is in many respects convenient for the Government and useful to the people. Entertaining this opinion, and deeply impressed with the belief that some of the powers and privileges possessed by the existing bank are unauthorized by the Constitution, subversive of the rights of the States, and dangerous to the liberties of the people, I felt it my duty at an early period of my Administration to call the attention of Congress to the practicability of organizing an institution combining all its advantages and obviating these objections. I sincerely regret that in the act before me I can perceive none of these modifications of the bank charter which are necessary, in my opinion, to make it compatible with justice, with sound policy, or with the Constitution of our country.

The present corporate body . . . enjoys an exclusive privilege of banking under the authority of the General Government, a monopoly of its favor and support, and, as a necessary consequence, almost a monopoly of the foreign and domestic exchange. The powers, privileges, and favors bestowed upon it in the original charter, by increasing the value of the stock far above its par value, operated as a gratuity of many millions to the stockholders. . . .

The act before me proposes another gratuity to the holders of the same stock. . . . On all hands it is conceded that its passage will increase at least 20 or 30 per cent more the market price of the stock, subject to the payment of the annuity of $200,000 per year secured by the act, thus adding in a moment one-fourth to its par value. It is not our own citizens only

From James D. Richardson, ed., *A Compilation of the Messages and Papers of the Presidents* (Government Printing Office, Washington, D.C., 1897–1907), II: 217–218.

who are to receive the bounty of our Government. More than eight millions of the stock of this bank are held by foreigners. By this act the American Republic proposes virtually to make them a present of some millions of dollars. For these gratuities to foreigners and to some of our own opulent citizens the act secures no equivalent whatever. . . .

Every monopoly and all exclusive privileges are granted at the expense of the public, which ought to receive a fair equivalent. The many millions which this act proposes to bestow on the stockholders of the existing bank must come directly or indirectly out of the earnings of the American people. It is due to them, therefore, if their Government sell monopolies and exclusive privileges, that they should at least exact for them as much as they are worth in open market. . . .

The modifications of the existing charter proposed by this act are not such, in my view, as make it consistent with the rights of the States or the liberties of the people. The qualification of the right of the bank to hold real estate, the limitation of its power to establish branches, and the power reserved to Congress to forbid the circulation of small notes are restrictions comparatively of little value or importance. All the objectionable principles of the existing corporation, and most of its odious features, are retained without alleviation. . . .

Is there no danger to our liberty and independence in a bank that in its nature has so little to bind it to our country? The president of the bank has told us that most of the State banks exist by its forbearance. Should its influence become concentrated, as it may under the operation of such an act as this, in the hands of a self-elected directory whose interests are identified with those of the foreign stockholders, will there not be cause to tremble for the purity of our elections in peace and for the independence of our country in war? Their power would be great whenever they might choose to exert it; but if this monopoly were regularly renewed every fifteen or twenty years on terms proposed by themselves, they might seldom in peace put forth their strength to influence elections or control the affairs of the nation. But if any private citizen or public functionary should interpose to curtail its powers or prevent a renewal of its privileges, it can not be doubted that he would be made to feel its influence. . . .

If we must have a bank with private stockholders, every consideration of sound policy and every impulse of American feeling admonishes that it should be *purely American*. Its stockholders should be composed exclusively of our own citizens, who at least ought to be friendly to our Government and willing to support it in times of difficulty and danger. . . .

The principle is conceded that the States can not rightfully tax the operations of the General Government. They can not tax the money of the Government deposited in the State banks, nor the agency of those banks in remitting it; but will any man maintain that their mere selection to perform this public service for the General Government would exempt the State banks and their ordinary business from State taxation? Had the United

States, instead of establishing a bank at Philadelphia, employed a private banker to keep and transmit their funds, would it have deprived Pennsylvania of the right to tax his bank and his usual banking operations? . . .

It can not be *"necessary"* to the character of the bank as a fiscal agent of the Government that its private business should be exempted from that taxation to which all the State banks are liable, nor can I conceive it *"proper"* that the substantive and most essential powers reserved by the State shall be thus attacked and annihilated as a means of executing the powers delegated to the General Government. It may be safely assumed that none of those sages who had an agency in forming or adopting our Constitution ever imagined that any portion of the taxing power of the States not prohibited to them nor delegated to Congress was to be swept away and annihilated as a means of executing certain powers delegated to Congress. . . .

The bank is professedly established as an agent of the executive branch of the Government, and its constitutionality is maintained on that ground. Neither upon the propriety of present action nor upon the provisions of this act was the Executive consulted. It has had no opportunity to say that it neither needs nor wants an agent clothed with such powers and favored by such exemptions. There is nothing in its legitimate functions which makes it necessary or proper. Whatever interest or influence, whether public or private, has given birth to this act, it can not be found either in the wishes or necessities of the executive department, by which present action is deemed premature, and the powers conferred upon its agent not only unnecessary, but dangerous to the Government and country. . . .

There are no necessary evils in government. Its evils exist only in its abuse. If it would confine itself to equal protection, and, as Heaven does its rains, shower its favors alike on the high and the low, the rich and the poor, it would be an unqualified blessing. In the act before me there seems to be a wide and unnecessary departure from these just principles. . . .

Experience should teach us wisdom. Most of the difficulties our Government now encounters and most of the dangers which impend over our Union have sprung from an abandonment of the legitimate objects of Government by our national legislation, and the adoption of such principles as are embodied in this act. Many of our rich men have not been content with equal protection and equal benefits, but have besought us to make them richer by act of Congress. By attempting to gratify their desires we have in the results of our legislation arrayed section against section, interest against interest, and man against man, in a fearful commotion which threatens to shake the foundations of our Union. It is time to pause in our career to review our principles, and if possible revive that devoted patriotism and spirit of compromise which distinguished the sages of the Revolution and the fathers of our Union.

24

◆

TO THE FARTHEST SHORES

When James K. Polk ran for president in 1844, the Democrats campaigned for the reannexation of Texas and the reoccupation of Oregon. Texas, they insisted, had been acquired by the Louisiana Purchase of 1803 and had been unwisely returned to Spain in a later treaty. The Oregon country, too, they maintained, had become part of the United States by virtue of American settlements there in the early nineteenth century; they felt that British claims were unjustified. Polk agreed heartily with the Democratic platform on both issues.

Polk compromised with Britain on Oregon, signing a treaty in 1846 fixing the boundary at the 49th parallel. But his administration went to war with Mexico from 1846 to 1848 over Texas and ended by acquiring California and the Southwest for the United States. Polk's territorial conquests produced a lively debate over the meaning of expansionism for the United States. Some people, especially in New England, thought the Mexican War had been inspired by Southern planters (like Polk himself) greedy for new lands into which to extend slavery. Others saw both Oregon and the Southwest as tokens in a Northern drive for more farmland and for harbors on the West Coast for the China trade. Another group, perhaps the largest, saw expansion in terms of "manifest destiny," the right of a teeming, vigorous American nation to fill up a continent either empty or held by "inferior" peoples and thus destined almost by nature itself to be absorbed.

One of the most articulate representatives of the manifest destiny school was Senator Thomas Hart Benton of Missouri, a long-time supporter of Jackson, Polk, and the Democratic party. Benton was a tireless promoter of midwestern agricultural and commercial interests that looked favorably on the acquisition of new lands and ports. But he also took the "higher" ground of national destiny. Benton, born in North Carolina in 1782, briefly attended the University of North Carolina before moving to Tennessee, where he practiced law and served in the militia under Andrew Jackson. In 1815 he moved to St. Louis, Missouri, on the raw frontier. Here Benton prospered as a lawyer, newspaper editor, and land speculator. In 1820 he was elected to the Senate, where he remained, a champion of the Midwest and of Jackson and the Democratic party, until 1850. In that year his growing opposition to slavery cost him his Senate seat. The same stand also cost him the Missouri governor's race in 1856, the year in which he published his masterpiece of political autobiography, *Thirty Years' View*. A loyal Democrat to the end, Benton died in Washington, D.C., in 1858.

Questions to Consider. By placing expansionism within a context of age-old population movements, did Benton make it seem inevitable and irresistible and therefore not really open to political criticism? By explaining expansionism in terms of white superiority, did he encourage Americans to think according to racial categories about all issues, including slavery and political rights for dark-skinned people in the United States? Did he encourage Americans to pursue their destiny still further? Did his trans-Pacific vision involve conquest and colonization as well as trade? In what sense would Americans and Asians be common foes of the "great Powers of Europe"? How, precisely, would the "van of the Caucasian race" wake up the "torpid body of old Asia"? Does this prediction in any way modify Benton's racism?

◆

The Destiny of the Race (1846)

THOMAS HART BENTON

Since the dispersion of man upon earth, I know of no human event, past or present, which promises a greater, a more beneficent change upon earth than the arrival of the van of the Caucasian race (the Celtic-Anglo-Saxon division) upon the border of the sea which washes the shore of eastern Asia. The Mongolian, or Yellow race, is there, four hundred million in number, spreading almost to Europe; a race once the foremost of the human family in the arts of civilization, but torpid and stationary for thousands of years. It is a race far above the Ethiopian, or Black—above the Malay, or Brown (if we must admit five races)—and above the American Indian, or Red; it is a race far above all these, but still, far below the White; and, like all the rest, must receive an impression from the superior race whenever they come in contact. It would seem that the White race alone received the divine command, to subdue and replenish the earth! for it is the only race that has obeyed it—the only one that hunts out new and distant lands, and even a New World, to subdue and replenish. Starting from western Asia, taking Europe for their field, and the Sun for their guide, and leaving

From *The Congressional Globe*, May 28, 1846.

the Mongolians behind, they arrived, after many ages, on the shores of the Atlantic, which they lit up with the lights of science and religion, and adorned with the useful and the elegant arts. Three and a half centuries ago, this race, in obedience to the great command, arrived in the New World, and found new lands to subdue and replenish. For a long time, it was confined to the border of the new field (I now mean the Celtic-Anglo-Saxon division); and even fourscore years ago the philosophic Burke was considered a rash man because he said the English colonists would top the Alleghenies, and descend into the valley of the Mississippi, and occupy without parchment if the Crown refused to make grants of land.

What was considered a rash declaration eighty years ago, is old history, in our young country, at this day. Thirty years ago I said the same thing of the Rocky Mountains and the Columbia: it was ridiculed then: it is becoming history to-day. The venerable Mr. Macon [North Carolina senator] has often told me that he remembered a line low down in North Carolina, fixed by a royal governor as a boundary between the whites and the Indians: where is the boundary now? The van of the Caucasian race now top the Rocky Mountains, and spread down to the shores of the Pacific. In a few years a great population will grow up there, luminous with the accumulated lights of European and American civilization. Their presence in such a position cannot be without its influence upon eastern Asia. The sun of civilization must shine across the sea: socially and commercially, the van of the Caucasians, and the rear of the Mongolians, must intermix. They must talk together, and trade together, and marry together. Commerce is a great civilizer—social intercourse as great—and marriage greater. The White and Yellow races can marry together, as well as eat and trade together. Moral and intellectual superiority will do the rest: the White race will take the ascendant, elevating what is susceptible of improvement—wearing out what is not. The Red race has disappeared from the Atlantic coast: the tribes that resisted civilization, met extinction. This is a cause of lamentation with many. For my part, I cannot murmur at what seems to be the effect of divine law. I cannot repine that this Capitol has replaced the wigwam—this Christian people, replaced the savages—white matrons, the red squaws—and that such men as Washington, Franklin, and Jefferson, have taken the place of Powhattan, Opechonecanough, and other red men, howsoever respectable they may have been as savages.

Civilization, or extinction, has been the fate of all people who have found themselves in the track of the advancing Whites, and civilization, always the preference of the Whites, has been pressed as an object, while extinction has followed as a consequence of its resistance. The Black and the Red races have often felt their ameliorating influence. The Yellow race, next to themselves in the scale of mental and moral excellence, and in the beauty of form, once their superiors in the useful and elegant arts, and in learning, and still respectable though stationary; this race cannot fail to receive a new impulse from the approach of the Whites, improved so much since so many ages ago they left the western borders of Asia. The apparition of the van of the Caucasian race, rising upon them in the east after having left them on the west, and after having completed the circumnavigation of the globe, must wake up and reanimate the torpid body of the old Asia. Our position and policy will commend us to their hospitable reception: political considerations will aid the action of social and commercial influences. Pressed upon by the great Powers of Europe—the same that press upon us—they must in our approach see the advent of friends, not of foes—of benefactors, not of invaders. The moral and intellectual superiority of the White race will do the rest: and thus the youngest people, and the newest land, will become the reviver and the regenerator of the oldest.

Mob scene during a race riot. One of many pre-Civil War skirmishes in which African-Americans and their abolitionist supporters defended themselves against efforts to return them to the South in compliance with the Fugitive Slave Law.

CHAPTER FOUR

◆

The Age of Reform

25

◆

A CALL TO ARMS

With the publication in Boston of the first issue of William Lloyd Garrison's *Liberator* in January 1831, the antislavery movement turned toward militancy. But Garrison's call for immediate emancipation was preceded by David Walker's *Appeal to the Coloured Citizens of the World*, published in September 1829. In one place in his impassioned pamphlet, not appearing in the excerpt below, Walker called African-Americans the "most wretched, degraded, and abject sort of beings that ever lived since the world began." He blasted American whites for their condescension, insensitivity, and cruelty and demanded that they end slavery and begin treating blacks as human beings with all the rights of other citizens. "Treat us like men," he cried, "and we will be friends."

In composing his *Appeal* Walker knew whereof he wrote. A free black man born in North Carolina in 1785, he managed to get an education. He traveled widely in the South observing slavery before he settled in Boston in 1827 and opened a shop that sold old clothes. When *Freedom's Journal*, the first American black newspaper, began publication in New York in 1827, Walker began contributing articles to it; he also lectured against slavery to small groups in Boston. He wrote his *Appeal* at high speed, printed it at his own expense, and saw to it that copies made their way into the South. The reaction to the *Appeal* was not surprising. Prominent Southerners demanded its suppression; even Bostonians called it "wicked and inflammatory." Garrison himself praised its "impassioned and determined spirit," but regretted its publication; later he changed his mind and reprinted most of it in the *Liberator*. Though there were threats on his life, Walker prepared new editions of his *Appeal*. But on June 28, 1830, he was found dead near the doorway of his shop, possibly the victim of poisoning.

Questions to Consider. Why do you suppose Walker's *Appeal* shocked even those whites opposed to slavery? To whom was he addressing his plea: to slaves, free blacks, or whites? Do you think he was exaggerating the misery of blacks in the United States? How radical does his *Appeal* sound today? What kind of action did he call upon black Americans to take? What part did religion play in his view of things?

◆

Appeal to the Coloured Citizens of the World (1829)

DAVID WALKER

I know that the blacks, take them half enlightened and ignorant, are more humane and merciful than the most enlightened and refined European that can be found in all the earth. Let no one say that I assert this because I am prejudiced on the side of my colour, and against the whites or Europeans. For what I write, I do it candidly, for my God and the good of both parties: Natural observations have taught me these things; there is a solemn awe in the hearts of the blacks, as it respects *murdering* men; whereas the whites (though they are great cowards) where they have the advantage, or think that there are any prospects of getting it, they murder all before them, in order to subject men to wretchedness and degradation under them. This is the natural result of pride and avarice. . . . Should the lives of such creatures be spared? Are God and Mammon in league? What has the Lord to do with a gang of desperate wretches, who go *sneaking about the country like robbers*—light upon his people wherever they can get a chance, binding them with chains and handcuffs, beat and murder them as they would *rattle-snakes?* Are they not the Lord's enemies? Ought they not be destroyed? Any person who will save such wretches from destruction, is fighting against the Lord, and will receive his just recompense. . . . The whites have had us under them for more than three centuries, murdering, and treating us like brutes; and, as Mr. Jefferson wisely said, they have never *found us out*—they do not know, indeed, that there is an unconquerable disposition in the breasts of the blacks, which, when it is fully awakened and put in motion, will be subdued, only with the destruction of the animal existence. Get the blacks started, and if you do not have a gang of tigers and lions to deal with, I am a deceiver of the blacks and of the whites.

Now, I ask you, had you not rather be killed than to be a slave to a tyrant, who takes the life of your mother, wife, and dear little children? Look upon your mother, wife and children, and answer God Almighty; and believe this, that it is no more harm for you to kill a man, who is trying to kill you, than it is for you to take a drink of water when thirsty; in fact, the man who will stand still and let another murder him, is worse than an infidel, and, if he has common sense, ought not to be pitied. . . . Oh! coloured people of these United States, I ask you, in the name of that God who made us, have we, in consequence of oppression, nearly lost the spirit

From David Walker, *Walker's Appeal, in Four Articles; Together with a Preamble to Coloured Citizens of the World* (D. Walker, Boston, 1830), 11–87.

CREDIT SALE OF A CHOICE GANG OF 41
SLAVES!
COMPRISING MECHANICS, LABORERS, ETC,
FOR THE SETTLEMENT OF A CO-PARTNERSHIP OF RAILROAD CONTRACTORS
BY J. A. BEARD & MAY, J. A. BEARD, AUCT'R.
WILL BE SOLD AT AUCTION, AT BANKS' ARCADE, MAGAZINE STREET,
ON TUESDAY, FEBRUARY 5th, 1856,
AT 12 O'CLOCK,
A VERY VALUABLE GANG OF SLAVES,

Belonging to a co-partnership, and sold to close the same. The said slaves comprise a gang of 41 choice Negroes. On the list will be found a good Blacksmith, one superior Bricklayer, Field Hands, Laborers, one Tanner, one Cooper, and a first rate woman Cook.

LEWIS, a black man, aged		32	good field hand and laborer.
SHELLY,	do	26	do do
PHILIP,	do	30	fair bricklayer.
HENRY,	do	24	fair cooper.
JACOB BATES,	do	22	good field hand and laborer.
BOB STAKELEY	do	35	do do
COLUMBUS,	do	21	do do
MARTIN,	do	25	do do
GEORGE,	do	30	No. 1 blacksmith.
WESTLY, a griff,		24	a fine tanner and bricklayer.
NELSON, a black man,		30	a good field hand and laborer.
DOCK,	do	28	do do
BIG FRED,	do	24	do do
LITTLE SOL,	do	22	do do
ALFRED, a griff,		28	do do
SIMON, a black man,		21	do do
WATT,	do	30	do do
JIM LEAVY,	do	24	do do
JIM ALLEN,	do	26	do do
FRANK GETTYS, a griff,		26	do do
JERRY GETTYS, a black,		23	do do
BILL GETTYS,	do	23	do do
GRANDERSON,	do	24	do do
LITTLE FED,	do	23	do do
FRANK HENRY, a griff,		23	do do
EDMOND,	do	21	do do
ANDERSON, a black man,		24	a No. 1 bricklayer and mason.
BOB SPRIGS, a griff,		25	a good field hand and laborer.
ELIJAH, a black man,		35	do do
JACK,	do	30	do do
REUBEN,	do	28	unsound.
STEPHEN,	do	22	a good field hand and laborer.
YELLOW JERRY, a griff,		28	a good teamster.
BIG SOL, a black man,		26	a good field hand and laborer.
BILL COLLINS,	do	28	do do
JESS,	do	26	do do
JUDGE,	do	30	do do
JERRY CARTER,	do	28	do do

LOUISA, a griff, 38 years, a good Cook and seamstress, and an excellent servant.
ROBERT, 13 years old, defect in one toe.
JASPAR, 24 years old, an extra No. 1 laborer, driver and coachman.
The slaves can be seen four days previous to the day of sale. They are fully guarantied against the vices and maladies prescribed by law, and are all selected slaves.

TERMS OF SALE—One year's credit for approved city accept-
ances or endorsed paper, with interest at 7 per cent. from date, and mortgage on the slaves if required
ACTS OF SALE BEFORE WM. SHANNON, NOTARY PUBLIC, AT THE EXPENSE OF THE PURCHASERS.

After the sale of the above list of Slaves, will be sold Another lot of Negroes, comprising Field Hands, House servants and Mechanics. A full description of the same will be given at the sale. The slaves can be seen two days previous to the sale.

Slavery poster. Slavery in its grimmest terms, a commonplace in the antebellum South. (Chicago Historical Society) of man, and, in no very trifling degree, adopted that of brutes? Do you answer, no? I ask you, then, what set of men can you point me to, in all the world, who are so abjectedly employed by their oppressors, as we are by our *natural enemies?* How can, Oh! how can those enemies but say that we and our children are not of the HUMAN FAMILY, but were made by our Creator to be an inheritance to them and theirs for ever? How can the slaveholders but say that they can bribe the best coloured person in the country, to sell his brethren for a trifling sum of money, and take that atrocity to confirm them in their avaricious opinion, that we were made to be slaves to them and their children? . . .

I aver, that when I look over these United States of America, and the world, and see the ignorant deceptions and consequent wretchedness of my brethren, I am brought ofttimes solemnly to a stand, and in the midst of my reflections I exclaim to my God, "Lord didst thou make us to be slaves to our brethren, the whites?" But when I reflect that God is just, and that millions of my wretched brethren would meet death with glory— yea, more, would plunge into the very mouths of cannons and be torn into particles as minute as the atoms which compose the elements of the earth, in preference to a mean submission to the lash of tyrants, I am with streaming eyes, compelled to shrink back into nothingness before my Maker, and exclaim again, thy will be done, O Lord God Almighty.

Men of colour, who are also of sense, for you particularly is my APPEAL designed. Our more ignorant brethren are not able to penetrate its value. I call upon you therefore to cast your eyes upon the wretchedness of your brethren, and to do your utmost to enlighten them—*go to work and enlighten your brethren!*—Let the Lord see you doing what you can to rescue them and yourselves from degradation. Do any of you say that you and your family are free and happy, and what have you to do with the wretched slaves and other people? So can I say, for I enjoy as much freedom as any of you, if I am not quite as well off as the best of you. Look into our freedom and happiness, and see of what kind they are composed!! They are of the very lowest kind—they are the very *dregs!*—they are the most servile and abject kind, that ever a people was in possession of! If any of you wish to know how FREE you are, let one of you start and go through the southern and western States of this country, and unless you travel as a slave to a white man (a servant is a *slave* to the man whom he serves) or have your free papers (which if you are not careful they will get from you) if they do not take you up and put you in jail, and if you cannot give good evidence of your freedom, sell you into eternal slavery, I am not a living man: or any man of colour, immaterial who he is, or where he came from, if he is *the fourth from the negro race!!* (as we are called) the white Christian of America will serve him the same they will sink him into wretchedness and degradation for ever while he lives. And yet some of you have the hardihood to say that you are free and happy! May God have mercy on your freedom and happiness!! I met a coloured man in the street a short time since, with a string of boots on his shoulders; we fell into conversation, and in the course of which, I said to him, what a miserable set of people we are! He asked, why?—Said I, we are so subjected under the whites, that we cannot obtain the comforts of life, but by cleaning their boots and shoes, old clothes, waiting on them, shaving them &c. Said he, (with the boots on his shoulders) "I am completely happy!!! I never want to live any better or happier than when I get a plenty of boots and shoes to clean!!!" Oh! how can those who are actuated by avarice only, but think, that our Creator made us to be an inheritance to them for ever, when they see that our greatest glory is centered in such mean and low objects? Understand me, brethren, I do not mean to speak against the occupations by which we acquire enough and sometimes scarcely that, to render ourselves and families comfortable through life. I am subjected to the same inconvenience, as you all. —My objections are, to our *glorying* and being *happy* in such low employments; for if we are men, we ought to be thankful to the Lord for the past, and for the future. Be looking forward with thankful hearts to higher attainments than *wielding the razor* and *cleaning boots and shoes.* The man whose aspirations are not *above,* and even *below* these, is indeed, ignorant and wretched enough. I advanced it therefore to you, not as a *problematical,* but as an unshaken and for ever immovable *fact,* that your full glory and happiness, as well as all other coloured people under Heaven, shall never be fully consummated, but with the *entire emancipation of your enslaved brethren all over the world.* You may therefore, go to work and do what you can to rescue, or join in with tyrants to oppress them and yourselves, until the Lord shall come upon you all like a thief in the night. For I believe it is the will of the Lord that our greatest happiness shall consist in working for the salvation of our whole body. When this is accomplished a burst of glory will shine upon you, which will indeed astonish you and the world. Do any of you say this never will be done? I assure you that God will accomplish it—if nothing else will answer, he will hurl tyrants and devils into *atoms* and make way for his people. But O my brethren! I say unto you again, you must go to work and prepare the way of the Lord.

26

◆

FREEDOM NOW

David Walker's militant call to arms in 1829 failed to influence most white abolitionists, who wanted to end slavery through persuasion, not violence. Yet, after the rapid spread of the Cotton Kingdom had made slavery so profitable, persuading significant numbers of slaveholders to free their slaves seemed hopeless. It became virtually impossible when Southern states passed laws that outlawed public debates on the issue of slavery and made manumission [voluntarily freeing one's slaves] illegal.

Furthermore, persuading Northerners to support nonviolent abolitionism was almost as difficult as persuading Southerners. The cause appeared hopelessly impractical. In addition, most white Northerners considered blacks inferior and did not want them around, free or otherwise. Recognizing this difficulty, the American Colonization Society had tried—unsuccessfully—to encourage gradual manumission by raising money to send freed slaves to Africa. The problem remained when William Lloyd Garrison of Boston founded the militant American Anti-Slavery Society in 1833. His chief goals were to persuade Northerners on two points: that immediate abolition was feasible; and that slaves, once free, would make acceptable citizens and neighbors.

Women played a major role in nineteenth-century reform movements, including the antislavery struggle. They helped sensitize the Protestant churches to the evils of slavery and organized petition drives urging Congress to abolish the slave trade. At a time when the male-dominant mainstream culture of the United States was intolerant of women who commented on political issues, they wrote and sometimes spoke out against slavery. One of their great early successes was Lydia Maria Child's *An Appeal in Favor of That Class of Americans Called Africans,* which appeared in 1833. Child's book (excerpted below) blended anecdote, logic, and historical scholarship and was written in a clear, compelling style. It helped convert thousands of wavering Northerners to the cause of immediate abolitionism and thus significantly strengthened the role of the Garrisonians in the unfolding antislavery crusade.

Born in 1802 into a family of Massachusetts Unitarians, Lydia Maria Child was, at age 31, already the best-known woman writer in America when *An Appeal* appeared. She had several novels and domestic "how-to" works to her credit and had founded the country's first children's magazine, the *Juvenile Miscellany,* in 1826. Though influential with reformers, Child's *Appeal* badly damaged this popularity. Sales of her books fell sharply, and the *Juvenile Miscellany* foundered in 1834. From 1840 to 1849 she and her husband edited the *National Anti-Slavery Standard* in New York City. In 1852 they moved to a Massachusetts farm, where Lydia wrote extensively on religion, women's rights, capital punishment, slavery, and, following the Civil War, the plight of the freedmen. She died in Wayland, Massachusetts, in 1880.

Questions to Consider. It was an article of faith for most Americans in the early nineteenth century that women were different from men— that they saw the world differently and expressed themselves differently. Does Lydia Maria Child's *Appeal* seem "feminine" to you? Did she raise points or use arguments that a man might not have? Many Americans of the time thought abolitionists were humorless and self-righteous. Does Child seem to have been humorless? What was her primary method of persuasion? Why did she discuss the slave trade so extensively? What did she mean when she said that efforts to regulate slavery were like efforts to regulate murder?

———————◆———————

That Class of Americans Called Africans (1833)

LYDIA MARIA CHILD

A judicious and benevolent friend lately told me the story of one of her relatives, who married a slave-owner, and removed to his plantation. The lady in question was considered very amiable, and had a serene, affectionate expression of countenance. After several years' residence among her slaves, she visited New England. "Her history was written in her face," said my friend; "its expression had changed into that of a fiend. She brought but few slaves with her; and those few were of course compelled to perform additional labor. One faithful negro-woman nursed the twins of her mistress, and did all the washing, ironing, and scouring. If, after a sleepless night with the restless babes, (driven from the bosom of their own mother,) she performed her toilsome avocations with diminished activity, her mistress, with her own lady-like hands, applied the cowskin, and the neigh-

From Lydia Maria Child, *An Appeal in Favor of That Class of Americans Called Africans* (New York, 1833), 28–37, 141–146.

borhood resounded with the cries of her victim. The instrument of punishment was actually kept hanging in the entry, to the no small disgust of her New-England visiters. For my part," continued my friend, "I did not try to be polite to her; for I was not hypocrite enough to conceal my indignation."

The following occurred near Natchez, and was told to me by a highly intelligent man, who, being a diplomatist and a courtier, was very likely to make the best of national evils: A planter had occasion to send a female slave some distance on an errand. She did not return so soon as he expected, and he grew angry. At last he gave orders that she should be severely whipped when she came back. When the poor creature arrived, she pleaded for mercy, saying she had been so very ill, that she was obliged to rest in the fields; but she was ordered to receive another dozen lashes, for having had the impudence to speak. She died at the whipping-post; nor did she perish alone—a new-born baby died with her. The gentleman who told me this fact, witnessed the poor creature's funeral. It is true, the master was universally blamed and shunned for the cruel deed; but the laws were powerless.

I shall be told that such examples as these are of rare occurrence; and I have no doubt that instances of excessive severity are far from being common. I believe that a large proportion of masters are as kind to their slaves as they can be, consistently with keeping them in bondage; but it must be allowed that this, to make the best of it, is very stinted kindness. And let it never be forgotten that the negro's fate depends entirely on the character of his master; and it is a mere matter of chance whether he fall into merciful or unmerciful hands; his happiness, nay, his very life, depends on chance. . . .

But it is urged that it is the interest of planters to treat their slaves well. This argument no doubt has some force; and it is the poor negro's only security. But it is likewise the interest of men to treat their cattle kindly; yet we see that passion and short-sighted avarice do overcome the strongest motives of interest. Cattle are beat unmercifully, sometimes unto death; they are ruined by being over-worked; weakened by want of sufficient food; and so forth. Besides, it is sometimes directly *for* the interest of the planter to work his slaves beyond their strength. When there is a sudden rise in the prices of sugar, a certain amount of labor in a given time is of more consequence to the owner of a plantation than the price of several slaves; he can well *afford* to waste a few lives. This is no idle hypothesis— such calculations are gravely and openly made by planters. Hence, it is the slave's prayer that sugars may be cheap. When the negro is old, or feeble from incurable disease, is it his master's *interest* to feed him well, and clothe him comfortably? Certainly not: it then becomes desirable to get rid of the human brute as soon as convenient. It is a common remark, that it is not quite safe, in most cases, for even parents to be entirely dependant on the generosity of their children; and if human nature be such, what has the slave to expect, when he becomes a mere bill of expense? . . .

Among other apologies for slavery, it has been asserted that the Bible does not forbid it. Neither does it forbid the counterfeiting of a bank-bill. It is the *spirit* of the Holy Word, not its particular *expressions*, which must be a rule for our conduct. How can slavery be reconciled with the maxim, "Do unto others, as ye would that others should do unto you?" Does not the command, "Thou shalt not *steal*," prohibit *kidnapping?* And how does whipping men to death agree with the injunction, "Thou shalt do no *murder?*" Are we not told "to loose the bands of wickedness, to undo the heavy burdens, to let the oppressed go free, and to break every yoke?" It was a Jewish law that he who stole a man, or sold him, or he in whose hands the stolen man was found, should suffer death; and he in whose house a fugitive slave sought an asylum was forbidden to give him up to his master. Modern slavery is so unlike Hebrew servitude, and its regulations are so diametrically opposed to the rules of the Gospel, which came to bring deliverance to the captive, that it is idle to dwell upon this point. . . .

I shall perhaps be asked why I have said so much about the slave-*trade*, since it was long ago abolished in this country? There are several good reasons for it. In the first place, it is a part of the system; for if there were no slaves, there could be no slave-trade; and while there are slaves, the slave-trade *will* continue. In the next place, the trade is still briskly carried on in Africa, and slaves are smuggled into these States through the Spanish colonies. In the third place, a very extensive internal slave-trade is carried on in this country. The breeding of negro-cattle for the foreign markets, (of Louisiana, Georgia, Alabama, Arkansas, and Missouri,) is a very lucrative branch of business. Whole coffles of them, chained and manacled, are driven through our Capital on their way to auction. Foreigners, particularly those who come here with enthusiastic ideas of American freedom, are amazed and disgusted at the sight. A troop of slaves once passed through Washington on the fourth of July, while drums were beating, and standards flying. One of the captive negroes raised his hand, loaded with irons, and waving it toward the starry flag, sung with a smile of bitter irony, "Hail Columbia! *happy* land!". . .

A free man of color is in constant danger of being seized and carried off by these slave-dealers. Mr. Cooper, a Representative in Congress from Delaware, told Dr. Torrey, of Philadelphia, that he was often afraid to send his servants out in the evening, lest they should be encountered by kidnappers. Wherever these notorious slave-jockeys appear in our Southern States, the free people of color hide themselves, as they are obliged to do on the coast of Africa. . . .

Finally, I have described some of the horrors of the slave-trade, because when our constitution was formed, the government pledged itself not to abolish this traffic until 1808. We began our career of freedom by granting a twenty years' lease of iniquity—twenty years of allowed invasion of other men's rights—twenty years of bloodshed, violence, and fraud! And this will be told in our annals—this will be heard of to the end of time!

While the slave-trade was allowed, the South could use it to advance their views in various ways. In their representation to Congress, five slaves counted the same as three freemen; of course, every fresh cargo was not only an increase of property, but an increase of *political power*. Ample time was allowed to lay in a stock of slaves to supply the new slave states and territories that might grow up; and when this was effected, the prohibition of foreign commerce in human flesh, operated as a complete *tariff*, to protect the domestic supply.

Every man who buys a slave promotes this traffic, by raising the value of the article; every man who owns a slave, indirectly countenances it; every man who allows that slavery is a lamentable *necessity*, contributes his share to support it; and he who votes for admitting a slave-holding State into the Union, fearfully augments the amount of this crime. . . .

The abolitionists think it a duty to maintain at all times, and in all places, that slavery *ought* to be abolished, and that it *can* be abolished. When error is so often repeated it becomes very important to repeat the truth; especially as good men are apt to be quiet, and selfish men are prone to be active. They propose no *plan*—they leave that to the wisdom of Legislatures. But they never swerve from the *principle* that slavery is both wicked and un-necessary. —Their object is to turn the public voice against this evil, by a plain exposition of facts.

The Anti-Slavery Society is loudly accused of being seditious, fanatical, and likely to promote insurrections. It seems to be supposed, that they wish to send fire and sword into the South, and encourage the slaves to hunt down their masters. Slave-owners wish to have it viewed in this light, because they know the subject will not bear discussion; and men here, who give the tone to public opinion, have loudly repeated the charge—some from good motives, and some from bad. I once had a very strong prejudice against anti-slavery;—(I am ashamed to think *how* strong—for mere prejudice should never be stubborn,) but a candid examination has convinced me, that I was in an error. I made the common mistake of taking things for granted, without stopping to investigate.

Ridicule and reproach has been abundantly heaped upon the laborers in this righteous cause. Power, wealth, talent, pride, and sophistry, are all in arms against them; but God and truth is on their side. The cause of anti-slavery is rapidly gaining ground. Wise heads as well as warm hearts, are joining in its support. In a few years I believe the opinion of New-England will be unanimous in its favor. Maine, which enjoys the enviable distinction of never having had a slave upon her soil, has formed an Anti-Slavery Society composed of her best and most distinguished men. Those who are determined to be on the popular side, should be cautious how they move just now: It is a trying time for such characters, when public opinion is on the verge of a great change.

Men who *think* upon the subject, are fast coming to the conclusion that slavery can never be much ameliorated, while it is allowed to exist. What Mr. Fox said of the *trade* is true of the *system*—"you may as well try to *regulate* murder."

27

◆

RISING GENERATIONS

The era from the 1830s until the Civil War was marked by intense reform movements, especially in the Northeast. "In the history of the world," exclaimed Ralph Waldo Emerson, "the doctrine of Reform had never such a scope as at the present hour." Most reformers were deeply religious; they took seriously Christianity's emphasis on the spiritual equality of all human beings and Jesus' special concern for the lowly and humble. They were also inspired by the Declaration of Independence with its insistence on unalienable rights, and were eager to make its social and political ideas a reality. Many reformers believed that human nature was perfectible, and that with better social arrangements men and women would be able to live more fully and freely than they ever had before.

During the Age of Reform the antislavery movement became important; so did the temperance movement (against alcohol consumption), the struggle for women's rights, more humane prisons and asylums, and improved conditions for working people. Horace Mann, a Boston lawyer and politician, took an interest in all these reforms, but he was especially interested in the development of public elementary education, or the "common schools." So absorbed did Mann become with expanding and improving the schools that he stunned his friends by quitting the law and resigning from the Massachusetts senate to become secretary of the state's fledgling board of education.

At the time Mann began his labors, Massachusetts already had a notable educational tradition deriving chiefly from the Puritan insistence that as many people as possible should be able to read the Bible. By the early 1800s most districts of the state had rudimentary schools and a fair amount of somewhat haphazard instruction. But reformers, finding this thoroughly unsatisfactory, worked assiduously to persuade towns and villages to build more and better schools; to fill them with comfortable desks, blackboards, books, maps, blocks, and writing materials; to establish standards and train professional (mostly female) teachers; and to make elementary education compulsory.

The common (public) school "revivalists," as they called themselves, had little power save persuasion. Public schools then as now were almost wholly the responsibility of local governments. Yet the revivalists were astoundingly successful, particularly in the North. By the time of the Civil War, the United States, even with meager results in the South, had educated more of its children for a longer period than any other country in the world, with the possible exception of Prussia. But unlike Prussia and most other countries, the United States, accomplished this widespread education almost wholly through local initiative—prodded, to be sure, by Horace Mann and his fellow re-formers, but local nonetheless.

The fact that the so-called schoolmen usually had to persuade local districts to do something might help explain why their writing seems overblown and excessive to modern ears. Horace Mann achieved real impact only by painting a dire picture of the schools, and he was obviously not at all reluctant to do so. But something else was going on here, too. The nineteenth century was a golden age of American oratory, a period in which public figures—politicians, ministers, and reformers alike—took tremendous pride in entertaining and moving throngs of listeners. Public speakers worked hard on producing and delivering noteworthy speeches, and tried, usually with success, to have them published with all their original rhetorical flourishes intact. Most of the famous essays of Ralph Waldo Emerson were public lec-tures before they were works of literature, and Senator Daniel Webster, the "Godlike Dan'l" himself, once captivated 20,000 Bostonians with a two-hour address on municipal water systems! Horace Mann clearly reveled in this kind of expressive rhetoric. But what sounds ridiculously overheated to us would have seemed just comfortably warm in the nineteenth century.

Mann, most famous and influential of the school reformers, was born in the village of Franklin, Massachusetts, in 1796. Although his family was poor, Mann was able to pursue his education by means of various scholarships and eventually graduated from Brown University at the age of twenty-three. After serving for twelve years as secretary of the Massachusetts board of education, the post for which he gave up politics and the law, he left to replace John Quincy Adams in the U.S. House of Representatives for a term. In 1852 he became the first president of Antioch College in Ohio, where he died in 1859.

Questions to Consider. In this report, Mann was trying to describe society as he saw it and also to suggest what the future might bring without major school reform. What features of Massachusetts society—its economy, its institutions, its class structure, the habits and view-points of its people, and its tensions and conflicts—emerge most clearly from Mann's report? Are you surprised at any of the topics he in-cluded—or failed to include? What special problems did he perceive in the education of factory children as opposed to farm children, and of girls as opposed to boys? When Mann peered into the future, what did he see? Why did he seem to hold the English city of Manchester in such horror? What did he mean by "barbarism"?

◆

Report on the Public Schools (1840)

HORACE MANN

I feel fully justified in affirming, that the prospects of the rising generation are daily growing brighter, by means of the increasing light which is shed upon them from our Common Schools. . . . Stronger feelings and firmer convictions of the importance of our Common Schools are taking possession of the public mind, and where they have not yet manifested themselves in any outward and visible improvement, they are silently and gradually working to that end. . . .

It must not, however, be inferred, that the most extensive reform is not still necessary in regard to those edifices, where the business of education, for the great mass of the children in the State, is carried on. . . . Every other class of edifices, whether public or private, has felt the hand of reform. Churches, courthouses, even jails and prisons, are rebuilt, or remodelled, great regard being paid, in most cases to ornament, and in all cases to health, to personal convenience and accommodation. But the schoolhouse, which leads directly towards the church, or rather may be considered as its vestibule, and which furnishes to the vast majority of our children, the only public means they will ever enjoy, for qualifying themselves to profit by its counsels, its promises, its warnings, its consolations;—the schoolhouse, which leads directly from the courthouse, from the jail and from the prison, and is, for the mass of our children, the great preventive and safeguard against being called or forced into them, as litigants or as criminals;—this class of buildings, all over the State, stands in afflicting contrast with all the others. The courthouses, which are planned and erected under the advice and control of the county authorities, and of the leading men in the county for themselves and in which they spend but a few terms in the year, and the meeting-houses, where the parents spend but a few hours in a week, are provided with costly embellishments, and with every appurtenance, that can gratify taste or subserve comfort; but the houses where the children, in the most susceptible period of their lives, spend from thirty to forty hours in a week, seem to be deserted by all public care, and abandoned to cheerlessness and dilapidation. . . .

If, in a portion of the manufacturing districts in the State, a regular and systematic obedience is paid to the law, while, in other places, it is regularly and systematically disregarded, the inevitable consequences to the latter will be obvious, upon a moment's reflection. The neighborhood or town where the law is broken will soon become the receptacle of the poorest,

From Horace Mann, *Third Annual Report of the Secretary of the Board of Education* (Boston: Dutton and Wentworth, 1840), 35–36, 39–40, 43–48, 96.

New England schoolroom, 1857. Horace Mann's reform efforts succeeded to an astonishing degree in the towns and villages of the Northern states. By modern standards, however, even the new and newly refurbished schools were sometimes stark and gloomy, as this photograph of a girls' class suggests. Even when teachers were better trained and paid, they relied on strict discipline and drill to educate their students. (Daguerrotype by Southworth and Hawes; The Metropolitan Museum of Art)

most vicious and abandoned parents, who are bringing up their children to be also as poor, vicious and abandoned as themselves. The whole class of parents, who cannot obtain employment for their children, at one place, but are welcomed at another, will circulate through the body politic, until at last, they will settle down as permanent residents, in the latter; like the vicious humors of the natural body, which, being thrown off by every healthy part, at last accumulate and settle upon a diseased spot. Every breach of this law, therefore, inflicts direct and positive injustice, not only upon the children employed, but upon all the industrious and honest communities in which they are employed; because its effect will be to fill those communities with paupers and criminals;—or, at least, with a class of persons, who, without being absolute, technical paupers, draw their subsistence in a thousand indirect ways, from the neighborhood, where they reside; and without being absolute criminals in the eye of the law, still commit a thousand injurious, predatory acts, more harassing and annoying to the peace and security of a village, than many classes of positive crimes.

While water-power only is used for manufacturing purposes, a natural limit is affixed, in every place, to the extension of manufactories. The power being all taken up, in any place, the further investment of capital and the employment of an increased number of operatives, must cease. While we restrict ourselves to the propulsion of machinery by water, therefore, it is impossible, that we should have such an extensive manufacturing district as, for instance, that of Manchester in England, because we have no streams of sufficient magnitude for the purpose. But Massachusetts is already the greatest manufacturing State in the Union. Her best sites are all taken up, and yet her disposition to manufacture appears not to be checked. Under such circumstances, it seems not improbable, that steam-power will be resorted to. . . ; and, if steam is employed, there is no assignable limit to the amount of a manufacturing population, that may be gathered into a single manufacturing district. If, therefore, we would not have, in any subsequent time, a population like that of the immense city of Manchester, where great numbers of the laboring population live in the filthiest streets, and mostly in houses, which are framed back to back, so that in no case is there any yard behind them, but all ingress and egress, for all purposes, is between the front side of the house and the public street,—if we would not have such a population, we must not only have preventive laws, but we must see that no cupidity, no contempt of the public welfare for the sake of private gain, is allowed openly to violate or clandestinely to evade them. It would, indeed, be most lamentable and self-contradictory, if, with all our institutions devised and prepared on the hypothesis of common intelligence and virtue, we should rear a class of children, to be set apart and, as it were, dedicated to ignorance and vice. . . .

It is obvious, that children of ten, twelve, or fourteen years of age, may be steadily worked in our manufactories, without any schooling, and that this cruel deprivation may be persevered in for six, eight, or ten years, and yet, during all this period, no very alarming outbreak shall occur to rouse the public mind from its guilty slumber. The children are in their years of minority, and they have no control over their own time, or their own actions. The bell is to them, what the water-wheel and the main shaft are to the machinery, which they superintend. The wheel revolves and the machinery must go; the bell rings and the children must assemble. In their hours of work, they are under the police of the establishment; at other times, they are under the police of the neighborhood. Hence this state of things may continue for years, and the peace of the neighborhood remain undisturbed, except, perhaps, by a few nocturnal or sabbath-day depredations. The ordinary movements of society may go on without any shocks or collisions,—as, in the human system, a disease may work at the vitals and gain a fatal ascendancy there, before it manifests itself on the surface. But the punishment for such an offence, will not be remitted, because its infliction is postponed. The retribution, indeed, is not postponed, it only awaits the full completion of the offence; for this is a crime of such magnitude, that it requires years for the criminal to perpetrate it in, and to finish it off thoroughly, in all its parts. But when the children pass from the condition of restraint to that of freedom,—from years of enforced but impatient servitude to that independence for which they have secretly pined, and to which they have looked forward, not merely as the period of emancipation, but of long-delayed indulgence;—when they become strong in the passions and propensities that grow up spontaneously, but are weak in the moral powers that control them, and blind in the intellect which foresees their tendencies;—when, according to the course of our political institutions, they go, by one bound, from the political nothingness of a child, to the political sovereignty of a man,—then, for that people, who so cruelly neglected and injured them, there will assuredly come a day of retribution. . . .

But by far the most important subject, respecting which I have sought for information, during the year, remains to be noticed. While we are in little danger of over-estimating the value of Common Schools, yet we shall err egregiously, if we regard them as ends, and not as means. A forgetfulness of this distinction would send the mass of our children of both sexes into the world, scantily provided either with the ability or the disposition to perform even the most ordinary duties of life. Common Schools derive their value from the fact, that they are an instrument, more extensively applicable to the whole mass of the children, than any other instrument ever yet devised. They are an instrument, by which the good men in society can send redeeming influences to those children who suffer under the calamity of vicious parentage and evil domestic associations. The world is full of lamentable proofs, that the institution of the family may exist for an indefinite number of generations, without mitigating the horrors of barbarism. But the institution of Common Schools is the offspring of an advanced state of civilization, and is incapable of coexisting with barbarian life, because, should barbarism prevail, it would destroy the schools, should the schools prevail, they would destroy barbarism. They are the only civil institution; capable of extending its beneficent arms to embrace and to cultivate in all parts of its nature, every child that comes into the world. . . .

Young men, it may be said, have a larger circle of action; they can mingle more in promiscuous society,—at least, they have a far wider range of business occupations,—all of which stimulate thought, suggest inquiry and furnish means for improvement. But the sphere of females is domestic. Their life is comparatively secluded. The proper delicacy of the sex forbids them from appearing in the promiscuous marts of business, and even from mingling, as actors, in those less boisterous arenas, where mind is the acting agent, as well as the object to be acted upon. If then, she is precluded from these sources of information, and these incitements to inquiry; if, by the unanimous and universal opinion of civilized nations, when she breaks away from comparative seclusion and retirement, she leaves her charms behind her; and if, at the same time she is debarred from access to books, by what means, through what channels, is she to obtain the knowledge so indispensable for the fit discharge of maternal and domestic duties, and for rendering herself an enlightened companion for intelligent men? Without books, except in cases of extraordinary natural endowment, she will be doomed to relative ignorance and incapacity. . . .

The State, in its sovereign capacity, has the deepest interest in this matter. If it would spread the means of intelligence and self-culture over its entire surface, making them diffusive as sunshine, causing them to penetrate into every hamlet and dwelling, and, like the vernal sun, quickening into life the seeds of usefulness and worth, wherever the prodigal hand of nature may have scattered them;—it would call into existence an order of men, who would establish a broader basis for its prosperity, and give a brighter lustre to its name,—who would improve its arts, impart wisdom to its counsels, and extend the beneficent sphere of its charities. Yet, not for its own sake only, should it assume this work. It is a corollary from the axioms of its constitution, that every child, born within its borders, shall be enlightened. . . . Here are an inconceivable extent and magnitude of interests, sympathies, obligations;—here are all the great instincts of humanity, working out their way to a greater or less measure of good, according to the light they enjoy;—and, compared with this wide and deep mass of unrecorded life, all that emerges into history and is seen of man, is as nothing.

28

♦

UTOPIANS

The Brook Farm Association was established in 1841 in a rural area nine miles from Boston. One of many utopian communities that sprang up in the United States in the first part of the nineteenth century, Brook Farm was an experiment in cooperative living. Of the two hundred cooperative colonies that flowered from New England to Utah, Brook Farm was probably the most famous because of its proximity to a large city and because many well-known literary people were associated with it. The "Farmers," dedicated to "plain living and high thinking," engaged in agriculture, lived communally, operated an excellent school, and held dances, games, picnics, plays, lectures, and discussions. It was, said one visitor, "rich in cheerful buzz." The community was praised by Ralph Waldo Emerson for its experimentalism but disparaged by Henry David Thoreau for its conformity. Like many other utopians, the Brook Farmers emphasized the equality of the sexes and the rights and dignity of labor. In 1844, the association adopted Fourierism, a socialist doctrine originating in France. They introduced more organization into their community and published *The Harbinger,* a Fourierist journal with a nationwide circulation. In 1847 a fire destroyed the main building at Brook Farm; the association, which was heavily in debt, disbanded soon after. Elizabeth Palmer Peabody wrote the following account of Brook Farm for *The Dial,* the leading journal of New England transcendentalism, a few months after the Farm's establishment.

Born in Massachusetts in 1804, Elizabeth Palmer Peabody was precociously literate. She founded two schools and was a confidante of such writers as William Ellery Channing, Ralph Waldo Emerson, and Nathaniel Hawthorne (who married her sister, Sophia). In 1839 Peabody opened a Boston bookshop that quickly became a notable center of American letters and reform and the place from which *The Dial* was published. She was a sympathetic observer of the doings at Brook Farm, where she frequently taught. After 1845, Peabody devoted herself chiefly to education, writing a widely adopted history textbook and founding one of the earliest kindergartens in the United States. She was also a popular lecturer and donated most of her fees to further the education of Native Americans. She died in Jamaica Plain, Massachusetts, in 1894.

Questions to Consider. Why were communities like Brook Farm called "utopian"? What did Peabody mean by "Embryo University"? Why did the Brook Farmers feel the need to "come out from the world" to live a religious and moral life? Why did this life take the form of a community of property located in the country? Why did Peabody emphasize the equality of bodily and intellectual labor? What sort of people do you think Peabody expected to apply for admission to Brook Farm? Of the first hundred, for example, how many might have been writers and teachers, or mechanics and agricultural laborers, or young businessmen? Why might Peabody have thought that Brook Farm would have special appeal to ministers? What did she mean by "sordid passion" and "the spirit of coterie"?

◆

Plan of Brook Farm (1842)

ELIZABETH PALMER PEABODY

A few individuals, who, unknown to each other, under different disciplines of life, reacting from different social evils, but aiming at the same object,—of being wholly true to their natures as men and women; have been made acquainted with one another, and have determined to become the Faculty of the Embryo University.

In order to live a religious and moral life worthy the name, they feel it is necessary to come out in some degree from the world, and to form themselves into a community of property, so far as to exclude competition and the ordinary rules of trade;—while they reserve sufficient private property, or the means of obtaining it, for all purposes of independence, and isolation at will. They have bought a farm, in order to make agriculture the basis of their life, it being the most direct and simple in relation to nature.

A true life, although it aims beyond the highest star, is redolent of the healthy earth. The perfume of clover lingers about it. The lowing of cattle is the natural bass to the melody of human voices.

On the other hand, what absurdity can be imagined greater than the institution of cities? They originated not in love, but in war. It was war that drove men together in multitudes, and compelled them to stand so close, and build walls around them. This crowded condition produced wants of an unnatural character, which resulted in occupations that regenerated the evil, by creating artificial wants. . . .

The plan of the Community, as an Economy, is in brief this: for all who have property to take stock, and receive a fixed interest thereon; then to

The Dial II (Jan. 1842), 361–371.

keep house or board in commons, as they shall severally desire, at the cost of provisions purchased at wholesale, or raised on the farm; and for all to labor in community, and be paid at a certain rate an hour, choosing their own number of hours, and their own kind of work. With the results of this labor, and their interest, they are to pay their board, and also purchase whatever else they require at cost, at the warehouses of the Community, which are to be filled by the Community as such. To perfect this economy, in the course of time they must have all trades, and all modes of business carried on among themselves, from the lowest mechanical trade, which contributes to the health and comfort of life, to the finest art which adorns it with food or drapery for the mind.

All labor, whether bodily or intellectual, is to be paid at the same rate of wages; on the principle, that as the labor becomes merely bodily, it is a greater sacrifice to the individual laborer, to give his time to it; because time is desirable for the cultivation of the intellect, in exact proportion to ignorance. Besides, intellectual labor involves in itself higher pleasures, and is more its own reward, than bodily labor.

Another reason, for setting the same pecuniary value on every kind of labor, is, to give outward expression to the great truth, that all labor is sacred, when done for a common interest. Saints and philosophers already know this, but the childish world does not; and very decided measures must be taken to equalize labors, in the eyes of the young of the community, who are not beyond the moral influences of the world without them. . . .

Minds incapable of refinement will not be attracted into this association. It is an Ideal community, and only to the ideally inclined will it be attractive; but these are to be found in every rank of life, under every shadow of circumstance. Even among the diggers in the ditch are to be found some, who through religious cultivation, can look down, in meek superiority, upon the outwardly refined, and the book-learned.

Besides, after becoming members of this community, none will be engaged merely in bodily labor. . . . This community aims to be rich, not in the metallic representative of wealth, but in the wealth itself, which money should represent; namely, LEISURE TO LIVE IN ALL THE FACULTIES OF THE SOUL. As a community, it will traffic with the world at large, in the products of Agricultural labor; and it will sell education to as many young persons as can be domesticated in the families, and enter into the common life with their own children. In the end, it hopes to be enabled to provide—not only all the necessaries, but all the elegances desirable for bodily and for spiritual health; books, apparatus, collections for science, works of art, means of beautiful amusement. These things are to be common to all; and thus that object, which alone gilds and refines the passion for individual accumulation, will no longer exist for desire, and whenever the Sordid passion appears, it will be seen in its naked selfishness. In its ultimate success, the community will realize all the ends which selfishness seeks, but involved in spiritual blessings, which only greatness of soul can aspire after. . . .

This principle, with regard to labor, lies at the root of moral and religious life; for it is not more true that "money is the root of all evil," than that *labor is the germ of all good.*

All the work is to be offered for the free choice of the members of the community, at stated seasons, and such as is not chosen, will be hired. But it is not anticipated that any work will be set aside to be hired, for which there is actual ability in the community. It is so desirable that the hired labor should be avoided, that it is believed the work will all be done freely, even though at voluntary sacrifice. If there is some exception at first, it is because the material means are inadequate to the reception of all who desire to go. They cannot go, unless they have shelter; and in this climate, they cannot have shelter unless they can build houses; and they cannot build houses unless they have money. It is not here as in Robinson Crusoe's Island. . . .

The known accomplishments of many of the members of this association have already secured it an interest in the public mind, as a school of literary advantages quite superior. Most of the associates have had long practical experience in the details of teaching, and have groaned under the necessity of taking their method and law from custom and caprice, when they would rather have found it in the nature of the thing taught, and the condition of the pupil to be instructed. . . .

There are some persons who have entered the community without money. It is believed that these will be able to support themselves and dependents, by less work, more completely, and with more ease than elsewhere; while their labor will be of advantage to the community. It is in no sense an eleemosynary establishment,[1] but it is hoped that in the end it will be able to receive all who have the spiritual qualifications. . . .

It should be understood also, that after all the working and teaching, which individuals of the community may do, they will still have leisure, and in that leisure can employ themselves in connexion with the world around them. Some will not teach at all; and those especially can write books, pursue the Fine Arts, for private emolument if they will, and exercise various functions of men.—From this community might go forth preachers of the gospel of Christ, who would not have upon them the odium, or the burthen, that now diminishes the power of the clergy. And even if *pastors* were to go from this community, to reside among congregations as now, for a salary given, the fact that they would have something to retreat upon, at any moment, would save them from that virtual dependence on their congregations, which now corrupts the relation.

Now there can be only one way of selecting and winnowing their company. The power to do this must be inherent in their constitution; they must keep sternly true to their principles.

In the first place, they must not compromise their principle of labor, in receiving members. Every one, who has any personal power, whether

1. **Eleemosynary establishment:** one that is supported by alms.—*Eds.*

bodily or mental, must bring the contribution of personal service, no matter how much money he brings besides. . . .

Another danger which should be largely treated is the spirit of coterie.[2] The breadth of their platform, which admits all sects; and the generality of their plan, which demands all degrees of intellectual culture to begin with, is some security against this. But the ultimate security must be in numbers. Some may say, "already this taint has come upon them, for they are doubtless *transcendentalists*." But to mass a few protestants together and call them transcendentalists, is a popular cant. Transcendentalism belongs to no sect of religion, and no social party. It is the common ground to which all sects may rise, and be purified of their narrowness; for it consists in seeking the spiritual ground of all manifestations. As already in the pages of this periodical, Calvinist, and Unitarian, and Episcopalian, and Baptist, and Quaker, and Swedenborgian, have met and spoken in love and freedom on this common basis; so it would be seen, if the word were understood, that transcendentalism, notwithstanding its name is taken in vain by many moonshiny youths and misses who assume it, would be the best of all guards against the spirit of coterie.

2. **Coterie:** A small group of people who habitually associate with each other.—*Eds.*

29

◆

BALM FOR THE AFFLICTED

Dorothea L. Dix, a Boston schoolteacher, was interested in most ante-bellum reforms but especially in the treatment of the mentally ill. One Sunday, in March 1841, she went to the House of Correction in East Cambridge to hold a Sunday school class for the women inmates. She was horrified by the filth, neglect, and misery she discovered among the insane who were kept in the jail.

Dix's experience in East Cambridge turned her into an earnest re-former. She persuaded local authorities to improve conditions in the jail. She also began touring Massachusetts—visiting jails, almshouses, and houses of correction—to gather information about the treatment of the mentally ill. Having gathered a shocking collection of facts, she drew up a tract entitled *Memorial to the Legislature of Massachusetts,* which called for drastic reforms, and had it presented to the Massa-chusetts legislature in January 1843. The memorial raised a storm; Dix was called a sensationalist, a troublemaker, and a liar. But leading humanitarians supported her and, in the end, the lawmakers appro-priated money for enlarging and improving the state hospital for the insane in Worcester.

Dorothea L. Dix, born in Hampden, Maine, in 1802, and brought up by her grandmother in Boston, had never intended to be a reformer. Shy and sickly as a young woman, she taught in a girls' school, wrote children's stories and books on religious subjects, and led a retired life. But she was a friend and disciple of the great Unitarian preacher William Ellery Channing, who believed human nature could be bet-tered, and she also knew reformers like Samuel Gridley Howe, who ran a school for the blind and agitated for prison reform. There was something natural, then, about her turn to activism after her Sunday morning in East Cambridge in 1841. After the Massachusetts legislature responded affirmatively to her 1843 petition, she was in the field of reform for good. She continued her crusade for better asylums until the end of her life. She went from one state to another, following the procedure she had used in Massachusetts: gathering facts, drawing up petitions, winning public opinion over to the need for reform, and persuading states to do something about it. "I have travelled over more than ten thousand miles in the last three years," she wrote in 1845.

"Have visited eighteen state penitentiaries, three hundred county jails and houses of correction, more than five hundred almshouses and other institutions, besides hospitals and houses of refuge." Altogether she was responsible for the founding or enlarging of thirty-two mental hospitals in the United States and abroad. Her success owed much, no doubt, to the public's desire to control social deviants. But her own motivations were profoundly humanitarian. By the time she died in 1887, in a New Jersey hospital founded by her efforts, she was regarded as one of the most distinguished women in the nation.

Questions to Consider. Notice the method that Dix employed in her *Memorial* to rouse the interest of the Massachusetts legislators and persuade them to take action—that is, reporting in horrendous detail the conditions she had uncovered. Do you think the technique is convincing? Are there any similarities between Dix's method and those of investigative reporters today? For what reasons were the mentally ill badly treated? Why did Dix think the mentally ill should be separated from criminals? To what motives in the legislators did she appeal in her call for action? What did she reveal about her own motivations and outlook?

◆

Memorial on Asylums (1843)

DOROTHEA DIX

Gentlemen,—I respectfully ask to present this Memorial, believing that the cause, which actuates to and sanctions so unusual a movement, presents no equivocal claim to public consideration and sympathy. . . .

About two years since leisure afforded opportunity and duty prompted me to visit several prisons and almshouses in the vicinity of this metropolis, I found, near Boston, in the jails and asylums for the poor, a numerous class brought into unsuitable connection with criminals and the general mass of paupers. I refer to idiots and insane persons, dwelling in circumstances not only adverse to their own physical and moral improvement, but productive of extreme disadvantages to all other persons brought into association with them. I applied myself diligently to trace the causes of these evils, and sought to supply remedies. As one obstacle was surmounted, fresh difficulties appeared. Every new investigation has given depth to the conviction that it is only by decided, prompt, and vigorous

From D. L. Dix, *Memorial to the Legislature of Massachusetts* (Munroe and Francis, Boston, 1843), 3–32.

Dorothea Lynde Dix. (Portrait by Seth Cheney, courtesy The Boston Athenaeum)

legislation the evils to which I refer, and which I shall proceed more fully to illustrate, can be remedied. I shall be obliged to speak with great plainness, and to reveal many things revolting to the taste, and from which my woman's nature shrinks with peculiar sensitiveness. But truth is the highest consideration. *I tell what I have seen*—painful and shocking as the details often are—that from them you may feel more deeply the imperative obligation which lies upon you to prevent the possibility of a repetition or continuance of such outrages upon humanity. . . .

I come to present the strong claims of suffering humanity. I come to place before the Legislature of Massachusetts the condition of the miserable, the desolate, the outcast. I come as the advocate of helpless, forgotten, insane, and idiotic men and women; of beings sunk to a condition from which the most unconcerned would start with real horror; of beings wretched in our prisons, and more wretched in our almshouses. . . .

I must confine myself to few examples, but am ready to furnish other and more complete details, if required.

If my pictures are displeasing, coarse, and severe, my subjects, it must be recollected, offer no tranquil, refined, or composing features. The condition of human beings, reduced to the extremest states of degradation and misery cannot be exhibited in softened language, or adorn a polished page.

I proceed, gentlemen, briefly to call your attention to the *present state of* insane persons confined within this Commonwealth, *in cages, closets, cellars, stalls, pens! Chained, naked, beaten with rods,* and *lashed* into obedience. . . .

It is the Commonwealth, not its integral parts, that is accountable for most of the abuses which have lately and do still exist. I repeat it, it is defective legislation which perpetuates and multiplies these abuses. In illustration of my subject, I offer the following extracts from my Note-book and Journal:—

Springfield. In the jail, one lunatic woman, furiously mad, a State pauper, improperly situated, both in regard to the prisoners, the keepers, and herself. It is a case of extreme self-forgetfulness and oblivion to all the decencies of life, to describe which would be to repeat only the grossest scenes. She is much worse since leaving [the asylum of] Worcester. In the almshouse of the same town is a woman apparently only needing judicious care, and some well-chosen employment, to make it unnecessary to confine her in solitude, in a dreary unfurnished room. Her appeals for employment and companionship are most touching, but the mistress replied "she had no time to attend to her." . . .

Lincoln. A woman in a cage. *Medford.* One idiotic subject chained, and one in a close stall for seventeen years. *Pepperell.* One often doubly chained, hand and foot; another violent; several peaceable now. *Brookfield.* One man caged, comfortable. *Granville.* One often closely confined; now losing the use of his limbs from want of exercise. *Charlemont.* One man caged. *Savoy.*

One man caged. *Lenox*. Two in the jail, against whose unfit condition there the jailer protests.

Dedham. The insane disadvantageously placed in the jail. In the alms-house, two females in stalls, situated in the main building; lie in wooden bunks filled with straw; always shut up. One of these subjects is supposed curable. The overseers of the poor have declined giving her a trial at the hospital, as I was informed, on account of expense.

Besides the above, I have seen many who, part of the year, are chained or caged. The use of cages all but universal. Hardly a town but can refer to some not distant period of using them; chains are less common; negligences frequent; wilful abuse less frequent than sufferings proceeding from ignorance, or want of consideration. I encountered during the last three months many poor creatures wandering reckless and unprotected through the country. . . . But I cannot particularize. In traversing the State, I have found hundreds of insane persons in every variety of circumstance and condition, many whose situation could not and need not be improved; a less number, but that very large, whose lives are the saddest pictures of human suffering and degradation.

I give a few illustrations; but description fades before reality.

Danvers. November. Visited the almshouse. A large building, much out of repair. Understand a new one is in contemplation. Here are from fifty-six to sixty inmates, one idiotic, three insane; one of the latter in close confinement at all times.

Long before reaching the house, wild shouts, snatches of rude songs, imprecations and obscene language, fell upon the ear, proceeding from the occupant of a low building, rather remote from the principal building to which my course was directed. Found the mistress, and was conducted to the place which was called "the home" of the *forlorn* maniac, a young woman, exhibiting a condition of neglect and misery blotting out the faintest idea of comfort, and outraging every sentiment of decency. She had been, I learnt, "a respectable person, industrious and worthy. Disappointments and trials shook her mind, and, finally, laid prostrate reason and self-control. She became a maniac for life. She had been at Worcester Hospital for a considerable time, and had been returned as incurable." The mistress told me she understood that, "while there, she was comfortable and decent." Alas, what a change was here exhibited! She had passed from one degree of violence to another, in swift progress. There she stood, clinging to or beating upon the bars of her caged apartment, the contracted size of which afforded space only for increasing accumulations of filth, a *foul* spectacle. There she stood with naked arms and dishevelled hair, the unwashed frame invested with fragments of unclean garments, the air so extremely offensive, though ventilation was afforded on all sides save one, that it was not possible to remain beyond a few moments without retreating for recovery to the outward air. Irritation of body, produced by utter filth and exposure, incited her to the horrid process of tearing off her skin by inches. Her face, neck, and person were thus disfigured to hideousness. To my exclamation of horror, the mistress replied: "Oh, we can't help it. Half the skin is off sometimes. We can do nothing with her; and it makes no difference what she eats, for she consumes her own filth as readily as the food which is brought her."

Men of Massachusetts, I beg, I implore, I demand pity and protection for these of my suffering, outraged sex. Fathers, husbands, brothers, I would supplicate you for this boon; but what do I say? I dishonor you, divest you at once of Christianity and humanity, does this appeal imply distrust. If it comes burdened with a doubt of your righteousness in this legislation, then blot it out; while I declare confidence in your honor, not less than your humanity. Here you will put away the cold, calculating spirit of selfishness and self-seeking; lay off the armor of local strife and political opposition; here and now, for once, forgetful of the earthly and perishable, come up to these halls and consecrate them with one heart and one mind to works of righteousness and just judgment. . . .

Injustice is also done to the *convicts;* it is certainly very wrong that they should be doomed day after day and night to listen to the ravings of madmen and madwomen. This is a kind of punishment that is not recognized by our statutes, and is what the criminal ought not to be called upon to undergo. The confinement of the criminal and of the insane in the same building is subversive of that good order and discipline which should be observed in every well-regulated prison. I do most sincerely hope that more permanent provision will be made for the pauper insane by the State, either to restore Worcester Insane Asylum to what it was originally designed to be or else make some just appropriation for the benefit of this very unfortunate class of our "fellow-beings."

Gentlemen, I commit to you this sacred cause. Your action upon this subject will affect the present and future condition of hundreds and of thousands. In this legislation, as in all things, may you exercise that "wisdom which is the breath of the power of God."

30

◆

WOMEN'S FREEDOM

In March 1776, when the Continental Congress in Philadelphia was beginning to contemplate independence from Britain, Abigail Adams wrote her husband, John, from Braintree, Massachusetts: "I long to hear that you have declared an independency. And, by the way," she added, "in the new code of laws which I suppose it will be necessary for you to make, I desire you would remember the ladies and be more generous and favorable to them than your ancestors. Do not put un-limited power into the hands of the husbands. Remember, all men would be tyrants if they could. If particular care and attention is not paid to the ladies, we are determined to foment a rebellion, and will not hold ourselves bound by any laws in which we have no voice or representation. That your sex are naturally tyrannical is a truth so thoroughly established as to admit of no dispute. . . ." Adams wrote back good-humoredly. "We are obliged to go fairly and softly," he told his wife, "and, in practice, you know we are the subjects. We have only the name of masters, and rather than give this up, which would completely subject us to the despotism of the petticoat, I hope General Washington and all our brave heroes would fight. . . ."[1]

Adams wasn't being accurate. American men had more than "the name of masters." The status of women in Adams's day and for many years afterward was distinctly inferior. Sir William Blackstone, the great eighteenth-century British legal authority, set the standard for the American view. "The husband and wife are one," he proclaimed, "and that one is the husband." Women were regarded as the wards of their husbands, were barred from professions like the law, medicine, and the ministry, and had few opportunities for higher education. According to a little verse composed in 1844:

> The father gives his kind command
> The mother joins, approves,
> And children all attentive stand,
> Then each, obedient, moves.

1. Charles Francis Adams, ed., *Familiar Letters of John Adams and His Wife During the Revolution* (New York, 1876), 149–150, 155.

Abigail Adams wasn't the only woman to chafe at the situation. In 1832 Lydia Maria Child published a two-volume *History of the Condition of Woman in All Ages,* deploring woman's subservience, and in 1843 Margaret Fuller published a long essay, later expanded and published as *Woman in the Nineteenth Century,* in which she declared: "What woman needs is not as a woman to act or rule, but as a nature to grow, as an intellect to discern, as a soul to live freely and unimpeded, to unfold such powers as were given her when we left our common home."

Born near Boston in 1810 to parents who emphasized intellectual development, Margaret Fuller became one of the most learned Americans of her time despite the fact that academies and colleges did not then admit women. Fuller taught school in the Boston area, wrote for literary journals, and conducted highly popular public "conversations" on the education of women while still in her twenties. In 1840 she became an editor of the *Dial.* In 1844 she took a position as a literary columnist at the *New York Tribune,* and she soon earned the reputation as a leading American critic. After the publication of *Women in the Nineteenth Century* in 1843 and *Papers on Literature and Art* in 1846, Fuller sailed for Europe, where she married Angelo Ossoli, an Italian revolutionary. In July 1850, the ship on which she and her husband and child were returning to the United States foundered off the coast of Long Island, drowning all passengers.

Questions to Consider. What aspect of women's position most distressed Margaret Fuller? How specifically did she expect that position to be changed? Did she believe men *could* not speak effectively on behalf of women, or that they *would* not? What audience does she seem to have been addressing in this passage? How important was religion in her argument? Was this statement conservative or radical in its implications? Would Fuller have endorsed the Seneca Falls Declaration of 1848?

◆

Woman in the Nineteenth Century (1845)

MARGARET FULLER

The gain of creation consists always in the growth of individual minds, which live and aspire as flowers bloom and birds sing in the midst of morasses; and in the continual development of that thought, the thought of human destiny, which is given to eternity adequately to express, and which ages of failure only seemingly impede.

Knowing that there exists in the minds of men a tone of feeling toward women as toward slaves, such as is expressed in the common phrase, "Tell that to women and children"; that the infinite soul can only work through them in already ascertained limits; that the gift of reason, Man's highest prerogative, is allotted to them in much lower degree; that they must be kept from mischief and melancholy by being constantly engaged in active labor, which is to be furnished and directed by those better able to think, &c., &c.—we need not multiply instances without recalling words which imply, whether in jest or earnest, these views or views like these—knowing this, can we wonder that many reformers think that measures are not likely to be taken in behalf of women, unless their wishes could be publicly represented by women?

"That can never be necessary," cry the other side. "All men are privately influenced by women; each has his wife, sister, or female friends, and is too much biased by these relations to fail of representing their interests; and if this is not enough, let them propose and enforce their wishes with the pen. The beauty of home would be destroyed, the delicacy of the sex be violated, the dignity of halls of legislation degraded by an attempt to introduce them there. Such duties are inconsistent with those of a mother"; and then we have ludicrous pictures of ladies in hysterics at the polls, and senate chambers filled with cradles.

But if in reply we admit as truth that Woman seems destined by nature rather for the inner circle, we must add that the arrangements of civilized life have not been as yet such as to secure it to her. Her circle, if the duller, is not the quieter. If kept from "excitement," she is not from drudgery. Not only the Indian squaw carries the burdens of the camp, but the favorites of Louis XIV accompany him in his journeys, and the washerwoman stands at her tub and carries home her work at all seasons and in all states of health. Those who think the physical circumstances of Woman would make a part in the affairs of national government unsuitable are by no means

From S. Margaret Fuller, *Woman in the Nineteenth Century* (New York: Greeley & McElrath, 1845), 14–15, 23–28, 52.

those who think it impossible for Negresses to endure field work even during pregnancy, or for seamstresses to go through their killing labors. . . .

While we hear from men who owe to their wives not only all that is comfortable or graceful but all that is wise in the arrangement of their lives the frequent remark, "You cannot reason with a woman"—when not one man in the million, shall I say? no, not in the hundred million, can rise above the belief that Woman was made *for Man*—when such traits as these are daily forced upon the attention, can we feel that Man will always do justice to the interests of Woman? Can we think that he takes a sufficiently discerning and religious view of her office and destiny *ever* to do her justice, except when prompted by sentiment? . . . The lover, the poet, the artist are likely to view her nobly. The father and the philosopher have some chance of liberality; the man of the world, the legislator for expediency none.

Under these circumstances, without attaching importance in themselves to the changes demanded by the champions of Woman, we hail them as signs of the times. We would have every arbitrary barrier thrown down. We would have every path laid open to Woman as freely as to Man. Were this done and a slight temporary fermentation allowed to subside, we should see crystallizations more pure and of more various beauty. We believe the divine energy would pervade nature to a degree unknown in the history of former ages, and that no discordant collision but a ravishing harmony of the spheres would ensue.

Yet then and only then will mankind be ripe for this, when inward and outward freedom for Woman as much as for Man shall be acknowledged as a *right*, not yielded as a concession. As the friend of the Negro assumes that one man cannot by right hold another in bondage, so should the friend of Woman assume that Man cannot by right lay even well-meant restrictions on Woman. If the Negro be a soul, if the woman be a soul, appareled in flesh, to one Master only are they accountable. There is but one law for souls, and if there is to be an interpreter of it, he must come not as man or son of man, but as son of God.

Were thought and feeling once so far elevated that Man should esteem himself the brother and friend, but nowise the lord and tutor, of Woman— were he really bound with her in equal worship—arrangements as to function and employment would be of no consequence. What Woman needs is not as a woman to act or rule, but as a nature to grow, as an intellect to discern, as a soul to live freely and unimpeded to unfold such powers as were given her when we left our common home. If fewer talents were given her, yet if allowed the free and full employment of these, so that she may render back to the giver his own with usury, she will not complain; nay, I dare to say she will bless and rejoice in her earthly birthplace, her earthly lot. . . .

It is not the transient breath of poetic incense that women want; each can receive that from a lover. It is not lifelong sway; it needs but to become a coquette, a shrew, or a good cook to be sure of that. It is not money nor notoriety nor the badges of authority which men have appropriated to themselves. If demands made in their behalf lay stress on any of these particulars, those who make them have not searched deeply into the need. The want is for that which at once includes these and precludes them; which would not be forbidden power, lest there be temptation to steal and misuse it; which would not have the mind perverted by flattery from a worthiness of esteem; it is for that which is the birthright of every being capable of receiving it—the freedom, the religious, the intelligent freedom of the universe to use its means, to learn its secret as far as Nature has enabled them, with God alone for their guide and their judge.

31

◆

WOMEN'S RIGHTS

In the first part of the nineteenth century, women in increasing numbers began asking for equality before the law and asserting their right to be educated, enter the professions, and participate in public affairs along with men. Some women became active in reform, participating in the temperance movement, the fight against slavery, and the crusade for world peace. But even as reformers they were required to take a subordinate position. When a woman tried to speak at a temperance convention in New York she was shouted down. One man yelled, "Shame on the woman, shame on the woman!" And when several women attended the World Anti-Slavery Convention in London in 1840, men refused to seat them as delegates and made them sit in a curtained enclosure out of the public view. Two delegates—Lucretia Mott and Elizabeth Cady Stanton—began talking of holding a convention to battle for their own rights.

In July 1848 the first organized meeting for women's rights ever held met in Seneca Falls, New York, attended by two hundred delegates, including thirty-two men. Stanton drew up the Declaration of Sentiments, using the Declaration of Independence as a model. She also drafted a series of resolutions that were adopted by the convention. Only one of her demands ran into trouble: the right to vote. Woman suffrage still seemed so outlandish that it took the eloquence of Frederick Douglass, a black abolitionist and journalist, to persuade the delegates to adopt it by a small majority. Many people were shocked by the Seneca Falls convention. They denounced the "Reign of Petticoats" and warned against the "Insurrection among Women." But many distinguished Americans—including Ralph Waldo Emerson, John Greenleaf Whittier, and William Lloyd Garrison—supported the movement.

Elizabeth Cady Stanton, who drafted the Seneca Falls Declaration, was born in Johnstown, New York, in 1815. She attended Emma Willard's seminary in Troy, and while studying law with her father, became aware of the injustices suffered by women from American legal practices. When she married the abolitionist lawyer Henry B. Stanton in 1840, she insisted that the word *obey* be omitted from the ceremony. At an antislavery convention that she attended with her husband the same year, she got to know Lucretia Mott, and the two of them began working together for women's rights. Following the Seneca Falls Conference, Stanton joined Mott (and later Susan B. Anthony) in sponsoring conventions, writing articles, delivering lectures, and appearing before legislative bodies on behalf of the cause. Despite Stanton's grace and charm, she was considered a dangerous radical for espousing woman suffrage and easier divorce laws for women. During the Civil War she helped organize the Women's Loyal National League and urged emancipation. After the war she resumed her work for woman suffrage, became president of the National Woman Suffrage Association, lectured on family life, wrote for *Revolution,* a women's rights weekly, and contributed to the three-volume *History of Woman Suffrage,* published in the 1880s. One of the most distinguished feminist leaders in the country, she died in New York City in 1902.

Questions to Consider. Many years passed before the women's rights movement in America began achieving some of its objectives. But the Seneca Falls convention marks the formal beginning of the organized movement to advance women's position, so it merits careful study. Do you think there were any advantages in using the Declaration of Independence as a model for the Declaration of Sentiments? Does the Seneca Falls Declaration emphasize legal, economic, or political rights? Were any rights overlooked? Some of those who signed the declaration withdrew their names when the suffrage resolution met with ridicule. Why do you suppose this happened? How radical do the Seneca Falls demands seem today? Which demands have been met by legislation since 1848?

◆

The Seneca Falls Declaration of 1848

ELIZABETH CADY STANTON

When, in the course of human events, it becomes necessary for one portion of the family of man to assume among the people of the earth a position different from that which they have hitherto occupied, but one to which the laws of nature and of nature's God entitle them, a decent respect to the opinions of mankind requires that they should declare the causes that impel them to such a course.

From Susan B. Anthony, Elizabeth Cady Stanton, and Matilda Joslyn Gage, eds., *History of Woman Suffrage* (3 v., Susan B. Anthony, Elizabeth Cady Stanton, and Matilda Joslyn Gage, Rochester, N.Y., 1889), I: 75–80.

We hold these truths to be self-evident: that all men and women are created equal; that they are endowed by their Creator with certain inalienable rights; that among these are life, liberty, and the pursuit of happiness; that to secure these rights governments are instituted, deriving their just powers from the consent of the governed. . . . But when a long train of abuses and usurpations, pursuing invariably the same object evinces a design to reduce them under absolute despotism, it is their duty to throw off such government, and to provide new guards for their future security. Such has been the patient sufferance of the women under this government, and such is now the necessity which constrains them to demand the equal station to which they are entitled.

The history of mankind is a history of repeated injuries and usurpations on the part of man toward woman, having in direct object the establishment of an absolute tyranny over her. To prove this, let facts be submitted to a candid world.

He has never permitted her to exercise her inalienable right to the elective franchise.

He has compelled her to submit to laws, in the formation of which she had no voice.

He has withheld from her rights which are given to the most ignorant and degraded men—both natives and foreigners.

Having deprived her of this first right of a citizen, the elective franchise, thereby leaving her without representation in the halls of legislation, he has opposed her on all sides.

He has made her, if married, in the eye of the law, civilly dead.

He has taken from her all right in property, even to the wages she earns.

He has made her, morally, an irresponsible being, as she can commit many crimes with impunity, provided they be done in the presence of her husband. In the covenant of marriage, she is compelled to promise obedience to her husband, he becoming, to all intents and purposes, her master—the law giving him power to deprive her of her liberty, and to administer chastisement.

He has so framed the laws of divorce, as to what shall be the proper causes, and in case of separation, to whom the guardianship of the children shall be given, as to be wholly regardless of the happiness of women—the law, in all cases, going upon a false supposition of the supremacy of man, and giving all power into his hands.

After depriving her of all rights as a married woman, if single, and the owner of property, he has taxed her to support a government which recognizes her only when her property can be made profitable to it.

He has monopolized nearly all the profitable employments, and from those she is permitted to follow, she receives but a scanty remuneration. He closes against her all the avenues to wealth and distinction which he considers most honorable to himself. As a teacher of theology, medicine, or law, she is not known.

He has denied her the facilities for obtaining a thorough education, all colleges being closed against her.

He allows her in Church, as well as State, but a subordinate position, claiming Apostolic authority for her exclusion from the ministry, and, with some exceptions, from any public participation in the affairs of the Church.

He has created a false public sentiment by giving to the world a different code of morals for men and women, by which moral delinquencies which exclude women from society, are not only tolerated, but deemed of little account in man.

He has usurped the prerogative of Jehovah himself, claiming it as his right to assign for her a sphere of action, when that belongs to her conscience and to her God.

He has endeavored, in every way that he could, to destroy her confidence in her own powers, to lessen her self-respect, and to make her willing to lead a dependent and abject life.

Now, in view of this entire disfranchisement of one-half the people of this country, their social and religious degradation—in view of the unjust laws above mentioned, and because women do not feel themselves aggrieved, oppressed, and fraudulently deprived of their most sacred rights, we insist that they have immediate admission to all the rights and privileges which belong to them as citizens of the United States.

In entering upon the great work before us, we anticipate no small amount of misconception, misrepresentation, and ridicule; but we shall use every instrumentality within our power to effect our object. We shall employ agents, circulate tracts, petition the State and National legislatures, and endeavor to enlist the pulpit and the press in our behalf. We hope this Convention will be followed by a series of Conventions embracing every part of the country.

Resolutions

WHEREAS, The great precept of nature is conceded to be, that "man shall pursue his own true and substantial happiness." Blackstone in his Commentaries remarks, that this law of Nature being coequal with mankind, and dictated by God himself, is of course superior in obligation to any other. It is binding over all the globe, in all countries and at all times; no human laws are of any validity if contrary to this . . . . therefore,

Resolved, That such laws as conflict, in any way, with the true and substantial happiness of woman, are contrary to the great precept of nature and of no validity, for this is "superior in obligation to any other."

Resolved, That all laws which prevent woman from occupying such a station in society as her conscience shall dictate, or which place her in a position inferior to that of man, are contrary to the great precept of nature, and therefore of no force or authority.

Resolved, That woman is man's equal—was intended to be so by the Creator, and the highest good of the race demands that she should be recognized as such.

Resolved, That the women of this country ought to be enlightened in regard to the laws under which they live, that they may no longer publish their degradation by declaring themselves satisfied with their present position, nor their ignorance, by asserting that they have all the rights they want.

Resolved, That inasmuch as man, while claiming for himself intellectual superiority, does accord to woman moral superiority, it is pre-eminently his duty to encourage her to speak and teach, as she has an opportunity, in all religious assemblies.

Resolved, That the same amount of virtue, delicacy, and refinement of behavior that is required of woman in the social state, should also be required of man, and the same transgressions should be visited with equal severity on both man and woman.

Resolved, That the objection of indelicacy and impropriety, which is so often brought against woman when she addresses a public audience, comes with a very ill-grace from those who encourage, by their attendance, her appearance on the stage, in the concert, or in feats of the circus.

Resolved, That woman has too long rested satisfied in the circumscribed limits which corrupt customs and a perverted application of the Scriptures have marked out for her, and that it is time she should move in the enlarged sphere which her great Creator has assigned her.

Resolved, That it is the duty of the women of this country to secure to themselves their sacred right to the elective franchise.

Resolved, That the equality of human rights results necessarily from the fact of the identity of the race in capabilities and responsibilities.

Resolved, therefore, That, being invested by the Creator with the same capabilities, and the same consciousness of responsibility for their exercise, it is demonstrably the right and duty of woman, equally with man, to promote every righteous cause by every righteous means; and especially in regard to the great subjects of morals and religion, it is self-evidently her right to participate with her brother in teaching them, both in private and in public, by writing and by speaking, by any instrumentalities proper to be used, and in any assemblies proper to be held; and this being a self-evident truth growing out of the divinely implanted principles of human nature, any custom or authority adverse to it, whether modern or wearing the hoary sanction of antiquity, is to be regarded as a self-evident falsehood, and at war with mankind.

32

◆

RACE, SLAVERY, AND THE CONSTITUTION

The spread of slavery during the early nineteenth century divided the nation and so fanned the flames of sectionalism that the United States was able to remain united only by careful political compromise between North and South. The Missouri Compromise of 1820 admitted Maine, a free state, and Missouri, a slave state, to the Union about the same time, thus preserving the balance between the two sections; it also barred slavery from all territories north of a line (36°30'N) drawn westward from Missouri's southern border. The Compromise of 1850 admitted California as a free state but organized New Mexico and Utah on the principle of popular sovereignty, with slavery left to the inhabitants' decision.

In 1854 Congress violated the Missouri Compromise line. By the Kansas-Nebraska Act of that year, sponsored by Illinois Senator Stephen A. Douglas, who wanted settlers to decide whether or not to have slavery, territory north of 36°30'N was opened to slavery on a "local option" basis. The result was a bloody conflict in Kansas between free-soil settlers opposed to slavery there and those favoring slavery. In 1857, moreover, Chief Justice Roger B. Taney's opinion in the Dred Scott case placed the Supreme Court squarely behind the institution of slavery. (A Missouri slave, Dred Scott, had sued his master for freedom, basing his case on the fact that they had lived for a time in free territory.) Speaking for the majority of the justices, Taney announced that blacks could not be American citizens and that Congress could not prohibit slavery even in territories under its direct jurisdiction. The Dred Scott decision made all previous compromises over slavery unconstitutional. It also exacerbated sectional tensions. Proslavery Southerners were anxious to extend slavery into new areas; antislavery Northerners were just as determined to do all they could to prevent the further expansion of human bondage despite the Court's ruling. Even Northerners who were not abolitionists opposed Taney's decision. They did not like the idea of Southerners bringing their slaves into the federal territories.

Roger Taney was born in 1777 in Maryland, where he practiced law for a time and then entered politics. An early supporter of Andrew Jackson, he became attorney general in 1831 and helped draft Jackson's message to Congress in 1832 vetoing the recharter bill for the

Bank of the United States. In 1836 Jackson made Taney chief justice of the Supreme Court. Taney's major opinion before Dred Scott was an antimonopoly decision in the Charles River Bridge case in 1837. After the Dred Scott decision, Taney's prestige declined rapidly, and it all but disappeared after the Republican victory in 1860. He died in Washington four years later.

Scott himself became free because when his master died, the widow married an abolitionist who arranged for Scott's freedom. Scott became a hotel porter in St. Louis and died there of tuberculosis a year after the Supreme Court decision.

Questions to Consider. The Dred Scott decision purports to cite historical facts as well as advance opinions about those facts. How accurate is Taney's statement that American blacks had never possessed any of the rights and privileges the U.S. Constitution confers on citizens? Why did he make a careful distinction between the rights of citizenship that a state may confer and the rights conferred by the federal Constitution? Do you think Taney's reference to the constitutional provision permitting the slave trade until 1808 strengthened his arguments? Note that, to find the Missouri Compromise unconstitutional, Taney maintained that the clause in the Constitution giving Congress power to regulate the federal territories applied only to territories belonging to the United States at the time the Constitution was adopted. Do you think he made a convincing case for this assertion? Would Taney's insistence that Congress cannot prohibit slavery in the federal territories logically apply to whites as well as blacks?

◆

Dred Scott v. *Sanford* (1857)

ROGER B. TANEY

The question is simply this: Can a negro, whose ancestors were imported into this country, and sold as slaves, become a member of the political community formed and brought into existence by the Constitution of the United States, and as such become entitled to all the rights, and privileges, and immunities, guaranteed by that instrument to the citizen? . . .

It will be observed, that the plea applies to that class of persons only whose ancestors were negroes of the African race, and imported into this country, and sold and held as slaves. The only matter in issue before the court, therefore, is whether the descendants of such slaves, when they

19 Howard 393 (1857)

Dred and Harriet Scott. It took eleven years for the federal courts to dispose of the freedom suit of Dred and Harriet Scott. During that time the couple became figures of considerable interest to the readers of popular periodicals, such as **Frank Leslie's Illustrated Newspaper,** where these drawings of the couple appeared. Only two years old when Chief Justice Taney handed down his decision, **Leslie's Illustrated** already had almost a hundred thousand readers, mostly middle-class, who enjoyed how Leslie "seized promptly and illustrated the passing events of the day." In covering the Dred Scott affair, **Leslie's** reported not only on Dred and Harriet but on their two daughters. Northerners greeted Taney's harsh decision with anger due in part to the influence of the popular press. (Library of Congress)

shall be emancipated, or who are born of parents who had become free before their birth, are citizens of a State, in the sense in which the word citizen is used in the Constitution of the United States. And this being the only matter in dispute on the pleadings, the court must be understood as speaking in this opinion of that class only, that is of persons who are the descendants of Africans who were imported into this country and sold as slaves. . . .

The words "people of the United States" and "citizens" are synonymous terms, and mean the same thing. They both describe the political body who, according to our republican institutions, form the sovereignty, and who hold the power and conduct the government through their representatives. They are what we familiarly call the "sovereign people," and every citizen is one of this people, and a constituent member of this sovereignty. The question before us is, whether the class of persons described in the plea in abatement[1] compose a portion of this people, and are constituent members of this sovereignty? We think they are not, and that they are not included, and were not intended to be included, under the word "citizens" in the Constitution, and can, therefore, claim none of the rights and privileges which that instrument provides for and secures to citizens of the United States. On the contrary, they were at that time considered as a subordinate and inferior class of beings, who had been subjugated by the dominant race, and whether emancipated or not, yet remained subject to their authority, and had no rights or privileges but such as those who held the power and the government might choose to grant them. . . .

In discussing this question, we must not confound the rights of citizenship which a state may confer within its own limits, and the rights of citizenship as a member of the Union. It does not by any means follow, because he has all the rights and privileges of a citizen of a State, that he must be a citizen of the United States. He may have all of the rights and privileges of a State, and yet not be entitled to the rights and privileges of a citizen in any other State. For, previous to the adoption of the Constitution of the United States, every State had the undoubted right to confer on whomsoever it pleased the character of a citizen, and to endow him with all its rights. But this character, of course, was confined to the boundaries of the State, and gave him no rights or privileges in other States beyond those secured to him by the laws of nations and the comity [mutual jurisdiction] of States. Nor have the several States surrendered the power of conferring these rights and privileges by adopting the Constitution of the United States. Each State may still confer them upon an alien, or any one it thinks proper, or upon any class or description of persons; yet he would not be a citizen in the sense in which that word is used in the Constitution of the United States, nor entitled to sue as such in one of its courts, nor to the privileges and immunities of a citizen in the other States. The rights which he would acquire would be restricted to the State which gave them. . . .

The question then arises, whether the provisions of the Constitution, in relation to the personal rights and privileges to which the citizen of a State should be entitled, embraced the negro African race, at that time in this country, or who might afterwards be imported, who had then or should afterwards be made free in any State; and to put it in the power of a single State to make him a citizen of the United States, and endue him with the full rights of citizenship in every other State without their consent. Does the Constitution of the United States act upon him whenever he shall be made free under the laws of a State, and raised there to the rank of a citizen, and immediately clothe him with all the privileges of a citizen in every other State, and in its own courts?

---

1. **The plea of abatement:** Dred Scott's lawsuit. —*Eds.*

The court think the affirmative of these propositions cannot be maintained. . . .

It is difficult at this day to realize the state of public opinion in relation to that unfortunate race, which prevailed in the civilized and enlightened portions of the world at the time of the Declaration of Independence, and when the Constitution of the United States was framed and adopted. . . .

They had for more than a century before been regarded as beings of an inferior order; and altogether unfit to associate with the white race, either in social or political relations; and so far inferior that they had no rights which the white man was bound to respect; and that the negro might justly and lawfully be reduced to slavery for his benefit. . . . This opinion was at that time fixed and universal in the civilized portion of the white race. It was regarded as an axiom in morals as well as in politics, which no one thought of disputing, or supposed to be open to dispute; and men in every grade and position in society daily and habitually acted upon it in their private pursuits, as well as in matters of public concern, without doubting for a moment the correctness of this opinion. . . .

But there are two clauses in the Constitution which point directly and specifically to the negro race as a separate class of persons, and show clearly that they were not regarded as a portion of the people or citizens of the Government then formed.

One of these clauses reserves to each of the thirteen States the right to import slaves until the year 1808, if he thinks it proper. And the importation which it thus sanctions was unquestionably of persons of the race of which we are speaking, as the traffic in slaves in the United States had always been confined to them. And by the other provision the States pledge themselves to each other to maintain the right of property of the master, by delivering up to him any slave who may have escaped from his service, and be found within their respective territories. . . . And these two provisions show, conclusively, that neither the description of persons therein referred to, nor their descendants, were embraced in any of the other provisions of the Constitution; for certainly these two clauses were not intended to confer on them or their posterity the blessings of liberty, or any of the personal rights so carefully provided for the citizen. . . .

Indeed, when we look to the condition of this race in the several States at the time, it is impossible to believe that these rights and privileges were intended to be extended to them. . . .

The Act of Congress, upon which the plaintiff relies, declares that slavery and involuntary servitude, except as a punishment for crime, shall be forever prohibited in all that part of the territory ceded by France, under the name of Louisiana, which lies north of thirty-six degrees thirty minutes north latitude, and not included within the limits of Missouri. And the difficulty which meets us at the threshold of this part of the inquiry is, whether Congress was authorized to pass this law under any of the powers granted to it by the Constitution; for if the authority is not given by that instrument, it is the duty of this court to declare it void and inoperative, and incapable of conferring freedom upon any one who is held as a slave under the laws of any one of the States.

The counsel for the plaintiff has laid much stress upon that article in the Constitution which confers on Congress the power "to dispose of and make all needful rules and regulations respecting the territory or other property belonging to the United States," but, in the judgment of the court, that provision has no bearing on the present controversy, and the power there given, whatever it may be, is confined, and was intended to be confined, to the territory which at that time belonged to, or was claimed by, the United States, and was within their boundaries as settled by the treaty with Great Britain, and can have no influence upon a territory afterwards acquired from a foreign Government. It was a special provision for a known and particular territory, and to meet a present emergency, and nothing more. . . .

The power of Congress over the person or property of a citizen can never be a mere discretionary power under our Constitution and form of Government. The powers of the Government and the rights and privileges of the Citizen are regulated and plainly defined by the Constitution itself. And when the Territory becomes a part of the United States, the Federal Government enters into possession in the character impressed upon it by those who created it. It enters upon it with its powers over the citizen strictly defined, and limited by the Constitution, from which it derives its own existence, and by virtue of which alone it continues to exist and act as a Government and sovereignty. It has no power of any kind beyond it; and it cannot, when it enters a Territory of the United States, put off its character, and assume discretionary or despotic powers which the Constitution has denied to it. It cannot create for itself a new character separated from the citizens of the United States, and the duties it owes them under the provisions of the Constitution. The Territory being a part of the United States, the Government and the citizen both enter it under the authority of the Constitution, with their respective rights defined and marked out; and the Federal Government can exercise no power over his person or property, beyond what that instrument confers, nor lawfully deny any right which it has reserved. . . .

The rights of private property have been guarded with equal care. Thus the rights of property are united with the rights of person, and placed on the same ground by the fifth amendment to the Constitution[2]. . . . An Act of Congress which deprives a person of the United States of his liberty or property merely because he came himself or brought his property into a particular Territory of the United States, and who had committed no offense against the laws, could hardly be dignified with the name of due process of law. . . .

---

2. **The Fifth Amendment:** "No person shall . . . be deprived of life, liberty, or property without due process of the law; nor shall private property be taken for public use without just compensation."

And this prohibition is not confined to the States, but the words are general, and extend to the whole territory over which the Constitution gives it power to legislate, including those portions of it remaining under territorial government, as well as that covered by States. It is a total absence of power everywhere within the dominion of the United States, and places the citizen of a territory, so far as these rights are concerned, on the same footing with citizens of the States; and guards them as firmly and plainly against any inroads which the general government might attempt, under the plea of implied or incidental powers. And if Congress itself cannot do this—if it is beyond the powers conferred on the Federal Government—it will be admitted, we presume, that it could not authorize a territorial government to exercise them. It could confer no power on any local government, established by its authority, to violate the provisions of the Constitution.

It seems, however, to be supposed, that there is a difference between property in a slave and other property, and that different rules may be applied to it in expounding the Constitution of the United States. And the laws and usages of nations, and the writings of eminent jurists upon the relation of master and slave and their mutual rights and duties, and the powers which governments may exercise over it, have been dwelt upon in the argument.

But . . . if the Constitution recognizes the right of property of the master in a slave, and makes no distinction between that description of property and other property owned by a citizen, no tribunal, acting under the authority of the United States, whether it be legislative, executive, or judicial, has a right to draw such a distinction, or deny to it the benefit of the provisions and guarantees which have been provided for the protection of private property against the encroachments of the Government.

Now . . . the right of property in a slave is distinctly and expressly affirmed in the Constitution. The right to traffic in it, like an ordinary article of merchandise and property, was guaranteed to the citizens of the United States, in every State that might desire it, for twenty years. And the Government in express terms is pledged to protect it in all future time, if the slave escapes from his owner. . . . And no word can be found in the Constitution which gives Congress a greater power over slave property, or which entitles property of that kind to less protection than property of any other description. The only power conferred is the power coupled with the duty of guarding and protecting the owner in his rights.

Upon these considerations, it is the opinion of the court that the Act of Congress which prohibited a citizen from holding and owning property of this kind in the territory of the United States north of the line therein mentioned, is not warranted by the Constitution, and is therefore void; and that neither Dred Scott himself, nor any of his family, were made free by being carried into this territory; even if they had been carried there by the owner, with the intention of becoming a permanent resident.

33

◆

LIBERTY AND UNION

The great vehicle for antislavery politics was the Republican party. Founded in Ripon, Wisconsin, in 1854, the new party rapidly absorbed members of earlier, smaller antislavery organizations by pledging itself to oppose the further extension of slavery in the United States. In the election of 1856, the Republicans showed amazing strength: their candidate, John C. Frémont, won 1,339,932 popular and 114 electoral votes to Democratic candidate James Buchanan's 1,832,955 popular and 174 electoral votes. During the next four years the party broadened its appeal so as to attract industrialists and workers as well as farmers, professional people, and religious leaders who were opposed to slavery. It also developed able party leaders and made impressive gains at the state and congressional levels.

The Republican party's 1860 platform not only upheld the Union and reiterated its stand against the extension of slavery but also contained a number of economic planks that would appeal to industrialists in the Northeast and farmers in the West. It favored a protective tariff, the building of a transcontinental railroad, and a homestead act giving free land to settlers. Adopted in Chicago in May 1860, the platform conformed closely to the views of such moderates as William H. Seward and Horace Greeley of New York, Benjamin F. Wade and Salmon P. Chase of Ohio, and its standard-bearer, Abraham Lincoln of Illinois. Only when leading abolitionists threatened to walk out of the convention did Republican leaders incorporate a reaffirmation of the Declaration of Independence into their platform. But though the Republicans took a moderate position in their platform, the victory of Lincoln in the 1860 election triggered secession and civil war.

Questions to Consider. To what did the Republican platform refer when it announced that events of the past four years had established the necessity of organizing a new party? Do you agree with the statement that the principles of the Declaration of Independence are "essential to the preservation of our Republican institutions"? Do you agree with the assertion that "threats of Disunion" are equivalent to "an avowal of contemplated treason"? In denouncing "the lawless invasion by armed force of the soil of any State or Territory," what did the platform makers have in mind? What did the platform say about Kansas and the Dred Scott decision? What dominated the platform, the slavery issue or economic issues? On balance, to whom was the platform supposed to appeal?

———————◆———————

The Republican Party Platform of 1860

Resolved, That we, the delegated representatives of the Republican electors of the United States, in Convention assembled, in discharge of the duty we owe to our constituents and our country, unite in the following declarations:

1. That the history of the nation, during the last four years, has fully established the propriety and necessity of the organization and perpetuation of the Republican party, and that the causes which called it into existence are permanent in their nature, and now, more than ever before, demand its peaceful and constitutional triumph.

2. That the maintenance of the principles promulgated in the Declaration of Independence and embodied in the Federal Constitution, "That all men are created equal; that they are endowed by their Creator with certain inalienable rights; that among these are life, liberty and the pursuit of happiness; that, to secure these rights, governments are instituted among men, deriving their just powers from the consent of the governed," is essential to the preservation of our Republican institutions, and that the Federal Constitution, the Rights of the States, and the Union of the States, must and shall be preserved.

3. That to the Union of the States this nation owes its unprecedented increase in population, its surprising development of material resources, its rapid augmentation of wealth, its happiness at home and its honor abroad; and we hold in abhorrence all schemes for Disunion, come from whatever source they may; And we congratulate the country that no Republican member of Congress has uttered or countenanced the threats of Disunion so often made by Democratic members, without rebuke and with applause from their political associates; and we denounce those threats of Disunion, in case of a popular overthrow of their ascendancy, as denying the vital principles of a free government, and as an avowal of contemplated treason, which it is the imperative duty of an indignant People sternly to rebuke and forever silence.

From Francis Curtis, *The Republican Party* (2 v., G. P. Putnam's Sons, New York, 1904), I: 355–358.

4. That the maintenance inviolate of the rights of the States, and especially the right of each State to order and control its own domestic institutions according to its own judgment exclusively, is essential to that balance of powers on which the perfection and endurance of our political fabric depends; and we denounce the lawless invasion by armed forces of the soil of any State or Territory, no matter under what pretext, as among the gravest of crimes.

5. That the present Democratic Administration has far exceeded our worst apprehensions, in its measureless subserviency to the exactions of a sectional interest, as especially evinced in its desperate exertions to force the infamous Lecompton constitution[1] upon the protesting people of Kansas; in construing the personal relation between master and servant to involve an unqualified property in persons; in its attempted enforcement, everywhere, on land and sea, through the intervention of Congress and of the Federal Courts of the extreme pretensions of a purely local interest; and in its general and unvarying abuse of the power intrusted to it by a confiding people. . . .

7. That the new dogma that the Constitution, of its own force, carries Slavery into any or all of the Territories of the United States, is a dangerous political heresy, at variance with the explicit provisions of that instrument itself, with contemporaneous exposition, and with legislative and judicial precedent; is revolutionary in its tendency, and subversive of the peace and harmony of the country.

8. That the normal condition of all the territory of the United States is that of freedom; That as our Republican fathers, when they had abolished slavery in all our national territory, ordained that "no person should be deprived of life, liberty, or property, without due process of law," it becomes our duty, by legislation, whenever such legislation is necessary, to maintain this provision of the Constitution against all attempts to violate it; and we deny the authority of Congress, of a territorial legislature, or of any individuals, to give legal existence to Slavery in any Territory of the United States.

9. That we brand the recent re-opening of the African slave-trade, under the cover of our national flag, aided by perversions of judicial power, as a crime against humanity and a burning shame to our country and age; and we call upon Congress to take prompt and efficient measures for the total and final suppression of that execrable traffic.

10. That in the recent vetoes, by their Federal Governors, of the acts of the Legislatures of Kansas and Nebraska, prohibiting Slavery in those territories, we find a practical illustration of the boasted Democratic principle of Non-Intervention and Popular Sovereignty embodied in the Kansas-

---

1. **Lecompton constitution:** A proslavery constitution adopted by a proslavery legislature in 1857 and not submitted to a popular vote.—*Eds.*

Nebraska bill, and a demonstration of the deception and fraud involved therein.

11. That Kansas should, of right, be immediately admitted as a State under the Constitution recently formed and adopted by her people, and accepted by the House of Representatives.

12. That, while providing revenue for the support of the General Government by duties upon imports, sound policy requires such an adjustment of these imposts as to encourage the development of the industrial interests of the whole country; and we commend that policy of national exchanges which secures to the working men liberal wages, to agriculture remunerating prices, to mechanics and manufacturers an adequate reward for their skill, labor and enterprise, and to the nation commercial prosperity and independence.

13. That we protest against any sale or alienation to others of the Public Lands held by actual settlers, and against any view of the Homestead policy which regards the settlers as paupers or supplicants for public bounty; and we demand the passage by Congress of the complete and satisfactory Homestead measure which has already passed the House.

14. That the Republican Party is opposed to any change in our Naturalization Laws or any State legislation by which the rights of our citizenship hitherto accorded to immigrants from foreign lands shall be abridged or impaired; and in favor of giving a full and efficient protection to the rights of all classes of citizens, whether native or naturalized, both at home and abroad.

15. That appropriations by Congress for River and Harbor improvements of a National character, required for the accommodation and security of an existing commerce, are authorized by the Constitution, and justified by the obligations of Government to protect the lives and property of its citizens.

16. That a Railroad to the Pacific Ocean is imperatively demanded by the interests of the whole country; that the Federal Government ought to render immediate and efficient aid in its construction; and that, as preliminary thereto, a daily Overland Mail should be promptly established.

Banner of the South Carolina Secession Convention. Maryland and Kentucky remained loyal to the Union; Missouri, bitterly divided, never passed a resolution of secession.

CHAPTER FIVE

◆

Rebels, Yankees, and Freedmen

34

◆

FLIGHT FROM UNION

The election of 1860 centered on slavery and the Union. The Republicans ran Abraham Lincoln for president on a platform opposing the further extension of slavery. The Democrats split over the issue. The Northern Democrats ran Illinois Senator Stephen A. Douglas on a platform calling for "popular sovereignty," that is, the right of people in the federal territories to decide for themselves whether they wanted slavery. The Southern Democrats ran Kentucky's John C. Breckenridge on a frankly proslavery platform demanding federal protection of slavery in the territories. A fourth party, the Constitutional Union party, which ran John Bell of Tennessee, tried to play down the slavery issue by emphasizing the preservation of the Union. This division of Lincoln's opponents made his victory an almost foregone conclusion. Though Lincoln did not win the majority of popular votes cast in the election, he won more popular votes than any of his three opponents and he also took the majority of electoral votes. But he received not one electoral vote in the South.

Even before Lincoln's election, Mississippi had contemplated withdrawing from the Union if the Republicans won. When Lincoln did win, Governor John J. Pettus issued a proclamation denouncing the "Black Republicans," held a conference with the state's congressional delegation, including Jefferson Davis, and recommended a state convention to take action on secession. Late in November 1860, the Mississippi legislature met in Jackson, received the governor's recommendation, and passed a bill providing for elections the following month for a convention to meet on January 7 "to consider the then existing relations between the government of the United States and the government and people of the State of Mississippi." It also passed a series of resolutions outlining the reasons for adopting secession as "the proper remedy" for the state's grievances.

On December 20, South Carolina seceded from the Union. Shortly afterward ten other states followed its lead: Mississippi, Florida, Alabama, Georgia, Louisiana, Texas, Virginia, Arkansas, Tennessee, and North Carolina. In February 1861, delegates from the seceding states met in Montgomery, Alabama, to adopt a constitution for the Confederate States of America. They chose Mississippi's Jefferson Davis as president. On April 12, the Civil War began.

Questions to Consider. The Mississippi resolutions contained a succinct summary of the outlook of Southern secessionists. To what extent did they depend on John C. Calhoun's "compact" theory of the Union? Were the resolutions correct in stating that the Northern states had "assumed a revolutionary position" toward the Southern states? Was the charge that the Northern states had violated the Constitution in their behavior toward the South valid? Was it accurate to say that Northerners sought an abolitionist amendment to the Constitution? To what "incendiary publications" do the resolutions refer? What "hostile invasion of a Southern State" did the drafters of the resolutions have in mind? Do you see any similarities between the arguments advanced here and those appearing in the Declaration of Independence?

◆

Mississippi Resolutions on Secession (1860)

Whereas, The Constitutional Union was formed by the several States in their separate sovereign capacity for the purpose of mutual advantage and protection;

That the several States are distinct sovereignties, whose supremacy is limited so far only as the same has been delegated by voluntary compact to a Federal Government, and when it fails to accomplish the ends for which it was established, the parties to the compact have the right to resume, each State for itself, such delegated powers;

That the institution of slavery existed prior to the formation of the Federal Constitution, and is recognized by its letter, and all efforts to impair its value or lessen its duration by Congress, or any of the free States, is a violation of the compact of Union and is destructive of the ends for which it was ordained, but in defiance of the principles of the Union thus established, the people of the Northern States have assumed a revolutionary position towards the Southern States;

That they have set at defiance that provision of the Constitution which was intended to secure domestic tranquillity among the States and promote their general welfare, namely: "No person held to service or labor in one State, under the laws thereof, escaping into another, shall, in consequence of any law or regulation therein, be discharged from such service or labor,

Reprinted by permission of Louisiana State University Press from *Mississippi in the Confederacy,* edited by John K. Bettersworth, copyright © 1961, pp. 22–24.

Confederate soldier. Tintype of Sergeant Thomas Jefferson Rushin, 12th Georgia Infantry. Killed September 17, 1962, in Sharpsburg, Maryland. (Courtesy
Georgia Department of Archives and History)

but shall be delivered up on claim of the party to whom such service or
labor may be due;"

That they have by voluntary associations, individual agencies and State
legislation interfered with slavery as it prevails in the slave-holding States;

That they have enticed our slaves from us, and by State intervention
obstructed and prevented their rendition under the fugitive slave law;

That they continue their system of agitation obviously for the purpose
of encouraging other slaves to escape from service, to weaken the institution in the slave-holding States by rendering the holding of such property
insecure, and as a consequence its ultimate abolition certain;

That they claim the right and demand its execution by Congress to
exclude slavery from the Territories, but claim the right of protection for
every species of property owned by themselves;

That they declare in every manner in which public opinion is expressed their unalterable determination to exclude from admittance into the Union any new State that tolerates slavery in its Constitution, and thereby force Congress to a condemnation of that species of property;

That they thus seek by an increase of abolition States "to acquire two-thirds of both houses" for the purpose of preparing an amendment to the Constitution of the United States, abolishing slavery in the States, and so continue the agitation that the proposed amendment shall be ratified by the Legislatures of three-fourths of the States;

That they have in violation of the comity of all civilized nations, and in violation of the comity established by the Constitution of the United States, insulted and outraged our citizens when travelling among them for pleasure, health or business, by taking their servants and liberating the same, under the forms of State laws, and subjecting their owners to degrading and ignominious punishment;

That to encourage the stealing of our property they have put at defiance that provision of the Constitution which declares that fugitives from justice (escaping) into another State, on demand of the Executive authority of that State from which he fled, shall be delivered up;

That they have sought to create domestic discord in the Southern States by incendiary publications;

That they encouraged a hostile invasion of a Southern State to excite insurrection, murder and rapine;

That they have deprived Southern citizens of their property and continue an unfriendly agitation of their domestic institutions, claiming for themselves perfect immunity from external interference with their domestic policy. . . .

That they have elected a majority of Electors for President and Vice-President on the ground that there exists an irreconcilable conflict between the two sections of the Confederacy in reference to their respective systems of labor and in pursuance of their hostility to us and our institutions, thus declaring to the civilized world that the powers of this Government are to be used for the dishonor and overthrow of the Southern Section of this great Confederacy. Therefore,

Be it resolved by the Legislature of the State of Mississippi, That in the opinion of those who now constitute the said Legislature, the secession of each aggrieved State is the proper remedy for these injuries.

35

◆

UNION INVIOLATE

Fifteen states had significant slave populations when Abraham Lincoln was elected president of the United States on November 6, 1860. One of these, South Carolina, seceded from the Union in late December; others appeared ready to follow early in the new year. To forestall this mass exit, various last-minute compromise proposals emerged in Congress, including the so-called Crittenden Plan. This plan called for two constitutional amendments, the first guaranteeing slavery forever in the states where it already existed, and the second dividing the territories between slavery and freedom. President-elect Lincoln had no objection to the first proposed amendment, but he was unalterably opposed to the second, which would have nullified the free-soil plank of the Republican Party. A territorial division, Lincoln wrote, would only encourage planter expansionism and thus "put us again on the highroad to a slave empire," and on this point "I am inflexible."

Taking this as their cue, five more states—Georgia, Florida, Alabama, Mississippi, and Louisiana—seceded in January 1861. Texas followed on February 1. Seven states were therefore already gone, at least by their own declaration, as Lincoln prepared to deliver his inaugural address on March 4. The stakes were enormously high. Eight slave states, all in the strategically significant upper South, still remained in the Union. Should war begin, their allegiance would be invaluable and the inaugural address could help achieve that. Moreover, in the event of war, the North would have to unite behind the goals of the new president and his party. The address could articulate those unifying goals.

Lincoln believed his first inaugural address could be the most important speech of his life. Like most American politicians, he was a lawyer by trade, and the numerous legalistic formulations of the speech perhaps reflect this background. But the crisis Lincoln faced was fundamentally a constitutional—that is, a legalistic—crisis: Could a nation permit secessionist activity and remain a nation? What compromise with basic principles was possible before constitutional rights were destroyed? Because these were questions partly of constitutional law, Lincoln addressed them partly in legal language. But, as always in his great speeches, he also relied on common sense, common sentiments of patriotism, and, particularly in his conclusion, common familiarity with the cadences of the single most popular work in nineteenth-century America—the King James Bible.

Born to a frontier farming family in Kentucky in 1809, Abraham Lincoln grew up in Indiana and Illinois. As a young man he worked as a farmer, rail-splitter, boatsman, and storekeeper before turning to law and politics. He was enormously successful as a lawyer and served several years in the Illinois legislature and one term in the House of Representatives. Largely a self-educated man, Lincoln read and reread such books as the Bible, Aesop's fables, the works of Shakespeare, and the poems of Robert Burns. He also developed great skill as a writer. In 1858, his debates with Stephen Douglas over slavery brought him national prominence and helped him win the Republican nomination for president in 1860. Although he made restoration of the Union his primary objective during the Civil War, in time he also made it clear that, eventually, it must be a Union without slavery. On April 14, 1865, while attending a performance at Ford's Theatre in Washington, he was shot by actor John Wilkes Booth, a Confederate sympathizer. Lincoln died the next morning.

Questions to Consider. In what ways did Lincoln try to reassure Southerners about his intentions? Could he have said more without compromising his principles? What *was* his basic operating principle in this crisis? What did Lincoln see as the "only substantial dispute" between North and South, and why did he think secession would only make this dispute worse? Was he right in thinking that "deliberate" would be better than "hurried"? To what impulse was Lincoln trying to appeal when he referred to "the better angels of our nature"?

◆

First Inaugural Address (1861)

ABRAHAM LINCOLN

I consider that in view of the Constitution and the laws, the Union is unbroken, and to the extent of my ability I shall take care, as the Constitution itself expressly enjoins me, that the laws of the Union be faithfully executed in all the States. Doing this I deem to be only a simple duty on my part, and I shall perform it so far as practicable unless my rightful masters, the American people, shall withhold the requisite means or in

From James D. Richardson, ed., *A Compilation of the Messages and Papers of the Presidents* (Government Printing Office, Washington, D.C., 1897–1907) VI: 6–12.

President-elect Abraham Lincoln, 1860. (Chicago Historical Society)

some authoritative manner direct the contrary. I trust this will not be regarded as a menace, but only as the declared purpose of the Union that it *will* constitutionally defend and maintain itself.

In doing this there needs to be no bloodshed or violence, and there shall be none unless it be forced upon the national authority. The power confided to me will be used to hold, occupy, and possess the property and places belonging to the Government and to collect the duties and imposts; but beyond what may be necessary for these objects, there will be no invasion, no using of force against or among the people anywhere. . . .

Plainly the central idea of secession is the essence of anarchy. A majority held in restraint by constitutional checks and limitations, and always changing easily with deliberate changes of popular opinions and sentiments, is the only true sovereign of a free people. Whoever rejects it does of necessity fly to anarchy or to despotism. Unanimity is impossible. The rule of a minority, as a permanent arrangement, is wholly inadmissible; so that, rejecting the majority principle, anarchy or despotism in some form is all that is left. . . .

One section of our country believes slavery is *right* and ought to be extended, while the other believes it is *wrong* and ought not to be extended. This is the only substantial dispute. The fugitive-slave clause of the Constitution and the law for the suppression of the foreign slave trade are each as well enforced, perhaps, as any law can ever be in a community where the moral sense of the people imperfectly supports the law itself. The great body of the people abide by the dry legal obligation in both cases, and a few break over in each. This, I think, can not be perfectly cured, and it would be worse in both cases *after* the separation of the sections than before. The foreign slave trade, now imperfectly suppressed, would be ultimately revived without restriction in one section, while fugitive slaves, now only partially surrendered, would not be surrendered at all by the other.

Physically speaking, we can not separate. We can not remove our respective sections from each other nor build an impassable wall between them. A husband and wife may be divorced and go out of the presence and beyond the reach of each other, but the different parts of our country can not do this. They can not but remain face to face, and intercourse, either amicable or hostile, must continue between them. Is it possible, then, to make that intercourse more advantageous or more satisfactory *after* separation than *before?* Can aliens make treaties easier than friends can make laws? Can treaties be more faithfully enforced between aliens than laws can among friends? Suppose you go to war, you can not fight always; and when, after much loss on both sides and no gain on either, you cease fighting, the identical old questions, as to terms of intercourse, are again upon you. . . .

My countrymen, one and all, think calmly and *well* upon this whole subject. Nothing valuable can be lost by taking time. If there be an object to *hurry* any of you in hot haste to a step which you would never take *deliberately*, that object will be frustrated by taking time; but no good object can be frustrated by it. Such of you as are now dissatisfied still have the old Constitution unimpaired, and, on the sensitive point, the laws of your own framing under it; while the new Administration will have no immediate power, if it would, to change either. If it were admitted that you who are dissatisfied hold the right side in the dispute, there still is no single good reason for precipitate action. Intelligence, patriotism, Christianity, and a firm reliance on Him who has never yet forsaken this favored land are still competent to adjust in the best way all our present difficulty.

In *your* hands, my dissatisfied fellow-countrymen, and not in *mine*, is the momentous issue of civil war. The Government will not assail *you*. You can have no conflict without being yourselves the aggressors. *You* have no oath registered in heaven to destroy the Government, while *I* shall have the most solemn one to "preserve, protect, and defend it."

I am loath to close. We are not enemies, but friends. We must not be enemies. Though passion may have strained it must not break our bonds of affection. The mystic chords of memory, stretching from every battlefield and patriot grave to every living heart and hearthstone all over this broad land, will yet swell the chorus of the Union, when again touched, as surely they will be, by the better angels of our nature.

36

◆

A DECLARATION OF FREEDOM

From the outset, the abolitionists urged Abraham Lincoln to make freeing the slaves the major objective of the war. But Lincoln declared: "My paramount object in this struggle is to save the Union." The Republican platform had promised to check the extension of slavery, but it also pledged not to interfere with slavery where it legally existed. Four border slave states—Maryland, Kentucky, Missouri, and Delaware—had remained in the Union, and Lincoln was afraid that an abolitionist policy would drive them into the Confederacy, with disastrous results for the Union cause. He was not convinced at first, moreover, that the majority of Northerners favored abolition.

As the Civil War progressed, Northern public opinion moved slowly in the direction of emancipation. At the same time it was becoming clear that a Union victory would mean the end of slavery. Whenever Union troops occupied any part of the Confederacy, the slaves promptly left the plantations and became camp followers of the Northern armies. Union generals began asking what policy to adopt toward slavery in the occupied parts of the South. In addition, the European public was becoming critical of the North for its failure to emancipate the slaves. Lincoln finally decided that the time had come to take action.

At a secret cabinet meeting on July 22, 1862, Lincoln presented a proclamation abolishing slavery, on which he had been working nearly a month. Secretary of State William H. Seward urged him not to issue it until after a Union victory. Then, on September 17, came the battle of Antietam, at which the Union armies of General George M. McClellan halted the advance of General Robert E. Lee's troops. On September 22, Lincoln officially proclaimed emancipation. In his capacity as commander in chief he announced that, "on the 1st day of January, A.D. 1863, all persons held as slaves within any State or designated part of a State the people whereof shall then be in rebellion against the United States shall be then, thenceforward, and forever free."

The Emancipation Proclamation did not immediately end slavery. It did not apply to the border states because they were not in rebellion. Nor did it apply to those parts of the Confederacy then held by Union troops. Nevertheless, in all Confederate territories subsequently occupied by Northern troops, the slaves became free by the terms of

Lincoln's proclamation. Furthermore, the proclamation led to the voluntary freeing of slaves in many places where it did not apply; Missouri and Maryland freed their slaves in 1863 and 1864. But it was the Thirteenth Amendment that ended slavery everywhere in the United States for all time. Introduced in Congress in December 1863 and adopted with Lincoln's energetic support in January 1865, it became part of the Constitution the following December when the necessary three-fourths of the states had ratified it.

Questions to Consider. The Emancipation Proclamation has been called as prosaic as a bill of lading. Do you think this is a fair appraisal? Do you think a statement more like the preamble to the Declaration of Independence would have been better? Why do you think Lincoln, a great prose master, avoided exalted language in writing the proclamation? On what constitutional powers as president did he depend in announcing his policy? In what ways does the proclamation demonstrate that Lincoln was a practical man? Reactions to the proclamation were varied. The London *Spectator* made fun of it. "The principle," sneered the editor, "is not that a human being cannot justly own another, but that he cannot own him unless he is loyal to the United States." Was the editor's comment justified? Not everyone agreed with the *Spectator*. Many abolitionists and most Southern blacks hailed the proclamation as a giant step on the road to freedom. Were they correct?

◆

The Emancipation Proclamation (1863)

ABRAHAM LINCOLN

Whereas on the 22d day of September, A.D. 1862, a proclamation was issued by the President of the United States, containing among other things, the following, to wit:

"That on the 1st day of January, A.D. 1863, all persons held as slaves within any State or designated part of a State the people whereof shall then be in rebellion against the United States shall be then, thenceforward, and forever free; and the executive government of the United States, including the military and naval authority thereof, will recognize and maintain the freedom of such persons and will do no act or acts to repress such persons, or any of them, in any efforts they may make for their actual freedom.

From John Nicolay and John Hay, eds., *Complete Works of Abraham Lincoln* (12 v., Lincoln Memorial University, n.p., 1894), VIII: 161–164.

"That the executive will on the 1st day of January aforesaid, by proclamation, designate the States and parts of States, if any, in which the people thereof, respectively, shall then be in rebellion against the United States; and the fact that any State or the people thereof shall on that day be in good faith represented in the Congress of the United States by members chosen thereto at elections wherein a majority of the qualified voters of such States shall have participated shall, in the absence of strong countervailing testimony, be deemed conclusive evidence that such State and the people thereof are not then in rebellion against the United States."

Now, therefore, I, Abraham Lincoln, President of the United States, by virtue of the power in me vested as Commander-in-Chief of the Army and Navy of the United States in time of actual armed rebellion against the authority and government of the United States, and as a fit and necessary war measure for suppressing said rebellion, do, on this 1st day of January, A.D. 1863, and in accordance with my purpose so to do, publicly proclaimed for the full period of one hundred days from the first day above mentioned, order and designate as the States and parts of States wherein the people thereof, respectively, are this day in rebellion against the United States the following, to wit:

Arkansas, Texas, Louisiana (except the parishes of St. Bernard, Plaquemines, Jefferson, St. John, St. Charles, St. James, Ascension, Assumption, Terrebonne, Lafourche, St. Mary, St. Martin, and Orleans, including the city of New Orleans), Mississippi, Alabama, Florida, Georgia, South Carolina, North Carolina, and Virginia (except the forty-eight counties designated as West Virginia, and also the counties of Berkeley, Accomac, Northhampton, Elizabeth City, York, Princess Anne, and Norfolk, including the cities of Norfolk and Portsmouth), and which excepted parts are for the present left precisely as if this proclamation were not issued.

And by virtue of the power and for the purpose aforesaid, I do order and declare that all persons held as slaves within said designated States and parts of States are, and henceforward shall be, free; and that the Executive Government of the United States, including the military and naval authorities thereof, will recognize and maintain the freedom of said persons.

And I hereby enjoin upon the people so declared to be free to abstain from all violence, unless in necessary self-defense; and I recommend to them that, in all cases when allowed, they labor faithfully for reasonable wages.

And I further declare and make known that such persons of suitable condition will be received into the armed service of the United States to garrison forts, positions, stations, and other places, and to man vessels of all sorts in said service.

And upon this act, sincerely believed to be an act of justice, warranted by the Constitution upon military necessity, I invoke the considerate judgment of mankind and the gracious favor of Almighty God.

37

◆

PEOPLE'S GOVERNMENT

Late in June 1863, General Robert E. Lee crossed the Potomac River and moved his Confederate army rapidly through Maryland into Pennsylvania. On July 1 his troops met the Union army, commanded by General George G. Meade, at Gettysburg, Pennsylvania. After three days of fierce fighting, with thousands of casualties, Lee's greatly weakened army began to retreat. Lincoln was disappointed that Lee's army was able to escape, but he realized that the Confederates had suffered a decisive defeat. "I am very grateful to Meade," he said, "for the great service he did at Gettysburg." The Gettysburg battle marked the peak of the Confederate effort. Never again were the Confederates able to invade the North, and they never came close to winning the war after that time.

Four months after the bloody encounter—on November 19, 1863—when a national cemetery was dedicated on the Gettysburg battlefield, Lincoln delivered perhaps his most famous address. Edward Everett, famed for his oratory, spoke first, talking for almost two hours. Lincoln's address lasted only a couple of minutes. Afterward, it is said, Everett took Lincoln's hand and told him, "My speech will soon be forgotten; yours never will be. How gladly I would exchange my hundred pages for your twenty lines!" Everett was right. His own speech was soon forgotten, whereas Lincoln's brief address came to be regarded as one of the most powerful statements of the democratic outlook ever made.

Questions to Consider. Why was Everett so impressed with Lincoln's address? Lincoln once said that his basic political ideas came from the Declaration of Independence. Do you think this influence appears in the Gettysburg Address? What in Lincoln's opinion was the basic meaning of the Civil War? To what extent was style, as well as substance, important in the address Lincoln wrote for the Gettysburg dedication?

The Gettysburg Address (1863)

ABRAHAM LINCOLN

Fourscore and seven years ago our fathers brought forth on this continent a new nation, conceived in liberty, and dedicated to the proposition that all men are created equal.

Now we are engaged in a great civil war, testing whether that nation, or any nation so conceived and so dedicated, can long endure. We are met on a great battle-field of that war. We have come to dedicate a portion of that field as a final resting-place for those who here gave their lives that that nation might live. It is altogether fitting and proper that we should do this.

But, in a larger sense, we cannot dedicate—we cannot consecrate—we cannot hallow—this ground. The brave men, living and dead, who struggled here, have consecrated it far above our poor power to add or detract. The world will little note nor long remember what we say here, but it can never forget what they did here. It is for us, the living, rather, to be dedicated here to the unfinished work which they who fought here have thus far so nobly advanced. It is rather for us to be here dedicated to the great task remaining before us—that from these honored dead we take increased devotion to that cause for which they gave the last full measure of devotion; that we here highly resolve that these dead shall not have died in vain; that this nation, under God, shall have a new birth of freedom; and that government of the people, by the people, for the people, shall not perish from the earth.

From John Nicolay and John Hay, eds., *Complete Works of Abraham Lincoln* (12 v., Lincoln Memorial University, n.p., 1894), IX: 209–210.

38

◆

BINDING WOUNDS

In June 1864, when the Republicans nominated Abraham Lincoln for a second term, the end of the war seemed as far away as ever. Northerners were shocked at the heavy casualties reported from battlefields in Virginia, and criticism of the administration had become so harsh that in mid-August Lincoln was convinced he would not be reelected. The Radical Republicans, who spoke for the antislavery faction of the party, condemned him as "politically, militarily, and financially a failure" and for a time backed John C. Frémont for the presidency. The Northern Democrats nominated General George B. McClellan, a former federal commander, and adopted a platform calling for the immediate cessation of hostilities and the restoration of the Union by a negotiated peace. Lincoln was so sure McClellan would defeat him that he wrote a secret memorandum explaining how he would cooperate with the new president after the election in order to save the Union.

But a series of federal victories—the closing of Mobile Bay, the capture of Atlanta, and the routing of Southern forces in the Shenandoah Valley—led public opinion to swing back rapidly to Lincoln. Republican newspapers began ridiculing the "war-is-a-failure" platform of the Democrats, and Frémont decided to drop out of the campaign. Lincoln's prediction that he would not be reelected proved wrong. On election day he won a plurality of nearly half a million votes and carried every state in the Union except Kentucky, Delaware, and New Jersey.

In his second inaugural address on March 4, 1865, Lincoln singled out slavery as the cause of the Civil War and stated that its eradication was inevitable. He expressed hope for a speedy end to the conflict, called for "malice toward none" and "charity for all," and looked forward to the day when Americans would achieve a "just and lasting peace" among themselves and with all nations. On April 9, Lee surrendered to Grant at Appomattox; two days later Lincoln made his last public address, outlining his reconstruction policy. He had never considered the South to be outside of the Union and hoped for a speedy reconciliation. On April 14, at his last cabinet meeting, he urged the cabinet members to put aside all thoughts of hatred and revenge. That evening he was shot.

Questions to Consider. Lincoln's second inaugural address is commonly regarded as one of the greatest addresses ever made by an American president. Why do you think this is so? What did he regard as the basic issue of the Civil War? What irony did he see in the attitude of the contestants? What use of the Bible did he make? Do you think this was likely to appeal to Americans in 1865?

◆

Second Inaugural Address (1865)

ABRAHAM LINCOLN

FELLOW-COUNTRYMEN:—At this second appearing to take the oath of the presidential office there is less occasion for an extended address than there was at the first. Then a statement somewhat in detail of a course to be pursued seemed fitting and proper. Now, at the expiration of four years, during which public declarations have been constantly called forth on every point and phase of the great contest which still absorbs the attention and engrosses the energies of the nation, little that is new could be presented. The progress of our arms, upon which all else chiefly depends, is as well known to the public as to myself, and it is, I trust, reasonably satisfactory and encouraging to all. With high hope for the future, no prediction in regard to it is ventured.

On the occasion corresponding to this four years ago all thoughts were anxiously directed to an impending civil war. All dreaded it, all sought to avert it. While the inaugural address was being delivered from this place, devoted altogether to *saving* the Union without war, insurgent agents were in the city seeking to *destroy* it without war—seeking to dissolve the Union and divide effects by negotiation. Both parties deprecated war, but one of them would *make* war rather than let the nation survive, and the other would *accept* war rather than let it perish, and the war came.

One eighth of the whole population was colored slaves, not distributed generally over the Union, but localized in the southern part of it. These slaves constituted a peculiar and powerful interest. All knew that this interest was somehow the cause of the war. To strengthen, perpetuate, and extend this interest was the object for which the insurgents would rend the Union even by war, while the Government claimed no right to do more than to restrict the territorial enlargement of it. Neither party expected for the war the magnitude nor the duration which it has already attained. Neither anticipated that the *cause* of the conflict might cease with or even before the conflict itself should cease. Each looked for an easier

From James D. Richardson, ed., *A Compilation of the Messages and Papers of the Presidents* (Government Printing Office, Washington, D.C., 1897–1907), VIII: 3477–3478.

End of the war. Anticipating the final triumph of Union arms, New York City stages a huge triumphal procession on March 6, 1865, two days after Lincoln's second inauguration. (Courtesy Dover Pictorial Archive Series, *New York in the 19th Century* by John Grafton, © 1980 Dover Publications, Inc.)

triumph, and a result less fundamental and astounding. Both read the same Bible and pray to the same God, and each invokes His aid against the other. It may seem strange that any men should dare to ask a just God's assistance in wringing their bread from the sweat of other men's faces, but let us judge not, that we be not judged. The prayers of both could not be answered. That of neither has been answered fully. The Almighty has His own purposes. "Woe unto the world because of offenses; for it must needs be that offenses come, but woe to that man by whom the offense cometh." If we shall suppose that American slavery is one of those offenses which, in the providence of God, must needs come, but which, having continued through His appointed time, He now wills to remove, and that He gives to both North and South this terrible war as the woe due to those by whom the offense came, shall we discern therein any departure from those divine attributes which the believers in a living God always ascribe to Him? Fondly do we hope, fervently do we pray, that this mighty scourge of war may speedily pass away. Yet, if God wills that it continue until all the wealth piled by the bondsman's two hundred and fifty years of unrequited toil shall be sunk, and until every drop of blood drawn with the lash shall be paid by another drawn with the sword, as was said three thousand years ago, so still it must be said, "The judgments of the Lord are true and righteous altogether."

With malice toward none, with charity for all, with firmness in the right as God gives us to see the right, let us strive on to finish the work we are in, to bind up the nation's wounds, to care for him who shall have borne the battle and for his widow and his orphan, to do all which may achieve and cherish a just and lasting peace among ourselves and with all nations.

39

◆

A HELPING HAND

The Thirteenth Amendment, which became part of the Constitution in 1865, freed about four million slaves in the South. But with freedom came uncertainty, insecurity, and perplexity. Unlike the peasants of France and Russia, who stayed on the land on which they had been working when they were freed from serfdom, the former American slaves were cast adrift at the end of the Civil War with no means of livelihood. They found themselves without property, legal rights, education, training, and any experience as independent farmers or laborers. Thousands began roaming the countryside looking for work and ways to survive. The first year of freedom brought hunger, disease, suffering, and death.

The freedmen did receive some assistance from the federal government after the war. In March 1865, Congress established the Bureau of Refugees, Freedmen, and Abandoned Lands (commonly called the Freedmen's Bureau) to provide them with food, clothing, shelter, and medical aid. Under the direction of General Oliver O. Howard (the "Christian General"), the Freedmen's Bureau also established schools and colleges for young blacks, founded savings banks, set up courts to protect their civil rights, and tried to get them jobs and fair contracts of employment. During its seven years of existence (1865–1872), the bureau spent more than $15 million for food and other aid and over $6 million on schools and educational work, and gave medical attention to nearly half a million patients. Bureau agents also registered black voters and encouraged political participation. The hostility of Southern whites and the growing indifference of whites in the North, however, negated much of the bureau's work.

The report excerpted below was written by Colonel Eliphalet Whittlesey, assistant bureau commissioner for North Carolina, in October 1865. Whittlesey later became a general and moved to Washington, where he served as a trustee of the national Freedman's Savings Bank. In North Carolina where blacks made up only a third of the population and therefore only a third of the potential voters, the Republican party and the national government soon began to lose political control. By 1871 the white Democratic party once again controlled the state, ending Reconstruction there.

Questions to Consider. Southern whites argued repeatedly that the fundamental objective of the Freedmen's Bureau was not to help the needy but to punish its foes by transforming Southern racial and economic relations. Does Whittlesey's report support this contention? Who received federal assistance in 1865? On what grounds was assistance given? Who made the decisions? Did Whittlesey sound like the commander of an occupying army? Of the bureau's four goals, which did he seem to feel were most urgent? Was he optimistic? Which of its goals was the bureau most likely to achieve in the short run?

◆

Report on the Freedmen's Bureau (1865)

On the 22d of June I arrived at Raleigh with instructions from you to take the control of all subjects relating to "refugees, freedmen, and the abandoned lands" within this State. I found these subjects in much confusion. Hundreds of white refugees and thousands of blacks were collected about this and other towns, occupying every hovel and shanty, living upon government rations, without employment and without comfort, many dying for want of proper food and medical supplies. A much larger number, both white and black, were crowding into the towns, and literally swarming about every depot of supplies to receive their rations. My first effort was to reduce this class of suffering and idle humanity to order, and to discover how large a proportion of these applicants were really deserving of help. The whites, excepting "loyal refugees," were referred to the military authorities. To investigate the condition of refugees and freedmen and minister to the wants of the destitute, I saw at once would require the services of a large number of efficient officers. As fast as suitable persons could be selected, application was made to the department and district commanders for their detail, in accordance with General Order No. 102, War Department, May 31, 1865. In many cases these applications were unsuccessful because the officers asked for could not be spared. The difficulties and delays experienced in obtaining the help needed for a proper organization of my work will be seen from the fact that upon thirty-four written requests, in due form, only eleven officers have been detailed by the department and district commanders. . . .

With this brief history of my efforts to organize the bureau, I proceed to state

From *Report of the Joint Committee on Reconstruction, 1st Session, 39th Congress* (Government Printing Office, Washington, D.C., 1866), II: 186–192.

An early class at Hampton Institute. Uniformed African-American students in class at Virginia's Hampton Institute, founded in 1868 with white philanthropic help to "train selected Negro youth who should go out and teach and lead their people." (The Museum of Modern Art, NY)

The Design and Work Proposed

In my circulars Nos. 1 and 2 (copies of which are herewith enclosed) the objects to be attained are fully stated. All officers of the bureau are instructed—

1. To aid the destitutes, yet in such a way as not to encourage dependence.
2. To protect freedmen from injustice.
3. To assist freedmen in obtaining employment and fair wages for their labor.
4. To encourage education, intellectual and moral.

Under these four divisions the operations of the bureau can best be presented.

Relief Afforded

It was evident at the outset that large numbers were drawing rations who might support themselves. The street in front of the post commissary's office was blocked up with vehicles of all the descriptions peculiar to North Carolina, and with people who had come from the country around, in some instances from a distance of sixty miles, for government rations. These were destitute whites, and were supplied by order of the department commander. Our own headquarters, and every office of the bureau, was besieged from morning till night by freedmen, some coming many miles on foot, others in wagons and carts. The rations issued would scarcely last till they reached home, and in many instances they were sold before leaving the town, in exchange for luxuries. To correct these evils, orders were issued that no able-bodied man or woman should receive supplies, except such as were known to be industrious, and to be entirely destitute. By constant inquiry and effort the throng of beggars was gradually removed. The homeless and helpless were gathered in camps, where shelter and food could be furnished, and the sick collected in hospitals, where they could receive proper care. . . .

Protection

Regarding this bureau as the appointed instrument for redeeming the solemn pledge of the nation, through its Chief Magistrate, to secure the rights of freedmen, I have made every effort to protect them from wrong. Suddenly set free, they were at first exhilarated by the air of liberty, and committed some excesses. To be sure of their freedom, many thought they must leave the old scenes of oppression and seek new homes. Others regarded the property accumulated by their labor as in part their own, and demanded a share of it. On the other hand, the former masters, suddenly stripped of their wealth, at first looked upon the freedmen with a mixture of hate and fear. In these circumstances some collisions were inevitable. The negroes were complained of as idle, insolent, and dishonest; while they complained that they were treated with more cruelty than when they were slaves. Some were tied up and whipped without trial; some were driven from their homes without pay for their labor, without clothing or means of support; others were forbidden to leave on pain of death, and a few were shot or otherwise murdered. All officers of the bureau were directed, in accordance with your circular No. 5, to investigate these difficulties between the two classes, to settle them by counsel and arbitration as far as possible, to punish light offences by fines or otherwise, and to report more serious cases of crime to the military authorities for trial. The exact number of cases heard and decided cannot be given; they have been so numerous that no complete record could be kept; one officer reported that he had heard and disposed of as many as 180 complaints in a single day. The method pursued may be best presented by citing a few cases and the action thereon. From the report of Captain James, for August, I quote the following:

"Reports had reached me of the way in which David Parker, of Gates county, treated his colored people, and I determined to ascertain for myself their truth. Accordingly, last Monday, August 20, accompanied by a guard of six men from this post, (Elizabeth City,) I proceeded to his residence, about forty miles distant. He is very wealthy. I ascertained, after due investigation, and after convincing his colored people that I was really their friend, that the worst reports in regard to him were true. He had twenty-three negroes on his farm, large and small. Of these, fourteen were fieldhands; they all bore unmistakable evidence of the way they had been worked; very much undersized, rarely exceeding, man or women, 4 feet 6 inches—men and women of thirty and forty years of age looking like boys and girls. It has been his habit for years to work them from sunrise to sunset, and often long after, only stopping one hour for dinner—food always cooked for them to save time. He had, and has had for many years, an old colored man, one-eyed and worn out in the service, for an overseer or 'over-looker,' as he called himself. In addition, he has two sons at home, one of whom has made it a point to be with them all summer long— not so much to superintend as to drive. The old colored overseer always went behind the gang with a cane or whip, and woe betide the unlucky wretch who did not continually do his part; he had been brought up to work, and had not the least pity for any one who could not work as well as he.

"Mr. Parker told me that he had hired his people for the season: that directly after the surrender of General Lee he called them up and told them they were free; that he was better used to them than to others, and would prefer hiring them; that he would give them board and two suits of clothing to stay with him till the 1st day of January, 1866, and one Sunday suit at the end of that time; that they consented willingly—in fact, preferred to remain with him, &c. But from his people I learned that though he did call them up, as stated, yet when one of them demurred at the offer his son James flew at him and cuffed and kicked him; that after that they were all 'perfectly willing to stay'; they were watched night and day; that Bob, one of the men, had been kept chained nights; that they were actually afraid to try to get away. There was no complaint of the food nor much of the clothing, but they were in constant terror of the whip. Only three days before my arrival, Bob had been stripped in the field and given fifty lashes for hitting Adam, the colored over-looker, while James Parker stood by with a gun, and told him to run if he wanted to, he had a gun there. About four weeks before, four of them who went to church and returned before sunset were treated to twenty-five lashes each. Some were beaten or whipped almost every day. Having ascertained these and other similar facts, I directed him to call them up and pay them for the first of May last up to the present time. I investigated each case, taking into consideration age, family, physical condition, &c., estimating their work from $8 down, and saw him pay them off then and there, allowing for clothing and medical bill. I then arrested him and his two sons, and brought them here, except Dr. Joseph Parker, whose sister is very sick, with all the colored people I thought necessary as witnesses, intending to send them to Newbern for trial. But on account of the want of immediate transportation I concluded to release them on their giving a bond in the sum of $2,000 to Colonel E. Whittlesey, assistant commissioner for the State of North Carolina, and to his successors in office, conditioned as follows:

"That whereas David Parker and James Parker have heretofore maltreated their colored people, and have enforced the compulsory system instead of the free labor system: Now, therefore, if they, each of them, shall hereafter well and kindly treat, and cause to be treated, the hired laborers under their or his charge, and shall adopt the free labor system in lieu of the compulsory system, then this bond to be void and of no effect; otherwise to remain in full force and effect, with good security."

Lieutenant Colonel Clapp, superintendent central district, reports three cases of cruel beating, which have been investigated, and the offenders turned over to the military authorities for trial; besides very many instances of defrauding freedmen of their wages. . . .

The following cases are taken from the report of Captain Barritt, assistant commissioner, at Charlotte:

"Morrison Miller charged with whipping a girl Hannah (colored.) Found guilty. Action: ordered to pay said Hannah fifty bushels of corn towards supporting herself and children, two of said children being the offspring of Miller.

"Wm. Wallace charged with whipping Martha (colored.) Plead guilty. Action: fined said Wallace $15, with assurance that if the above offence was repeated, the fine would be doubled.

"Council Best attempts to defraud six families of their summer labor, by offering to sell at auction the crop on his leased plantation. Action: sent military force and stopped the sale until contract with laborers was complied with."

A hundred pages of similar reports might be copied, showing, on the one side, that many freedmen need the presence of some authority to enforce upon them their new duties; and on the other, that so far from being true that "there is no county in which a freedman can be imposed upon," there is no county in which he is not oftener wronged; and these wrongs increase just in proportion to their distance from United States authorities. There has been great improvement, during the quarter, in this respect. The efforts of the bureau to protect the freedmen have done much to restrain violence and injustice. Such efforts must be continued until civil government is fully restored, just laws enacted, or great suffering and serious disturbance will be the result.

Industry

Contrary to the fears and predictions of many, the great mass of colored people have remained quietly at work upon the plantations of their former masters during the entire summer. The crowds seen about the towns in the early part of the season had followed in the wake of the Union army, to escape from slavery. After hostilities ceased these refugees returned to their homes, so that but few vagrants can now be found. In truth, a much larger amount of vagrancy exists among the whites than among the blacks. It is the almost uniform report of officers of the bureau that freedmen are industrious.

The report is confirmed by the fact that out of a colored population of nearly 350,000 in the State, only about 5,000 are now receiving support from the government. Probably some others are receiving aid from kind-hearted men who have enjoyed the benefit of their services from childhood. To the general quiet and industry of this people there can be no doubt that the efforts of the bureau have contributed greatly. I have visited some of the larger towns, as Wilmington, Newbern, Goldsborough, and both by public addresses and private instructions counselled the freedmen to secure employment and maintain themselves. Captain James has made an extensive tour through the eastern district for the same purpose, and has exerted a most happy influence. Lieutenant Colonel Clapp has spent much of his time in visiting the county seats of the central district, and everywhere been listened to by all classes with deep interest. Other officers have done much good in this way. They have visited plantations, explained the difference between slave and free labor, the nature and the solemn obligation of contracts. The chief difficulty met with has been a want of confidence between the two parties. The employer, accustomed only to the system of compulsory labor, is slow to believe that he can secure fruitful services by the stimulus of wages. The laborer is unwilling to trust the promises of those for whom he had toiled all his days without pay; hence but few contracts for long periods have been effected. The bargains for the present year are generally vague, and their settlement as the crops are gathered in requires much labor. In a great majority of cases the landowners seem disposed to do justly, and even generously; and when this year's work is done, and the proceeds divided, it is hoped that a large number of freedmen will enter into contracts for the coming year. They will, however, labor much more cheerfully for money, with prompt and frequent payments, than for a share of the crop, for which they must wait twelve months. A large farmer in Pitt county hires hands by the job, and states that he never saw negroes work so well. Another in Lenoir county pays monthly, and is satisfied so far with the experiment of free labor. Another obstacle to long contracts was found in the impression which had become prevalent to some degree, *i.e.*, that lands were to be given to freedmen by the government. To correct this false impression I published a circular, No. 3, and directed all officers of the bureau to make it as widely known as possible. From the statistical reports enclosed, it will be seen that during the quarter 257 written contracts for labor have been prepared and witnessed; that the average rate of wages, when paid in money, is from $8 to $10 per month; that 128 farms are under the control of the bureau and cultivated for the benefit of freedmen; that 8,540 acres are under cultivation, and 6,102 are employed. Many of the farms were rented by agents of the treasury as abandoned lands, previous to the establishing of this bureau, and were transferred to us with the leases upon them. Nearly all have been restored to their owners, under the President's proclamation of amnesty, and our tenure of the few that remain is so uncertain that I have not deemed it prudent to set apart any for use of refugees and freedmen, in accordance with the act of Congress approved March 3, 1865. But many freedmen are taking this matter into their own hands, and renting lands from the owners for one or more years. . . .

Education

The quarter has been one of vacation rather than active work in this department. Still some progress has been made, and much done to prepare for the coming autumn and winter. Rev. F. A. Fiske, a Massachusetts teacher, has been appointed superintendent of education, and has devoted himself with energy to his duties. From his report it will be seen that the whole number of schools, during the whole or any part of the quarter, is 63, the number of teachers 85, and the number of scholars 5,624. A few of the schools are self-supporting, and taught by colored teachers, but the majority are sustained by northern societies and northern teachers. The officers of the bureau have, as far as practicable, assigned buildings for their use, and assisted in making them suitable; but the time is nearly past when such facilities can be given. The societies will be obliged hereafter to pay rent for school-rooms and for teachers' homes. The teachers are engaged in a noble and self-denying work. They report a surprising thirst for knowledge among the colored people—children giving earnest attention and learning rapidly, and adults, after the day's work is done, devoting the evening to study. In this connexion it may be mentioned, as a result of moral instruction, that 512 marriages have been reported and registered, and 42 orphans provided with good homes.

40

◆

KLANSMEN OF THE CAROLINAS

Reconstruction developed in a series of moves and countermoves. In a white Southern backlash to Union victory and emancipation came the "black codes" for coercing black laborers and President Andrew Johnson's pardon of Confederate landowners. Then in a Northern backlash to these codes and pardons came the Civil Rights bills, the sweeping Reconstruction Acts of 1867, and the Fourteenth and Fifteenth Amendments, all designed to guarantee black political rights. White Southerners reacted to these impositions in turn with secret night-time terrorist or "night rider" organizations designed to shatter Republican political power. Congress tried to protect Republican voters and the freedmen with the Force Acts of 1870 allowing the use of the army to prevent physical assaults, but Northern willingness to commit troops and resources to the struggle was waning. By the mid-1870s only three states remained in Republican hands, and within three years racist Democrats controlled these, too. The night riders had turned the tide.

Although numerous secret societies for whites appeared in the Reconstruction South—including the Order of the White Camelia (Louisiana), the Pale Faces (Tennessee), the White Brotherhood (North Carolina), and the Invisible Circle (South Carolina)—the largest and most influential society, and the one that spawned these imitators, was the Ku Klux Klan, the so-called Invisible Empire. The Klan began in Tennessee in 1866 as a young men's social club with secret costumes and rituals similar to those of the Masons, the Odd-Fellows, and other popular societies. In 1867, however, following passage of the Reconstruction Acts, anti-Republican racists began to see the usefulness of such a spookily secret order, and the Klan was reorganized to provide for "dens," "provinces" (counties), and "realms" (states), all under the authority of a "Grand Wizard," who in 1867 was believed to have been Nathan B. Forrest, a former slave trader and Confederate general.

The Klan structure was probably never fully established because of the disorganized conditions of the postwar South. Other societies with different names emerged, and the Reconstruction-era "Ku-Klux" may have disbanded as a formal entity in the early 1870s. But it clearly survived in spirit and in loosely formed groups, continuing to terrorize

Republicans and their allies among the newly enfranchised freedmen into the 1870s and sowing fear among the black families who composed, after all, the labor force on which the white planters still depended. The excerpt reprinted below includes congressional testimony by David Schenck, a member of the North Carolina Klan seeking to portray it in the best possible light, followed by testimony from Elias Hill, a South Carolina black man victimized by a local "den" of the Klan. Schenck and Hill were testifying before a joint Senate-House committee concerned with antiblack terrorism.

Questions to Consider. The oath taken by David Schenck emphasizes the Klan's religious, constitutional, and benevolent qualities, whereas Elias Hill's story reveals its terrorist features. Are there elements in the Klan oath that seem to hint at or justify the use of violence? Why does the oath contain the phrases "original purity," "pecuniary embarrassments," and "traitor's doom"? What "secrets of this order" could deserve death? Klansmen later claimed that because they could terrorize the superstitious freedmen simply by using masks, odd voices, and ghostly sheets, no real violence was necessary. Opponents have claimed, on the other hand, that Klansmen were basically sadists acting out sexual phobias and deep paranoia. What light does Elias Hill's testimony shed on these conflicting claims? What position did Hill hold in the black community? Did the Klansmen seem to be assaulting him because of his condition or because of his position in the black community? Why did they ask Hill to pray for them? Would it be fair or accurate to call the Ku Klux Klan a terrorist organization that succeeded?

◆

Report of the Joint Committee on Reconstruction (1872)

A select committee of the Senate, upon the 10th of March, 1871, made a report of the result of their investigation into the security of person and property in the State of North Carolina. . . . A sub-committee of their number proceeded to the State of South Carolina, and examined witnesses in that State until July 29. . . .

David Schenck, esq., a member of the bar of Lincoln County, North Carolina . . . was initiated in October, 1868, as a member of the Invisible

From *Report of the Joint Select Committee to Inquire into the Condition of Affairs in the Late Insurrectionary States* (Government Printing Office, Washington, D.C., 1872), 25–27, 44–47.

Empire. . . . In his own words: "We were in favor of constitutional liberty as handed down to us by our forefathers. I think the idea incorporated was that we were opposed to the [fourteenth and fifteenth] amendments to the Constitution. I desire to explain in regard to that that it was not to be—at least, I did not intend by that that it should be—forcible resistance, but a political principle."

The oath itself is as follows:

> I, (name,) before the great immaculate Judge of heaven and earth, and upon the Holy Evangelist of Almighty God, do, of my own free will and accord, subscribe to the following sacred, binding obligation:
>
>   I. I am on the side of justice and humanity and constitutional liberty, as bequeathed to us by our forefathers in its original purity.
>
>   II. I reject and oppose the principles of the radical [Republican] party.
>
>   III. I pledge aid to a brother of the Ku-Klux Klan in sickness, distress, or pecuniary embarrassments. Females, friends, widows, and their households shall be the special objects of my care and protection.
>
>   IV. Should I ever divulge, or cause to be divulged, any of the secrets of this order, or any of the foregoing obligations, I must meet with the fearful punishment of death and traitor's doom, which is death, death, death, at the hands of the brethren. . . .

Elias Hill of York County, South Carolina, is a remarkable character. He is crippled in both legs and arms, which are shriveled by rheumatism; he cannot walk, cannot help himself . . .; was in early life a slave, whose freedom was purchased by his father. . . . He learned his letters and to read by calling the school children into the cabin as they passed, and also learned to write. He became a Baptist preacher, and after the war engaged in teaching colored children, and conducted the business correspondence of many of his colored neighbors. . . . We put the story of his wrongs in his own language:

"On the night of the 5th of May, after I had heard a great deal of what they had done in that neighborhood, they came . . . to my brother's door, which is in the same yard, and broke open the door and attacked his wife, and I heard her screaming and mourning. I could not understand what they said, for they were talking in an outlandish and unnatural tone, which I had heard they generally used at a negro's house. They said, 'Where's Elias?' She said, 'He doesn't stay here; yon is his house.' I had heard them strike her five or six licks. Someone then hit my door. . . .

"They carried me into the yard between the houses, my brother's and mine, and put me on the ground. . . . 'Who did that burning? Who burned our houses?' I told them it was not me. I could not burn houses. Then they hit me with their fists, and said I did it, I ordered it. They went on asking me didn't I tell the black men to ravish all the white women. No, I answered them. They struck me again. . . . 'Haven't you been preaching and praying about the Ku-Klux? Haven't you been preaching political sermons? Doesn't a [Republican Party newspaper] come to your house? Haven't you written letters?' Generally one asked me all the questions, but the rest were squatting over me—some six men I counted as I lay there. . . . I told them if they would take me back into the house, and lay me in the bed, which was close adjoining my books and papers, I would try and get it. They said I would never go back to that bed, for they were going to kill me. . . . They caught my leg and pulled me over the yard, and then left me there, knowing I could not walk nor crawl. . . .

"After they had stayed in the house for a considerable time, they came back to where I lay and asked if I wasn't afraid at all. They pointed pistols at me all around my head once or twice, as if they were going to shoot me. . . . One caught me by the leg and hurt me, for my leg for forty years has been drawn each year, more and more, and I made moan when it hurt so. One said, 'G–d d—n it, hush!' He had a horsewhip, [and] I reckon he struck me eight cuts right on the hip bone; it was almost the only place he could hit my body, my legs are so short. They all had disguises. . . . One of them then took a strap, and buckled it around my neck and said, 'Let's take him to the river and drown him.' . . .

"Then they said, 'Look here! Will you put a card in the paper to renounce all republicanism? Will you quit preaching?' I told them I did not know. I said that to save my life. . . . They said if I did not they would come back the next week and kill me. [After more licks with the strap] one of them went into the house where my brother and sister-and-law lived, and brought her to pick me up. As she stooped down to pick me up one of them struck her, and as she was carrying me into the house another struck her with a strap. . . . They said, 'Don't you pray against Ku-Klux, but pray that God may forgive Ku-Klux. Pray that God may bless and save us.' I was so chilled with cold lying out of doors so long and in such pain I could not speak to pray, but I tried to, and they said that would do very well, and all went out of the house. . . ."

Satisfied that he could no longer live in that community, Hill wrote to make inquiry about the means of going to Liberia. Hearing this, many of his neighbors desired to go also. . . . Others are still hoping for relief, through the means of this sub-committee.

41

◆

A KIND OF REUNION

Despite Congress's seizure of control over Reconstruction policy and Ulysses S. Grant's defeat of Andrew Johnson for the presidency in 1868, Radical Reconstruction—the garrisoning of the South, the disfranchisement of former rebels, and the control of Southern state governments by Republican votes—did not last long in most places. During President Grant's first term of office, the white-dominated Democratic Party gained control of North Carolina, Tennessee, and Virginia, the three ex-Confederate states with the lowest percentage of black population. During Grant's second term, Democrats seized control of Alabama, Arkansas, Georgia, Mississippi, and Texas. That left Republican governments (and federal troops) in Florida, Louisiana, and South Carolina, three states with large black populations.

Those states mattered greatly in national politics. During the election of 1876 both parties resorted to fraud. Two sets of electoral returns came in from the three states, and it was necessary for Congress to set up an electoral commission to decide whether Rutherford B. Hayes, the Republican candidate, or Samuel J. Tilden, the Democratic standard bearer, had won. By a strict party vote of 8 to 7, the commission awarded all 20 disputed electoral votes to the Republicans. Hayes became president, with 185 votes to Tilden's 184. In the end, Southern Democrats reached a compromise with Northern Republicans. The Democrats agreed to accept the commission's decision and the Republicans promised to withdraw the remaining federal troops from the South. In April 1877, the last federal soldiers left the South. Solid Democratic control—and stepped-up measures to disfranchise black voters—quickly followed.

Although political maneuvering was important in finally killing Republican Reconstruction, the underlying reason it died was simply that Northerners were losing the will to suppress an increasingly violent white South. The nation's approaching centennial celebration in 1876 triggered an especially strong outpouring of sentiment in favor of improving sectional feelings by withdrawing the troops, even if withdrawal meant the resurgence of the Democratic Party. That, in turn, would permit an overdue rebonding of the century-old republic. The following unsigned editorial ran in the August 1875 issue of *Scribner's*

Monthly, an influential, generally Republican, New York magazine. It expressed, with unusual eloquence, this emotional yearning for peace.

Questions to Consider. What was the occasion of the *Scribner's* editorial? Was this a natural time to consider troop withdrawals? What, in the view of the editor, was the major accomplishment of the Civil War? What specific political theory had been tested and defeated? When addressing the "men of the South," was the editor speaking to all Southern men? What did the phrase "brotherly sympathy" mean? Was it naive or was it realistic for the writer to think that the upcoming centennial could "heal all the old wounds" and "reconcile all the old differences"? Would Abraham Lincoln have agreed with the spirit of this editorial?

◆

"What the Centennial Ought to Accomplish" (1875)

SCRIBNER'S MONTHLY

We are to have grand doings next year. There is to be an Exposition. There are to be speeches, and songs, and processions, and elaborate ceremonies and general rejoicings. Cannon are to be fired, flags are to be floated, and the eagle is expected to scream while he dips the tip of either pinion in the Atlantic and the Pacific, and sprinkles the land with a new baptism of freedom. The national oratory will exhaust the figures of speech in patriotic glorification, while the effete civilizations of the Old World, and the despots of the East, tottering upon their tumbling thrones, will rub their eyes and sleepily inquire, "What's the row?" The Centennial is expected to celebrate in a fitting way—somewhat dimly apprehended, it is true—the birth of a nation.

Well, the object is a good one. When the old colonies declared themselves free, they took a grand step in the march of progress; but now, before we begin our celebration of this event, would it not be well for us to inquire whether we have a nation? In a large number of the States of this country there exists not only a belief that the United States do not constitute a nation, but a theory of State rights which forbids that they ever shall become one. We hear about the perturbed condition of the Southern mind. We hear it said that multitudes there are just as disloyal as they were during the civil war. This, we believe, we are justified in denying. Before the war they had a theory of State rights. They fought to establish that theory, and

From *Scribner's Monthly* 10 (August 1875), 509–510.

Miss Liberty's torch. A display at the great 1876 Centennial Exposition, Philadelphia. (National Portrait Gallery/ Smithsonian Institution, Washington, DC)

they now speak of the result as "the lost cause." They are not actively in rebellion, and they do not propose to be. They do not hope for the re-establishment of slavery. They fought bravely and well to establish their theory, but the majority was against them; and if the result of the war emphasized any fact, it was that *en masse* the people of the United States constitute a nation—indivisible in constituents, in interest, in destiny. The result of the war was without significance, if it did not mean that the United States constitute a nation which cannot be divided; which will not permit itself to be divided; which is integral, indissoluble, indestructible. We do not care what theories of State rights are entertained outside of this. State rights, in all the States, should be jealously guarded, and, by all legitimate means, defended. New York should be as jealous of her State prerogatives as South Carolina or Louisiana; but this theory which makes of the Union a rope of sand, and of the States a collection of petty nationalities that can at liberty drop the bands which hold them together, is forever exploded. It has been tested at the point of the bayonet. It went down in blood, and went down for all time. Its adherents may mourn over the fact, as we can never cease to mourn over the events which accompanied it, over the sad, incalculable cost to them and to those who opposed them. The great point with them is to recognize the fact that, for richer or poorer, in sickness and health, until death do us part, these United States constitute a nation; that we are to live, grow, prosper, and suffer together, united by bands that cannot be sundered.

Unless this fact is fully recognized throughout the Union, our Centennial will be but a hollow mockery. If we are to celebrate anything worth celebrating, it is the birth of a nation. If we are to celebrate anything worth celebrating, it should be by the whole heart and united voice of the nation. If we can make the Centennial an occasion for emphasizing the great lesson of the war, and universally assenting to the results of the war, it will, indeed, be worth all the money expended upon and the time devoted to it. If around the old Altars of Liberty we cannot rejoin our hands in brotherly affection and national loyalty, let us spike the cannon that will only proclaim our weakness, put our flags at half-mast, smother our eagles, eat our ashes, and wait for our American aloe to give us a better blossoming.

A few weeks ago, Mr. Jefferson Davis, the ex-President of the Confederacy, was reported to have exhorted an audience to which he was speaking to be as loyal to the old flag of the Union now as they were during the Mexican War. If the South could know what music there was in these words to Northern ears—how grateful we were to their old chief for them—it would appreciate the strength of our longing for a complete restoration of the national feeling that existed when Northern and Southern blood mingled in common sacrifice on Mexican soil. This national feeling, this national pride, this brotherly sympathy *must be restored;* and accursed be any Northern or Southern man, whether in power or out of power, whether politician, theorizer, carpet-bagger, president-maker or plunderer, who puts obstacles in the way of such a restoration. Men of the South, we want you. Men of the South, we long for the restoration of your peace and your prosperity. We would see your cities thriving, your homes happy, your plantations teeming with plenteous harvests, your schools overflowing, your wisest statesmen leading you, and all causes and all memories of discord wiped out forever. You do not believe this? Then you do not know the heart of the North. Have you cause of complaint against the politicians? Alas! so have we. Help us, as loving and loyal American citizens, to make our politicians better. Only remember and believe that there is nothing that the North wants so much to-day, as your recognition of the fact that the old relations between you and us are forever restored—that your hope, your pride, your policy, and your destiny are one with ours. Our children will grow up to despise our childishness, if we cannot do away with our personal hates so far, that in the cause of an established nationality we may join hands under the old flag.

To bring about this reunion of the two sections of the country in the old fellowship, should be the leading object of the approaching Centennial. A celebration of the national birth, begun, carried on, and finished by a section, would be a mockery and a shame. The nations of the world might well point at it the finger of scorn. The money expended upon it were better sunk in the sea, or devoted to repairing the waste places of the war. Men of the South, it is for you to say whether your magnanimity is equal to your valor—whether you are as reasonable as you are brave, and whether, like your old chief, you accept that definite and irreversible result of the war which makes you and yours forever members of the great American nation with us. Let us see to it, North and South, that the Centennial heals all the old wounds, reconciles all the old differences, and furnishes the occasion for such a reunion of the great American nationality, as shall make our celebration an expression of fraternal good-will among all sections and all States, and a corner-stone over which shall be reared a new temple to national freedom, concord, peace, and prosperity.

42

◆

AFTERMATH

Frederick Douglass regarded the Declaration of Independence as a "watchword of freedom." But he was tempted to turn it to the wall, he said, because its human rights principles were so shamelessly violated. A former slave himself, Douglass knew what he was talking about. Douglass thought that enslaving blacks fettered whites as well and that the United States would never be truly free until it ended chattel slavery. During the Civil War, he had several conversations with Lincoln, urging him to make emancipation his major aim. He also put unremitting pressure on the Union army to accept black volunteers, and after resistance to admitting blacks into the army gave way, he toured the country encouraging blacks to enlist and imploring the government to treat black and white soldiers equally in matters of pay and promotion.

Douglass had great hopes for his fellow blacks after the Civil War. He demanded they be given full rights—political, legal, educational, and economic—as citizens. He also wanted to see the wall of separation between the races crumble and see "the colored people of this country, enjoying the same freedom [as whites], voting at the same ballot-box, using the same cartridge-box, going to the same schools, attending the same churches, travelling in the same street cars, in the same railroad cars, on the same steam-boats, proud of the same country, fighting the same war, and enjoying the same peace and all its advantages." He regarded the Republican party as the "party of progress, justice and freedom" and at election time took to the stump and rallied black votes for the party. He was rewarded for these services by appointment as marshal of the District of Columbia in 1877, as recorder of deeds for the District in 1881, and as minister to Haiti in 1889. But he was also asked by Republican leaders to keep a low profile, was omitted from White House guest lists, and was excluded from presidential receptions even though one duty of the District marshal was to introduce the guests at White House state occasions.

Douglass was puzzled and then upset by the increasing indifference of Republican leaders to conditions among blacks after the Civil War. In 1883 he attended a convention of blacks in Louisville, Kentucky, which met to discuss their plight and reaffirm their demand for full civil rights. In his keynote address, which is reprinted here, Douglass vividly portrayed the discrimination and persecution his people encountered, but he continued to believe that "prejudice, with all its malign accomplishments, may yet be removed by peaceful means."

Born into slavery in Maryland in 1817, Frederick Augustus Washington Bailey learned to read and write despite efforts to keep him illiterate. In 1838 he managed to escape to freedom and adopted the name Frederick Douglass. Shortly afterward he became associated with William Lloyd Garrison and developed into such an articulate spokesman for the antislavery cause that people doubted he had ever been a slave. In 1845 he published his *Narrative of the Life of Frederick Douglass, an American Slave,* naming names, places, dates, and precise events to convince people he had been born in bondage. Douglass continued to be an articulate spokesman for the black cause throughout his life. Shortly before his death in 1895 a college student asked him what a young black could do to help the cause. "Agitate! Agitate! Agitate!" Douglass is supposed to have told him.

Questions to Consider. In the following address Douglass was speaking to a convention of blacks in Louisville, but his appeal was primarily to American whites. How did he try to convince them that blacks deserved the same rights and opportunities as all Americans? How powerful did he think the color line was? What outrages against his people did he report? What was his attitude toward the Republican party, which he had so faithfully served? Were the grievances he cited largely economic or were they social and political in nature?

◆

Address to the Louisville Convention (1883)

FREDERICK DOUGLASS

Born on American soil in common with yourselves, deriving our bodies and our minds from its dust, centuries having passed away since our ancestors were torn from the shores of Africa, we, like yourselves, hold ourselves to be in every sense Americans, and that we may, therefore, venture to speak to you in a tone not lower than that which becomes earnest men and American citizens. Having watered your soil with our tears, enriched it with our blood, performed its roughest labor in time of peace, defended it against enemies in time of war, and at all times been

From Philip Foner, ed., *The Life and Writings of Frederick Douglass* (4 v., International Publishers, New York, 1955), IV: 373–392. Reprinted by permission.

loyal and true to its best interests, we deem it no arrogance or presumption to manifest now a common concern with you for its welfare, prosperity, honor and glory. . . .

It is our lot to live among a people whose laws, traditions, and prejudices have been against us for centuries, and from these they are not yet free. To assume that they are free from these evils simply because they have changed their laws is to assume what is utterly unreasonable and contrary to facts. Large bodies move slowly. Individuals may be converted on the instant and change their whole course of life. Nations never. Time and events are required for the conversion of nations. Not even the character of a great political organization can be changed by a new platform. It will be the same old snake though in a new skin. Though we have had war, reconstruction and abolition as a nation, we still linger in the shadow and blight of an extinct institution. Though the colored man is no longer subject to be bought and sold, he is still surrounded by an adverse sentiment which fetters all his movements. In his downward course he meets with no resistance, but his course upward is resented and resisted at every step of his progress. If he comes in ignorance, rags, and wretchedness, he conforms to the popular belief of his character, and in that character he is welcome. But if he shall come as a gentleman, a scholar, and a statesman, he is hailed as a contradiction to the national faith concerning his race, and his coming is resented as impudence. In the one case he may provoke contempt and derision, but in the other he is an affront to pride, and provokes malice. Let him do what he will, there is at present, therefore, no escape for him. The color line meets him everywhere, and in a measure shuts him out from all respectable and profitable trades and callings. In spite of all your religion and laws he is a rejected man.

He is rejected by trade unions, of every trade, and refused work while he lives, and burial when he dies, and yet he is asked to forget his color, and forget that which everybody else remembers. If he offers himself to a builder as a mechanic, to a client as a lawyer, to a patient as a physician, to a college as a professor, to a firm as a clerk, to a Government Department as an agent, or an officer, he is sternly met on the color line, and his claim to consideration in some way is disputed on the ground of color.

Not even our churches, whose members profess to follow the despised Nazarene, whose home, when on earth, was among the lowly and despised, have yet conquered this feeling of color madness, and what is true of our churches is also true of our courts of law. Neither is free from this all-pervading atmosphere of color hate. The one describes the Deity as impartial, no respecter of persons, and the other the Goddess of Justice as blindfolded, with sword by her side and scales in her hand held evenly between high and low, rich and poor, white and black, but both are the images of American imagination, rather than American practices.

Taking advantage of the general disposition in this country to impute crime to color, white men *color* their faces to commit crime and wash off

Frederick Douglass. Douglass's greatest work came before and during the Civil War. One of the most eloquent and magnetic of all the abolitionist leaders, he contributed enormously to the antislavery cause. During the Civil War he pressed hard for the enlistment of blacks to fight in the Union armies on an equal footing with whites. After the war he continued his efforts for civil rights, including black suffrage. For his services to the Republican party he received appointments as secretary to the Santo Domingo commission, marshal and recorder of deeds for the District of Columbia, and U.S. minister to Haiti. (National Portrait Gallery, Smithsonian Institution/Washington, DC)

the hated color to escape punishment. In many places where the commission of crime is alleged against one of our color, the ordinary processes of law are set aside as too slow for the impetuous justice of the infuriated populace. They take the law into their own bloody hands and proceed to whip, stab, shoot, hang, or burn the alleged culprit, without the intervention of courts, counsel, judges, juries, or witnesses. In such cases it is not the business of the accusers to prove guilt, but it is for the accused to prove his innocence, a thing hard for him to do in these infernal Lynch courts. A man accused, surprised, frightened, and captured by a motley crowd, dragged with a rope about his neck in midnight-darkness to the nearest tree, and told in the coarsest terms of profanity to prepare for death, would be more than human if he did not, in his terror-stricken appearance, more confirm suspicion of guilt than the contrary. Worse still, in the presence of such hell-black outrages, the pulpit is usually dumb, and the press in the neighborhood is silent or openly takes side with the mob. There are occasional cases in which white men are lynched, but one sparrow does not make a summer. Every one knows that what is called Lynch law is peculiarly the law for colored people and for nobody else. If there were no other grievance than this horrible and barbarous Lynch law custom, we should be justified in assembling, as we have now done, to expose and denounce it. But this is not all. Even now, after twenty years of so-called emancipation, we are subject to lawless raids of midnight riders, who, with blackened faces, invade our homes and perpetrate the foulest of crimes upon us and our families. This condition of things is too flagrant and notorious to require specifications or proof. Thus in all the relations of life and death we are met by the color line.

While we recognize the color line as a hurtful force, a mountain barrier to our progress, wounding our bleeding feet with its flinty rocks at every step, we do not despair. We are a hopeful people. This convention is a proof of our faith in you, in reason, in truth and justice—our belief that prejudice, with all its malign accomplishments, may yet be removed by peaceful means; that, assisted by time and events and the growing enlightenment of both races, the color line will ultimately become harmless. When this shall come it will then only be used, as it should be, to distinguish one variety of the human family from another. It will cease to have any civil, political, or moral significance, and colored conventions will then be dispensed with as anachronisms, wholly out of place, but not till then. Do not marvel that we are discouraged. The faith within us has a rational basis, and is confirmed by facts. When we consider how deep-seated this feeling against us is; the long centuries it has been forming; the forces of avarice which have been marshaled to sustain it; how the language and literature of the country have been pervaded with it; how the church, the press, the play-house, and other influences of the country have been arrayed in its support, the progress toward its extinction must be considered vast and wonderful. . . .

We do not believe, as we are often told, that the Negro is the ugly child of the national family, and the more he is kept out of sight the better it will be for him. You know that liberty given is never so precious as liberty sought for and fought for. The man outraged is the man to make the outcry. Depend upon it, men will not care much for a people who do not care for themselves. Our meeting here was opposed by some of our members, because it would disturb the peace of the Republican party. The suggestion came from coward lips and misapprehended the character of that party. If the Republican party cannot stand a demand for justice and fair play, it ought to go down. We were men before that party was born, and our manhood is more sacred than any party can be. Parties were made for men, not men for parties.

The colored people of the South are the laboring people of the South. The labor of a country is the source of its wealth; without the colored laborer to-day the South would be a howling wilderness, given up to bats, owls, wolves, and bears. He was the source of its wealth before the war, and has been the source of its prosperity since the war. He almost alone is visible in her fields, with implements of toil in his hands, and laboriously using them to-day.

Let us look candidly at the matter. While we see and hear that the South is more prosperous than it ever was before and rapidly recovering from the waste of war, while we read that it raises more cotton, sugar, rice, tobacco, corn, and other valuable products than it ever produced before, how happens it, we sternly ask, that the houses of its laborers are miserable huts, that their clothes are rags, and their food the coarsest and scantiest? How happens it that the land-owner is becoming richer and the laborer poorer?

The implication is irresistible—that where the landlord is prosperous the laborer ought to share his prosperity, and whenever and wherever we find this is not the case there is manifestly wrong somewhere. . . .

Flagrant as have been the outrages committed upon colored citizens in respect to their civil rights, more flagrant, shocking, and scandalous still have been the outrages committed upon our political rights by means of bull-dozing and Kukluxing, Mississippi plans, fraudulent courts, tissue ballots, and the like devices. Three States in which the colored people outnumber the white population are without colored representation and their political voice suppressed. The colored citizens in those States are virtually disfranchised, the Constitution held in utter contempt and its provisions nullified. This has been done in the face of the Republican party and successive Republican administrations. . . .

This is no question of party. It is a question of law and government. It is a question whether men shall be protected by law, or be left to the mercy of cyclones of anarchy and bloodshed. It is whether the Government or the mob shall rule this land; whether the promises solemnly made to us in the constitution be manfully kept or meanly and flagrantly broken. Upon this vital point we ask the whole people of the United States to take notice that whatever of political power we have shall be exerted for no man of any party who will not, in advance of election, promise to use every power given him by the Government, State or National, to make the black man's path to the ballot-box as straight, smooth and safe as that of any other American citizen. . . .

We hold it to be self-evident that no class or color should be the exclusive rulers of this country. If there is such a ruling class, there must of course be a subject class, and when this condition is once established this Government of the people, by the people, and for the people, will have perished from the earth.